SO FAR FROM HOME

HOME

THE PEARL BRYAN MURDER

Robert Wilhelm

PEARL BRYAN
Traditional Ballad

In Greencastle lived a maiden
She was known the wide world o'er
She was murdered by Scott Jackson
Whom she fondly did adore.

Yes, she loved him very dearly
For she was both bright and gay,
And she trusted in him fully
And by him was led astray.

When she told him her sad story,
And he knew that it was true,
Then he grew so discouraged
That he knew not what to do.

Then he called on his friend Walling
For to seek advice and aid
And they held a consultation
And the daring plot was made

In a cab one rainy evening,
At the closing of the day
There came Walling and Scott Jackson
And with Pearl they drove away

Yes. they drove far from the city,
To a place so far from home,
There they left her body lying
Headless and all stained with blood

CONTENTS

AUTHOR'S NOTE

Newspapers from Ohio, Kentucky, and Indiana between 1896 and 1897 provided the source material for this story. All conversations and other statements in quotes were taken directly from interviews, police interrogations, and trial transcripts exactly as they appeared in the daily papers. All letters, telegrams, and official documents were taken verbatim from newspaper accounts.

INTRODUCTION

The headless corpse of a young woman was found lying in the woods in the Highlands of Northern Kentucky on February 1, 1896. The discovery, just four miles south of the Ohio River, with Cincinnati, Ohio, on the opposite shore, set lawmen and reporters from both states into a frantic search for missing women and possible suspects. When the body was identified as 22-year-old Pearl Bryan, daughter of a wealthy farmer from Greencastle, Indiana, and the prime suspects Scott Jackson and Alonzo Walling, two Cincinnati dental students, three states became involved, and the mystery deepened.

It was the age of yellow journalism when sensational murder cases drove newspaper circulation, and papers competed to publish lurid details. Readers followed the daily progress of police investigations and murder trials as if they were installments of serialized mystery stories. Local murders became national sensations, and the papers had plenty of source material. In 1892, readers pondered the guilt or innocence of Lizzie Borden in the daylight ax murder of her parents in Fall River, Massachusetts. The trial of Theo Durrant, in 1895, for the murder and mutilation of two women in a San Francisco Baptist Church became a national sensation and was briefly mentioned in Scott Jackson's trial for Pearl Bryan's murder. The notorious serial killer H.H. Holmes was awaiting execution in a Philadelphia prison as Jackson and Walling prepared for their trials.

The story of Pearl Bryan's murder would also unfold on front pages across the nation, accompanied by engraved illustrations of the victim and her killers. When the murder became national news, the Cincinnati Police received letters from people with no connection, hundreds of miles away, claiming to have uncovered the conspiracy of Pearl Bryan's murder, or learned in a dream the location of her missing head, or could tell by looking at his portrait that Scott Jackson was innocent.

Emotions ran high in Kentucky, Ohio, and Indiana; the call for vengeful justice was coupled with skepticism of the legal system's ability to deliver it. The people of Kentucky had a long history of distrust in the wheels of justice and often took matters into their own hands. In Cincinnati, a lenient verdict in a murder trial twelve years earlier had triggered the Courthouse Riot—three days of civil unrest that left 45 people dead. Even in normally staid Greencastle, Indiana, serious talk of a lynching drove a third suspect out of town. Pressure from the citizens of all three states was palpable, and the threat of violence was always present. The need to convict Pearl Bryan's killers was urgent and overwhelming, not only for the sake of justice but to maintain social order.

Investigating and prosecuting a murder case in 1896 relied on eyewitness testimony and circumstantial evidence. Much of the forensic science common today, such as fingerprinting and blood typing, would not become law enforcement tools until well into the twentieth century. The successful prosecution of suspects meant constructing a narrative of the crime that would convince a jury of their guilt. The Cincinnati Police believed they had a story that worked, and they were convinced they had the killers in custody. But neither man would confess or admit to any direct knowledge of Pearl's death, forcing the police into the arduous job of building a circumstantial case. They needed to prove cold-blooded murder in Kentucky—the only story that led to a legal execution—and they ignored any evidence that deviated from that story.

Cincinnati newspapers were not tied to a single story and were often at odds with the police as they followed every lead. While not every investigation paid off, the papers effectively pointed out the holes and flaws in the official story and challenged the veracity of the prosecution's witnesses. The press continued to raise doubts throughout the case, leaving readers unsure of who, if anyone, would hang for the murder of Pearl Bryan.

Within a year of the crime, three books were published on the murder: The Mysterious Murder of Pearl Bryan, Or: The Headless Horror; Pearl Bryan, Or: A Fatal Ending, and Headless Yet Identified. They run the gamut from somewhat inaccurate to mostly fiction. All three promote the official story, downplaying or ignoring anything that deviates, and giving the Cincinnati Police and the Sheriff of Campbell County, Kentucky, credit for closing the case. The accepted story of Pearl Bryan's murder became a simple mystery easily solved by dogged police work, with no mention of the doubt and turmoil that surrounded the case to the very end.

So Far from Home revisits the Pearl Bryan murder case as it was told in the daily newspapers at the time, when the mystery was fresh, the conclusion unknown, with clues that could lead anywhere. With all red herrings and blind alleys followed by reporters and the lies and contradictions relied upon by the police, the story is far from simple. A closer look at viable alternatives and possibilities will not provide a revised conclusion to the case but should revive the doubt and skepticism that surrounded every aspect when the story was new. This book does not attempt a new solution to the murder but reopens and shines new light on the forever insoluble mystery of Pearl Bryan's death.

PART ONE

1 TRAGEDY AND LUCK

They had been watching the house on Ninth Street since midafternoon, awaiting the killer's return. Cincinnati Police Detectives Bulmer and Witte were prepared to wait all night if necessary, but it was nearly ten o'clock, and they began to fear that Scott Jackson, the wanted man, might not return that night. They worried too, that the show at Robinson's Opera House, a few doors down, would be ending soon, and the crowd would fill the street just as they were about to arrest their man. Despite its name, Robinson's was a variety theater, playing vaudeville, not opera, and their audience was far from genteel. When they learned who was being arrested, they could become unruly— emotions ran high over this crime, and Cincinnati residents did not always trust their institutions to mete out justice. Matters could turn violent. It had happened before.

Scott Jackson's crime was particularly heinous. Just four days earlier, on the first of February 1896, the decapitated body of a young woman was found in the Kentucky Highlands, four miles south of Cincinnati, across the Ohio River. The entire Ohio Valley was in turmoil over the seemingly impossible task of identifying a headless corpse. Despite a rigorous search of the area, the head remained missing, and without it, identification seemed unlikely. But miraculously, earlier that day, February 5, a telegram from Cincinnati detectives in Greencastle, Indiana, proclaimed that the girl had been positively identified as Pearl Bryan of that city and her killer was likely Scott Jackson, known as "Dusty" in Greencastle, now a student at the Ohio College of Dental Surgery.

The college told the police that Jackson was living at 222 West Ninth Street, and detectives Bulmer and Witte hid in the shadows outside that address awaiting his return. Reporters from Cincinnati's major newspapers, who would never be far from the action, waited with them.

Shortly before ten o'clock, the detectives received word that Jackson was seen leaving the Palace Hotel, just a few blocks away on Sixth Street, and was believed to be on his way home.

A shadowy figure turned the corner from Elm to Ninth. It was too dark to make out the face, but the build matched the description in the telegram sent from Greencastle: Slender, about 5 feet, 7 inches tall. He was hardly menacing but a cold-blooded killer nonetheless, desperate and possibly armed.

Bulmer hushed the newsmen and waited, motionless, in the dark of the alley to see if his subject made his way to number 222. The man stopped in front of the house and looked up, as if checking for a light in the second-floor window, then he continued walking down Ninth toward Plum Street. Bulmer quietly rushed after him, motioning Witte to follow.

"Your name is Jackson, isn't it?" Bulmer called, "I want you."

Startled, Jackson cried, "My God, what is this for?"

Bulmer did not respond. The two detectives took Jackson firmly by the arms and walked him across Plum Street to the massive stone building that housed City Hall and the Central Police Station.

The arrest of Scott Jackson was a monumental achievement—in less than a week, the impossible case of the headless corpse in the Highlands had been solved. In days to come, the Cincinnati Police would be praised for their excellent detective work, but, in truth, police work had little to do with it. All the breakthroughs in the case had come from outside the force, and Jackson's arrest had been the result of an extended streak of good luck.

The discovery of the body itself had also been a stroke of luck. A young boy found the body the morning of February 1, 1896, less than twenty-four hours after the murder was committed, but it could have easily remained undiscovered for months. The headless corpse lay in a secluded section of woods in the Kentucky Highlands, south of Newport, not far from Fort Thomas, where the Army stationed about 300 soldiers. The intersection of Highland Avenue and Alexandria Pike formed an arrow pointing south with a wooded area between the roads. Along the Pike was a rail fence and behind that was a narrow path, overgrown with bushes. At one time, the path had been used by John Lock, the property owner, as a shortcut to his farmhouse. The body lay at the edge of a clearing in the woods along the path. Within walking distance of Fort Thomas, the spot was well-known to the soldiers who went there for secret trysts with prostitutes or sweethearts but never on a rainy, winter night. It would likely be another three months before any couple would venture there.

On his way to work at John Lock's farm that Saturday morning, 14-year-old John Huling got the shock of his life when he took a shortcut down the path and spotted the headless woman lying on her side down an embankment. Above the shoulders was a ragged edge of freshly cut flesh and bone. Blood was everywhere, saturating the ground beneath her, and even above the body, the undersides of privet leaves were spotted with blood as if they had been sprayed from below. Blood that soaked into the top of her dress was still wet; she had been murdered sometime during the previous night.

The boy frantically ran to tell his boss, and after seeing the body himself, John Lock took his wagon to Fort Thomas and used the fort's telephone to contact the Campbell County Sheriff's office. News of the discovery traveled quickly through Newport, Kentucky, and across the Ohio River to Cincinnati.

Reporters were the first to arrive, taking note of all they saw while corrupting the scene with their footprints in the mud near the body. Ruth Gottlieb of the *Covington Record*, one of the region's few female reporters, added to the confusion with footprints indistinguishable from those of the victim.

Mobs of curiosity seekers arrived soon after, eager for an exciting Saturday morning viewing a headless corpse. They went to work gathering souvenirs—clumps of bloody earth and privet leaves—corrupting the scene until the arrival of Campbell County Sheriff Jule Plummer, who took charge right away. Sheriff Plummer was lean and lanky with a drooping mustache and a gruff manner, recalling the Wild West sheriffs of dime novels. Seeing the potential hazard of the gathering crowds, Plummer wisely spread the word that the county would pay $50 to whoever found the missing head. The people then moved away from the one place they knew the head was not.

When Cincinnati Police detectives Cal Crim and Jack McDermott arrived, the lawmen drove reporters away from the body as well. Standing out of earshot, they discussed the situation with Sheriff Plummer and planned their investigation. Crim and McDermott often worked together in Cincinnati, but only a crime this shocking would send them across the Ohio River to aid a Kentucky sheriff.

The Cincinnati detectives looked so much alike they could be brothers. Both were big, barrel-chested men with close-cropped hair and full mustaches. Jack McDermott, the older of the two, was quieter but more in tune with the politics of the police force and the city. Cal Crim was a man of action and did most of the talking. He had been practically raised by the police department. Crim arrived alone in Cincinnati as a ten-year-old orphan, and the policemen who found the boy took him under their wing until he joined the force at age sixteen.

Crim and McDermott were good at what they did, but they were not the kind of detectives who solved mysteries. In Cincinnati, murder was a simple thing—an escalated quarrel, a domestic dispute, a robbery gone wrong—some everyday confrontation taken to extreme, usually fueled by alcohol. Get the straight story, and the killer's identity would be obvious. Crim and McDermott were used to getting the information they needed by force, or, more often, the threat of force. Their intimidating presence alone was usually enough to uncover their suspect and get him to confess. But force would not work in this case. They were not clear on how they would ever find the killer.

The lawmen examined the scene and canvased the neighbors, but they put most of their energy that day into finding the head, the only sure way of identifying the body. In addition to the civilian searchers, Sheriff Plummer brought in a team of champion bloodhounds owned by Arthur Carter of Indiana, considered the most effective tracking dogs in the region. Six men were currently behind bars due to the dogs' tracking abilities. A seventh, Indiana murderer, Bud Stone, had been hanged a month earlier.

Arthur Carter and the bloodhounds, Jack, Wheeler, and Stonewall, arrived at Lock's farm just before sundown, but Carter did not like what he saw. The noise of the crowd was making the dogs skittish, and even in the dark, it was apparent that any possible trail had been compromised by people stomping through the muddy ground. He saw little chance of success, but the Sheriff said to press on anyway and handed him a piece of the dead woman's clothing. After two tries, the dogs led Carter to the edge of a reservoir and began to howl. In the days that followed, the reservoir was completely drained in an unsuccessful search for the head.

John Lock heard nothing the previous night to disturb his sleep, but the detectives learned some of his neighbors had. Mrs. O'Neil, wife of the drum major at Fort Thomas, thought she heard a scream around midnight but decided it must have been animals fighting. Mrs. Hubert Cave said she and her husband had heard screams and cries for help around 4:00 a.m. She had been preparing his breakfast as he got ready for the early shift at work. She usually went back to bed after he left, but that day, she was too shaken to sleep.

Taking these stories at face value, the lawmen built a possible narrative of what had transpired the previous night. The girl and her killer arrived near Lock's farm sometime before midnight, when it began to rain. The rain was constant after that, but the ground was dry under the body, so the murder must have occurred before the rain started. From the footprints, they surmised that the murderer and his victim walked together to the clearing. There he turned on her, attacking her with a knife. She fought back, letting out the scream that Mrs. O'Neil heard, but she was overpowered and knocked to the ground. He stabbed her in the neck and left her for dead.

Several hours later, he began to worry about the consequences of the girl being identified, so he returned to the scene with the express purpose of cutting off her head to remove all possibility of identification. He straddled her and set his knife to the task, but she had only been unconscious, not dead, and the shock of the blade revived her. She screamed in terror—the cries heard by the Caves. In a frenzy, the killer continued his work removing the head while the girl was still alive.

When the work was done, the killer took her jewelry and anything else that might lead to identification. He also removed her corset and made sure it contained no hidden papers. He then wrapped the head in her coat and took it away with him. It was all conjecture, though, and it brought them no closer to the identity of the victim, or her killer.

In Newport, Kentucky, public opinion said that the victim must have come from across the river, a Cincinnati prostitute murdered by a soldier from Fort Thomas—as if any evil in Kentucky had to have come from out of state. The fort categorically denied the possibility that the killer was a soldier. Cincinnati brothels, though, were quick to supply names of missing girls - Fanny Palmer, Mamie Utter, and a girl identified only as Molly, not seen since Friday.

Like most American cities at the time, Cincinnati treated prostitution as a necessary evil. The current administration, controlled by the political machine of "Boss" George B. Cox, did not tolerate streetwalkers but sanctioned and taxed the bawdy houses, even providing routine medical examinations for the girls. The classiest brothels were located on Vine Street, Over-the-Rhine, the raucous entertainment district north of the Little Miami Canal. Brothels closer to the city center, on George and Longworth Streets, offered their services to those on a tighter budget. Approaching the river, through neighborhoods like Rat Row and Bucktown, price and quality diminished rapidly. The lowest, rankest cribs were on Front Street, the first street up from the Ohio River. Visible from the other side of the river, it was the reason Newport thought first of Cincinnati prostitutes.

Newport took a more provincial view of prostitution, and the Kentucky girls who serviced the fort tended to be more independent and less visible than their Ohio sisters. They worked the Midway, a half-mile strip of Highland Avenue near the fort, crowded with saloons, dancehalls, and card rooms. They were joined by non-professional local girls who enjoyed a dance and more with a soldier. Some of these girls were missing as well. Most notably, Mary Riggles, who was last seen Friday night at a Midway dancehall called Reidmatter's arguing with her boyfriend. They left together, and neither had been seen since. As these names came into circulation, they were investigated by reporters, and one by one, each was found alive and safe.

On Monday morning, Campbell County Coroner Walter Tingley, together with Dr. Caruthers of the Ohio Medical College, performed a post-mortem examination on the headless body. They could not conclusively determine the cause of death, but what the post-mortem did reveal resulted in a complete reassessment of the victim's profile and provided a motive for the crime. Contrary to early estimations, she was not middle-aged, but was a healthy young woman in her early twenties. She had a slight deformity on her feet – her toes were connected, almost to the tip, with a web of skin. The police were hopeful that this would help identify the body, or at least debunk false claims. But the most dramatic finding of the post-mortem forced both the police and the press to reassess the girl and rewrite her story—at the time of her death, she was five months pregnant.

Sensational as it was, this information was no help in identifying the headless corpse. But the police, with the aid of a few outsiders, were about to continue their run of good luck. If finding the body the morning after the murder had been a lucky break, what happened next was close to miraculous. The victim's clothing had no identifying marks, but inside her shoes was the imprint of a shoe store—Louis & Hayes, Greencastle, Indiana, followed by a series of numbers: 22 11 62358. Sheriff Plummer sent a telegram to the store with a description of the boot and the information inside it. The manager responded that indeed this pair of boots had been sold at their store, but there was no way to determine to whom. Their best guess for a customer who turned up dead in Kentucky was a member of an acting troupe that had passed through Greencastle the previous fall.

The shoes appeared to be another dead end until Louis Poock, a Newport shoe merchant, took it on himself to measure the woman's foot and examine her boots. The numbers 22 and 11, Poock knew, were the shoe size under the French System, a method of measurement favored by shoe dealers because it obscured the conventional size, allowing the salesman more leeway when fitting a difficult customer. A size of 22 11 would correspond to size 3B—a tiny shoe for a grown woman. The toes of the boots were stuffed with moss, indicating that the victim could have fit into a smaller size.

It was a well-made, cloth-topped boot with laces up the front—an expensive boot not likely purchased by an itinerant actress. Poock reasoned that the customer would have taken much care before deciding on such a purchase, and certainly, the salesman would remember this sale.

Prior to opening his own shoe store, Poock had spent nine years as a salesman traveling for the shoe trade, and he knew his business. From the stitching, he recognized that the shoe was not from the East Coast but was probably manufactured somewhere nearby. After visiting several Cincinnati shoe dealers, Poock determined that the shoes were manufactured by Drew, Selby, and Co., in Portsmouth, Ohio. Poock went to Portsmouth and visited the factory where he learned that the boot was part of an order sent to Louis and Hayes in Greencastle the previous September, and the order, lot number 62458, had included only one pair in that style and size.

Then a second, unrelated clue pointed to Greencastle. Word had reached Cincinnati that a young Greencastle woman, Mrs. Pearl Kesterson, had left her husband in September and run off with Francis J. Cooper, an army recruit assigned to Fort Thomas. Her family hadn't heard from her in several days. The shoes alone may have been enough to send the investigators to a small town in central Indiana, but a second story out of Greencastle clinched it.

Just before dawn on Tuesday morning, February 4, three Ohio Valley lawmen and at least as many reporters stepped off the train on the platform of the Vandalia depot in Greencastle, Indiana. They had left Cincinnati the previous afternoon and had hoped to arrive before midnight, but a blizzard had caused havoc throughout the state, and a derailed freight train had delayed them six hours.

The men checked into a hotel and grabbed what sleep they could before Greencastle came to life that morning. When the workday began, Detective Jack McDermott paid a call on Greencastle City Marshal William Starr, then he went in search of information on Mrs. Kesterson. In the meantime, Crim and Plummer, along with the reporters, descended on Louis and Hayes shoe store hoping to identify the girl who had purchased the boots.

Their work at the store turned out to be slow and tedious; the store kept records by customer name rather than date. Many of the store's customers were out-of-town students of DePauw University in Greencastle. They would mail in their orders, which the store could fill more readily if their details were already at hand.

Crim and Plummer checked each customer record looking for purchases between September and January, the most likely time for the sale. Then the style and size of each purchase was checked against the order list Poock had obtained from Drew and Selby. It was a laborious process, plowing through the big ledgers, and the hours went by slowly. By closing time, they had found all but three pairs from Poock's list, but none in a size 3.

From time to time throughout the day, a reporter or one of the lawmen would leave the shoe store and make their way to the Western Union office near the public square. They sent news of their progress back to Cincinnati and learned what was happening back home.

While progress in Indiana was interminably slow, the Kentucky investigation was still at full speed. Someone had identified the body as Francesca Englehart, a woman who had recently married a Dr. Kettner of Dakota. The doctor had allegedly murdered his new bride after she learned he already had a wife out West. Police had not yet interviewed Kettner, and the identification would later prove false.

It looked as though identifying the victim by the shoes would prove futile as well. Then the investigators received another stroke of good luck. Late that evening, the manager of the Greencastle Western Union office, A. W. "Gus" Early, approached a Cincinnati reporter who had come in to wire his paper. He said he had some information he thought might be useful to the police. Operators had full knowledge of telegraph messages sent and received in the office. Early said a telegram had been sent earlier in the week by Fred Bryan to a party in Indianapolis inquiring whether his sister Pearl had arrived safely. The response came later the same day saying that Pearl had not arrived; moreover, she had not been expected.

The reporter was not impressed. They had been tracking down missing girls for days, and here was another. But Early had more to tell. He was

7

friends with Pearl Bryan, and her cousin, Will Wood, had told him that Scott Jackson had been courting Pearl on the sly and had taken matters too far. Wood said that Pearl was pregnant, and he was going to send her to Cincinnati, where Jackson was to procure an abortion for her.

At first, Early had not given much credence to the story. He knew Wood to be a liar and a troublemaker who enjoyed spreading malicious rumors about Greencastle girls, including his cousin Pearl. But since the arrival of the police from Cincinnati, Early had given the matter more thought; maybe the reason Pearl was not in Indianapolis was that she had gone to Cincinnati. Early was very much afraid the headless girl in Kentucky might be Pearl Bryan.

The reporter immediately passed this latest information along to the lawmen. Late as it was, they went to the home of Mr. Spivey, the shoe clerk, and persuaded him to reopen the store. They needed to check the records for Pearl Bryan. Spivey was incredulous. The Bryans were one of the oldest and most respected families in the county, and Pearl was well known and highly regarded in Greencastle. The murdered girl could not be Pearl Bryan. But the men insisted, and Spivey reopened the store so that they could check.

The books he showed them earlier had mostly contained DePauw students, women from outside of Greencastle, who were far more likely than a local girl to be found dead in Kentucky. When they opened the book to the name of Pearl Bryan, there it was, the missing pair, ladies' cloth-top, button, size 3, 'B' last, sold to Pearl Bryan for $2.50 on November 18, 1895.

By now, it was after midnight, but any delay would only put more distance between the police and the killer. Sheriff Plummer, carrying a satchel containing the victim's bloodied clothes, hired a wagon to take them to the Bryans' home outside of town. The rattling of the wagon coming up the long drive woke those inside the house and lights came on in the windows before Sheriff Plummer reached the door.

An elderly man with a long gray beard answered the door, and Plummer asked if he was Alexander Bryan, father of Pearl Bryan. When the man said he was, Plummer, as gently as possible, delivered the terrible news.

Alarmed by the late-night visit, family members in their nightclothes gathered in the front room. Pearl's father and mother, an older sister, Mary, older brother Fred and younger brother Frank, stood in shocked silence and disbelief.

Sheriff Plummer turned to Pearl's mother and said he had a difficult task to ask of them; he wanted them to identify the dead girl's clothes. Piece by piece, he pulled each article of clothing, coated in dried blood, from the bag and showed it to the family.

Mrs. Bryan immediately began sobbing, "My Pearl, my Pearl."

There was no doubt they were Pearl's clothes; her sister could even tell them when and where each item had been purchased. The green checked dress, now stiff with bloodstains and mud, had been made by her mother for Pearl's sister Jennie, who had died of tuberculosis the previous summer. After that, Pearl had worn it as a dressing gown. Looking up wildly, Mary grasped desperately at the slightest straw of hope. Could there have been a mistake? Could Pearl have loaned the clothes to someone else?

Sheriff Plummer then told her that the murdered woman had toes connected almost to the tips by a thin web of skin.

"My God, it is Pearl!" Mary cried, "We used to tease her about those when she was little."

Pearl Bryan
Wikimedia Commons.

Pearl's mother broke into hysterical sobbing while the rest of the family tried to comfort her amid their own anguish and sorrow.

The following day when Mr. and Mrs. Bryan had regained their composure, they agreed to meet with reporters. Before answering their questions, the Bryans were anxious to learn all they could about the investigation and whether their daughter's head had been found yet.

"We don't want her grave pointed at as the grave of a headless woman," said Alexander Bryan. "Our sorrow is more than we can bear, yet we would rather stand over the grave of an innocent daughter lured to her ruin than that of her betrayer and assassin."

When asked about Scott Jackson, the Bryans said they were acquainted with him through their grandnephew, Will Wood, who occasionally brought him to the house, but if Jackson had been courting Pearl, it was without their knowledge. They spoke in the bitterest terms of Will Wood's treachery and made it clear that they held him equally responsible for their daughter's death.

When the news hit town the morning of February 6, Greencastle residents were shocked. They had followed the Fort Thomas tragedy in the newspapers, as much of the country had, but no one suspected for a moment that the victim might be one of their own. Pearl was well-known and popular in Greencastle, and the whole town was in mourning. Stores remained closed for the day, and townspeople gathered in the square to find solace in each other's company, sharing their grief and anger.

The only thing preventing a lynching in Greencastle that morning was the absence of anyone to lynch—Scott Jackson was in Cincinnati, and Will Wood had decided, a couple days before, to visit relatives in South Bend, Indiana.

Will Wood's father, The Reverend DeLoss Wood, Presiding Elder of the Methodist Episcopal Church, assured the lawmen that his son had nothing to do with Pearl Bryan's death. He had been in South Bend staying with his uncle since the previous week. But the detectives had gathered enough information in Greencastle to arrest both Scott Jackson and William Wood, and they were afraid that Wood, like Pearl Bryan, may have gone to Cincinnati instead of his stated destination. They sent this telegram to the Cincinnati Chief of Police, Colonel Phillip Deitsch:

> February 5, 1896. Arrest and charge with murder of Pearl Bryan, one Scott Jackson, student at Dental College, about 24 years old, 5 feet 7 or 8 inches high, weighs about 135 pounds, blonde, nearly sandy mustache, light complexion, may have beard of about six months growth, effeminate in appearance. Positive identification of clothing by family. Arrest if in Cincinnati, William Wood, friend of Jackson. Charge as accomplice. About 20 years, 5 feet 11 inches, light blond hair, smooth face, rather slender, weighs 165 pounds.

Then, taking Rev. Wood at his word, detectives Crim and McDermott, accompanied by Sheriff Plummer, took the next train to South Bend. They hoped to bring Will Wood back with them to Cincinnati. With three states now involved, extradition was likely to become an issue, so they made sure that Ohio and Kentucky were both represented.

Upon receipt of the telegram in Cincinnati, Colonel Deitsch contacted Judge Gregg, who issued arrest warrants for both Scott Jackson and William Wood. With Jackson's arrest imminent, Deitch and Mayor John Caldwell stayed late in the mayor's office. When they received the news that Jackson was in custody, the Mayor and the Chief were ecstatic. They had the killer and tomorrow Will Wood—either an accomplice of Jackson's or a witness against him—would arrive in Cincinnati. In less than a week, the impossible case was closed.

But the authorities had celebrated too soon. In coming days, the unfolding story would become increasingly complicated, with each new revelation prompting ever more questions and multiplying the possible answers. Instead of leading to certainty, the coming investigation would add increasing doubts as to how Pearl Bryan had met her terrible death, some of which would never be resolved. Scott Jackson's arrest was not the end of anything; it was only the beginning.

2 THE KILLER EXAMINED

The detectives led their frightened prisoner down the dark corridors of City Hall, followed by a pack of newspaper reporters. Late as it was, the policemen had orders to bring Jackson directly to the mayor's office, and as they approached, they could see light emanating from the bottom of the office door.

The mayor's large office was bright from the gas sconces around the walls. An oil lamp illuminated the papers on his desk, and a fire burning in a fireplace on the far wall filled the room with heat. The mayor and the police chief took their time as they looked Jackson over. Not much to him, a tiny man compared to the policemen who held him. He certainly fit the description in Crim and McDermott's telegram: Five foot seven, mid-twenties, light blonde hair. He wore a sandy-colored mustache, well-trimmed, and parted, accentuating a full lower lip. The telegram had not mentioned his eyes; they were pale blue in the office light, but strikingly radiant.

Scott Jackson
Courtesy of the *Cincinnati Inquirer*.

Mayor Caldwell motioned Jackson to take a seat on the sofa opposite his desk. Caldwell was a stately man in his late fifties with a full black mustache and deep-set eyes. As he took his seat in the high-backed chair behind the desk, he gave the impression of power and control. Deitsch stood beside him,

11

his arms folded. This was a man who always wore his police uniform and preferred to be addressed by his military rank of colonel. He was a few years older than the mayor and a bit stouter, but he had the look of a man not to be trifled with.

The reporters had followed the detectives into the office, and the policemen made no move to stop them. They gathered around the sofa and looked on as Mayor Caldwell and Colonel Deitsch took turns questioning the prisoner.

Jackson seemed to relax as he took his place on the sofa, sitting with one leg over the other, holding his derby in his right hand. But he grew pale trying to suppress his anxiety when the mayor began a very businesslike examination of his prisoner. Responding to the mayor's questions, he said his name was Scott Jackson, and his home was Greencastle, Indiana.

"Did you know a young woman named Pearl Bryan?" The mayor asked.

"Yes sir, I did," Jackson responded.

"When did you last see her?"

"It was during the holidays. I think on January 2."

"Have you seen her since?"

"I have not."

Referring to his notes, the mayor asked, "Do you know William Wood?"

"I do," said Jackson.

"What is his business?"

"I don't know." Jackson thought for a moment, "He used to be connected with the school at Greencastle. Saw him last about January 6."

The mayor nodded to Colonel Deitsch, who then read Jackson the telegram from his men in Greencastle charging Jackson and Wood with the murder of Pearl Bryan.

"What have you to say to that?"

Jackson responded frantically, "The charge is entirely false. I don't know anything about it."

"That's what everybody says who is arrested," said Colonel Deitsch, "but the identification of the clothes and other facts point to you as the man who took Pearl Bryan or her body to Fort Thomas. Where were you last Friday evening?"

"I must have been in my room," said Jackson, still excited, "I'm sure I was."

"What time did you go to your room?"

"I think I had supper at 7 o'clock and went home about 7:30."

"What did you do?"

"I studied in my room."

Colonel Deitsch asked Jackson to account for his time beginning with the Thursday before the murder. Speaking more calmly now, Jackson said he had spent his time studying every night except Saturday when he went to the theater with two friends from school and saw *La Tosca*. On the day of his arrest, he had been with a young lady. After supper, he went to the Palace Hotel to write some letters, using the stationery that the hotel provided free in the lobby. When arrested, he was on his way to the college to see if any of the students were dissecting.

"Did you read of the murder?" asked Colonel Deitsch.

"Part of it. It made me sick to my stomach."

"Didn't you take an interest in the murder when you read of Greencastle being the probable home of the murdered girl?" Deitsch could barely hide his disgust.

"There were so many theories that I didn't know what to think," said Jackson.

"When did Miss Bryan come up to Cincinnati?"

"Don't know. Didn't know she was here."

Jackson reiterated that he had last seen Pearl on January 2 when he was in Greencastle for the holidays. They were friends and he had seen Pearl at her home.

"You were in the habit of paying your respects to her?" Deitsch asked.

"I called on her a few times."

"Did you ever go out with her?"

"Once, I guess."

"Do you know any other men she kept company with?" Deitsch asked.

"Yes, but she never kept company with me," Jackson said emphatically.

Colonel Deitsch paused before taking another tack. Before his arrest, detectives had spoken with people in Jackson's neighborhood, including the owner of Legner's Saloon on the corner of Ninth Street and Central Avenue. Legner said that Jackson had left a valise in his saloon on Saturday night, picked it up on Monday morning, and left another. Jackson recalled leaving the valise, but said he picked it up the same day and did not leave another. He said he had since loaned it to a student named Hackelmen and denied any connection between the valise and the crime.

It was getting late, and Deitsch did not believe he would get any more from Jackson that night. He told Jackson once again that all evidence pointed to him as the murderer of Pearl Bryan.

"Well, Jackson," Deitsch said, "this is a serious charge. I will have to hold on to you."

"I don't see why you accuse me of this," Jackson said.

Detective Bulmer walked Jackson through the long corridor on the Eighth Street side of City Hall until they reached the receiving room of Central Police Station. There Lieutenant Corbin booked Jackson for murder, taking down his vital statistics: Age, 26; Occupation, dental student; Marital status, single; Place of birth, Wiscasset, Maine. Among his personal effects were three ladies' hand-worked lace handkerchiefs; a check for ten dollars drawn on the Citizen's National Bank of Greencastle, payable to one Edwin Post and endorsed to Scott Jackson; one pair of gloves; one black muffler; one white muffler; a gold watch and chain; two gentleman's handkerchiefs; six meal tickets; and two carriage tickets for the Central Newport Bridge. Jackson was taken downstairs and locked in a cell.

The reporters dispersed. Some left to write their stories, while a few accompanied the detectives Colonel Deitsch sent to the Ohio Dental College's dissecting room to see if Jackson had left any evidence there. Ed Anthony of the *Cincinnati Enquirer* stayed behind, following turnkey Curren, who led Jackson to his cell. After Jackson was locked in, Anthony stood outside his cell, waiting to see if Jackson had anything more to say.

Jackson removed his coat, vest, collar, and necktie, then called for the turnkey.

Curren walked back to the cell, "Well, what do you want?"

"I want you to get a chair and sit in front of my cell all night," Jackson said.

"Are you afraid of getting lynched?"

"Never mind that," said Jackson, "I prefer to be well guarded whether I'm in danger or not."

Curren assured Jackson he was well guarded then went back to his post. Ed Anthony stayed by the cell trying to get Jackson to talk, but the prisoner was reticent. Jackson lay down on his bunk and tried to sleep, but he was restless, rolling around, unable to relax. Anthony continued to wait, and his patience was rewarded.

Around 2:00 a.m., Jackson was up pacing his cell.

"Hasn't Walling been arrested yet?" He asked Anthony.

"Why should he be arrested?" Anthony responded. Alonzo Walling was Scott Jackson's roommate. The police who had watched their rooming house all day had not seen Walling, and following Jackson's arrest, had shown no interest in finding him.

"Oh nothing," Jackson said and continued pacing.

At that, Ed Anthony realized the police had made a mistake ignoring Walling and, for whatever reason, Jackson wanted to make sure Anthony knew it. He bid Jackson goodnight and quietly left the police station.

He briskly covered the short distance to 222 West Ninth. It was now well past midnight, but he pounded on the front door with his fist. The landlady, Miss McNevin, opened the door clutching her robe at her throat. Anthony loudly asked for Alonzo Walling.

A casual observer would not be likely to confuse Ed Anthony with a Cincinnati cop. Anthony was in his mid-forties with no hint of a policeman's build. He wore a high collar like a dandy and hid a receding hairline under his derby. His thin mustache was a mere shadow of the full walrus favored by Cincinnati policemen. But Anthony possessed the cocksure and commanding bearing of a cop, and Miss McNevin, who had been dealing with this posture all day, let him in unchallenged. She showed him to Walling's door on the second floor.

Anthony pounded on the door, and a groggy man, younger, taller, and stronger than Scott Jackson opened it. A country boy, Anthony thought, and one who could overpower him with little trouble if he wanted to.

When the boy confirmed that he was Alonzo Walling, Anthony told him he was under arrest.

Like Miss McNevin, Walling had no reason to believe that Anthony was not a policeman, and he put up no resistance.

They walked back to the Central Police Station, and Walling kept quiet the whole way. As hard as Anthony pressed him, Alonzo Walling would say nothing about Scott Jackson or Pearl Bryan.

3 THREE STORIES

When Colonel Deitsch arrived at Central Station the next morning, he found a crowd gathered at the west end of City Hall waiting for Police Court to open. News of the Fort Thomas killer's capture quickly spread through Cincinnati, and rumor said he would be arraigned that morning. Scott Jackson would not be appearing in Police Court that day, but the crowd was slow to disperse. Everyone hoped for a look at the monster.

Deitsch was surprised to learn that a second man had been arrested in connection with the murder. Though there was no evidence against Alonzo Walling, he was already referred to as Scott Jackson's accomplice. The chief had questions for Walling, but first he wanted to finish what he had started the night before. Maybe a night in jail and the news of his partner's arrest would make Jackson see the futility of continuing to lie.

Newspaper reporters, at the time, had virtually unlimited access to the Cincinnati police station. Several reporters who had been waiting with the crowd outside followed Deitsch in and were present in his office when Jackson was brought up from the cells. Deitsch showed the prisoner to a seat in front of his desk, and as the night before, he sat surrounded by newsmen anxious to take down his every word. Jackson looked drained. It was apparent the prisoner had gotten little or no sleep that night. His face was dirty and flushed, his clothing disarranged, and his hair unkempt. He was trembling slightly, but his cold blue eyes were bright and alive as they scanned the room, taking in each face.

"Well, Dusty, how are you feeling this morning?" Colonel Deitsch asked.

"As well as possible, under the circumstances," said Jackson.

"Have you anything to say this morning?"

Jackson hesitated, "Well, I don't know what I can say."

By this point, Jackson was aware that Alonzo Walling had been arrested and had probably heard that Will Wood was on his way from Indiana for questioning. He realized that he could no longer plead ignorance. His best

16

chance was to tell his version of the story before the others told theirs, but he was still not anxious to say anything.

Deitsch grew impatient, "Now, I want to know about your connection with this case."

"I was simply going to do what I thought a favor for a friend." Jackson stammered a bit, unsure where to start. "The last time I saw her was in January when I was at home for the holidays."

He took a breath and gathered his thoughts. Jackson explained that after he returned to Cincinnati, he received a letter from his friend William Wood. Pearl was pregnant, it said, and Wood was responsible. He desperately wanted Jackson to help him out. Jackson had no experience in this area, so he asked his roommate, Alonzo Walling.

"Why, tell him to give her some ergot." Walling said.

Jackson forwarded the information to Wood. A few days later Jackson received another letter from Wood. The medicine had not worked, and Wood was in more trouble than ever. Walling said the best thing to do was have the girl come to Cincinnati for an operation and Jackson passed on the suggestion.

Wood sent word that Pearl was coming to Cincinnati on Monday but neglected to say what train line she was taking and when she would arrive. Jackson went to one depot and Walling went to another, but they both missed her. The next day Jackson received word that she had arrived and was staying at the Indiana House, registered as Mabel Stanley. Jackson and Walling went to see her that afternoon.

"The next day I fixed it for Walling to meet her at Fourth and Race Streets at 1 o'clock." Jackson said, "I never heard of her after that."

"Well, what killed the girl?" Deitsch asked

"I guess the abortion did," Jackson said.

Colonel Deitsch continued to question Jackson, pressing him for details. Jackson repeated his story several times and rephrased his answer but with little new information. He had tried to help his friend William Wood who had gotten Pearl Bryan pregnant. When it became clear that she would need an abortion, he had Walling make the arrangements. They both had agreed it was better if Jackson did not know the details. They met her on Tuesday and arranged for her to go with Walling on Wednesday. Jackson thought she must have died from the abortion but had no first-hand knowledge of what had happened. He did not know where she was between Wednesday afternoon and Saturday morning when her body was found.

Deitsch sent Jackson back to his cell but brought him to his office a second time that morning after a man named John Kugel, who owned a saloon on the block where Jackson lived, brought in a valise he said had been left in his saloon by a man with a blonde mustache on Monday night. Deitsch believed that this was the same valise that Jackson had left in Legner's saloon on Saturday night. Kugel did not know the man by name, but when Jackson entered Deitsch's office, Kugel confirmed that he was the man.

It was a brown leather hand satchel about 15 inches long. Deitsch told Jackson to pick it up, and Jackson took a seat with the valise in his lap.

"Open it," said Deitsch, "What is in there?"

"Nothing that I can see, except that it is stained," said Jackson.

"What is it stained with?"

"It looks like blood."

Jackson flushed and was visibly nervous as Deitch angrily accused him of carrying Pearl Bryan's head in the valise. Jackson acknowledged that the valise had been Pearl's, but it had held only her clothes when he carried it. He said he had planned to pick it up from Kugel's and dispose of the clothing. Jackson did not think that the valise ever contained Pearl Bryan's head, but if it did, it was while Walling had it.

When he was through with Jackson, Deitsch had Walling brought up from the cells. Walling was more relaxed than Jackson had been and entered the office with the air of a man who had been the victim of some bureaucratic error that would soon be made right. Jackson had been returned to his cell, but the reporters were still in the room.

Colonel Deitsch saw a boy with half the brains of Scott Jackson and twice the strength. He had waves of dark hair and wore a small black mustache, and despite his boyish face, he looked more capable of violence than Jackson did.

"Well, now Walling, your friend Jackson has been up here talking," Deitsch said, "and he told me an awful lot of bad stuff about you."

"What did he say?" Walling asked.

Alonzo Walling
Courtesy of the *Cincinnati Inquirer.*

"He said you killed the girl."

"Well, I didn't," Walling tensed up, spoke quickly. "The only time I saw Miss Bryan was when he told me to meet her at Fourth and Race Streets and tell her that he was busy with a class and could not see her, but would meet her later."

"Never saw her again, eh?"

"No, that is the last time I saw her."

"Didn't you ever say anything to him about it?"

"Yes, when I read in the paper about the murder, I thought there was something wrong. I said to Jackson, 'What about this?' He said, 'Oh, I'm tired. If it wasn't for those damned shoes, I'd be all right.'"

Walling told Deitsch that he had been in his room all night on Friday, but Jackson had left at around 11:00 p.m. and did not return until around 1:00. He said he had nothing to do with the murder, and he could prove it. Deitsch asked a few more questions, but Walling had little more to say. He only saw Pearl Bryan once. He thought Scott Jackson killed her, but he didn't know anything about it.

As Walling got up to leave, Deitsch noticed a gold ring on Walling's little finger. It did not look like a man's ring.

"Where did you get that?" Deitsch asked, pointing to the ring.

Walling hesitated for a moment and said, "Miss Smith, of Louisville, gave it to me."

"Take it off."

Walling took off the ring and handed it to Colonel Deitsch, who would see if the Bryans could identify it.

When Mayor Caldwell arrived at his office, he was elated to learn that Jackson's accomplice had been arrested despite the embarrassment of having that accomplice arrested by a newspaperman. Before being elected mayor, John Caldwell was a city prosecutor, and knew from experience an accused man had little incentive to confess his crime without evidence, and a strong-willed prisoner could dig in his heels and withstand almost any level of interrogation. But if the police had his partner in another room, one could be played against the other, and with the right pressure, one man would invariably lay blame on his partner. The other man is likely to do the same. This game could be ratcheted up until the police had either two indictments or one unimpeachable witness towards an easy conviction of the other. Jackson and Walling were already accusing each other. The game had begun.

The mayor wanted to start his questioning with both men together, see how they behaved around each other. He brought Walling into his office, and when Jackson arrived, they were immediately at each other's throats.

"You are the murderer!" cried Walling when Jackson entered the room.

"You lie, and you know you lie," Jackson shouted back.

"You show in your eyes that you are lying," Walling shouted.

Detectives subdued the prisoners, then joined Mayor Caldwell and Colonel Deitsch as they interrogated Jackson and Walling for two hours without reporters.

In the coming days, there were many such sessions, some including reporters, some private, with Jackson and Walling—alone and together— all ending the same way, with the same two versions of the story. Jackson and Walling agreed on what happened between Monday night when Pearl arrived until that Wednesday afternoon when both men claimed to have lost track of her. Jackson maintained that he left Pearl in Walling's care to transport her to a location unknown to him to undergo an abortion. Walling insisted the only time he saw Pearl was Wednesday afternoon when she was waiting on the street corner. Jackson had asked him to relay a message, but Walling did not go over to her. He passed by instead and never saw her again.

Jackson told him that Pearl was coming to Cincinnati, and that he intended to "fix" her. Walling took that to mean he planned to murder her. He was sure that Jackson killed Pearl in cold blood and related in detail how Jackson had planned to do it—giving her poison, then cutting the body into pieces, which he would dispose of in outhouse vaults throughout the city. But Walling could offer no hard evidence that his roommate had followed through with his plans.

It soon became clear the mayor's strategy of persuading each man to bring evidence against the other was not going to work. While each was ready to blame the other, both professed ignorance as to what actually happened, and neither could or would offer concrete evidence. Caldwell and Deitsch were convinced that both men were guilty, but neither man was going to confess, and neither would inform on the other. Though they never relented in their attempts to force a confession, they resolved to build a case on circumstantial evidence and set the Cincinnati police force to find out what happened those three missing days between Wednesday and Saturday.

A search of Walling's locker at the college turned up an old pair of black trousers wrapped in newspaper, covered with mud and blood from the knees down. They were too small to be Walling's pants, and when shown to Jackson, he identified them as his but said he had not worn them for some time. He believed that Walling must have worn them the night Pearl died.

Clara Bates, who ran a brothel on Longworth Street, brought to the police a pair of rubbers spotted with blood that had been left in her house by a man called Doc. "Doc" was Scott Jackson's Cincinnati nickname, but she identified Walling as the man who left the rubbers in her house.

Cincinnati reporters began their own investigations of the prisoners' movements, uncovering some strange occurrences in the days surrounding the murder. Students at the dental college had been surprised the Monday after the murder to see Scott Jackson in class without the beard he had worn since school started that fall. Fred Albion, a barber who lived in the same rooming house as Jackson and Walling, said that he shaved it off on Friday afternoon—the day of the murder. Jackson came into the shop for a haircut, and when Albion suggested that he might look better without the beard, Jackson told him to go ahead and shave it.

Walling's behavior also had some quirks. On Thursday night, for some unknown reason, he did not sleep in his room at Miss McNevin's, but checked into Heider's Hotel at 3 a.m. The night clerk said that Walling did not sign the register when he checked in and was gone by 8 a.m. Friday morning. Jackson and Walling usually took their meals at Heider's, but neither slept there before.

Rose McNevin, the landlady at 222 West Ninth Street, was fond of both Jackson and Walling, and pleased to have them in her house. They were polite and thoughtful, even offering dental treatment when one of her nieces had a toothache. The boys kept late hours, but Miss McNevin prided herself on knowing who among her roomers was in the house and who was out at any given time. Jackson and Walling had predictable habits, but she could not account for the strange movements that week.

"I noticed last week that Jackson and Walling, who were before almost inseparable, seemed to act coolly toward each other," Rose McNevin told reporters, "and I asked Walling what the trouble was. He told me that Jackson had got into the habit of going out by himself whenever he had any money, and it had turned him against him. On Thursday night, Walling came in about 10 o'clock with some apples. He sat in the dining room where I was reading until about 10:30 o'clock. Their room is just over the dining room, and he called my attention to the creaking of a rocking chair in his room. He said, 'Jackson is up there now; do you hear him?'

"I said 'yes,' and then he said he wasn't going to bed until after Jackson had. He went out, as I supposed, to his room, but I have since learned that he had slept at Heider's Hotel that evening. Now, I don't know what they meant by acting as they did, but I now think it was done for effect."

She said she saw Scott Jackson on Friday; he came in when she was with her sister Minnie and her two nieces. It was the first time they had seen him without his beard, and they all commented on how odd he looked. Jackson borrowed a bottle of ink, then went to his room. She did not believe that he left that night. She had been in the dining room until midnight and would have seen him if he went out.

Reporters confirmed something strange was afoot that week but had come no closer to determining what happened than the police had.

As police and reporters investigated events in Cincinnati, Detectives Crim and McDermott were in South Bend, Indiana, talking with another person of interest—Pearl Bryan's 19-year-old second cousin, Will Wood. He was staying with his uncle, Rev. Dr. A. A. Gee, and preparing to study medicine with a South Bend doctor.

As with the prisoners, Wood's whereabouts at the time of the murder were uncertain. Investigators knew he left Greencastle on Thursday and did not arrive in South Bend until the following Monday. He said he stopped to visit a friend in Plymouth, Indiana, and stayed with the family of County Clerk J. W. Wiltfong. When it was suggested that Wood had gone to Cincinnati, possibly accompanying Pearl, before going to South Bend, Wood vehemently denied it. He said he had never been to Cincinnati and had no involvement in the affair beyond the knowledge that Pearl had gone there for an abortion and that Scott Jackson was the reason.

Will Wood
Greencastle Democrat, February 15, 1896

Sheriff Plummer, aware he could not force Will Wood to leave Indiana, requested that the boy voluntarily accompany the lawmen back to Cincinnati, where he could provide testimony for their investigation of the murder. Wood was willing, but his uncle strongly objected, and relented only after telegraphing Wood's father, who agreed to meet them in Indianapolis with a lawyer.

On the train to Indianapolis, Wood sat beside his uncle, with Crim and McDermott in the seat in front of them, and Sheriff Plummer in the seat behind. As the train rattled through the countryside, Wood's uncle handed him several letters that had come for him in the morning's post. After reading one particular letter, Wood surreptitiously tore it up under cover of the noise of the train and disposed of the pieces before anyone could notice. The letter was from Scott Jackson.

In Indianapolis, the party was joined by Wood's father, the Reverend Delos Wood, his attorney A. W. Grand, and Mr. A. R. Colburn, whose role was unclear; apparently, he was a wealthy man from Michigan City, Indiana. Aside from Will, who looked decidedly modern, the Indiana group seemed to have emerged from an earlier time. Delos Wood, like Alexander Bryan, wore a long, gray Old Testament beard. Both he and Reverend Gee wore long frock coats.

The Wood entourage arrived at the mayor's office in Cincinnati at around 11:30am on February 6. As with the first interviews of Jackson and Walling, reporters were present in the mayor's office as well. Will Wood strutted in with the natural cockiness he would soon be famous for. He felt protected in Cincinnati, surrounded as he was by the church, the bar, and big money.

Mayor Caldwell began the interview with a few formalities, some facts for the record—name, William Wood; age, 19; home, Greencastle, Indiana.

"You knew Pearl Bryan?" the mayor asked.

"Yes, sir." Said Wood.

"Very well?"

"Yes. She was a second cousin of mine."

"Explain the relationship," the mayor continued in the same matter-of-fact fashion.

"Her mother is an aunt of my mother."

"Does your family visit the Bryans?"

"Yes, sir. We exchange calls every two or three days."

"Were you intimate with the girl?"

The question took the group by surprise; the boy was a witness, not a suspect. They expected questions about Scott Jackson's private life, not Will's. Reverend Wood was about to object, but Attorney Grand stopped him. He wanted to let Will deny it now, on the record.

"No, sir." Wood answered emphatically.

"Did you know that she had been betrayed?"

"Yes, sir," Wood was quieter now. He said Scott Jackson had told him over the holidays that he and Pearl had been together that September and he had gotten her pregnant. In January, he received a letter from Jackson saying he would arrange for an abortion. Wood had discussed the matter with Pearl as well and she was willing to have the operation. She told him she would go to Indianapolis herself for an abortion if she had the money.

"You took a great deal of interest in the case, did you not?" asked the mayor

"Yes, I would have done the same if she had been my own sister." Wood replied.

"What arrangement did Jackson say he had made when he wrote to you?"

"He said that he had procured a room in Cincinnati and that she would be taken care of by an old woman. The operation would be performed by a doctor and chemist, who was an old hand at that kind of business."

"Did he mention the name of the doctor?"

"No, he said the party was a friend of Walling."

Wood said he had planned to accompany Pearl to Cincinnati, but his father asked him to do something that necessitated his staying at home. He needed to pick up his father at the depot, which explained his presence there when Pearl was leaving. She would, in fact, be boarding the same train that Delos Wood arrived on. Wood said Pearl was overjoyed to be on her way to Cincinnati and the end of her troubles. He was with her when the train arrived, but Wood vehemently denied taking Pearl to the depot as if this would somehow lessen his involvement in Pearl's abortion and subsequent death.

The mayor changed the focus of his questions to get Wood talking about Scott Jackson and Alonzo Walling.

"Do you know Walling?" The mayor asked.

"No, sir."

"Never saw him?"

"I saw a tintype of him when Jackson was up home."

"Would you recognize that picture if you were to see it?"

"I think I would."

At this point, the mayor interrupted the formal questioning and sent an officer to fetch the police photograph of Alonzo Walling. The occupants of the room began to talk quietly among themselves. An *Enquirer* reporter tried to have a few private words with Will Wood, but Attorney Grant intervened and would not allow it. The reporter asked him why he couldn't speak with the boy.

Grant responded, "Because I have just learned that an affidavit has been sworn against him, and I did not know that until just now."

The room erupted. Sheriff Plummer had promised Reverend Wood, in the presence of his attorney, that Will was needed in Cincinnati only to bring testimony against Scott Jackson and that he was not a suspect. Colonel Deitsch explained that a warrant had been issued for Wood's arrest two days prior, and he had heard enough from Will Wood's own mouth to charge him with aiding a criminal operation.

Delos Wood and his attorney argued that they had come to Cincinnati voluntarily on the condition that Will would not be arrested. Sheriff Plummer, his reputation at stake, sided with the Indiana faction. The mayor argued that a Cincinnati warrant would not be ignored, regardless of promises made by a Kentucky sheriff. Judge Gregg issued the warrant, and only he could stop its enforcement.

The mayor agreed to telephone Judge Gregg, who, after hearing both sides, proposed a compromise. Will Wood was to be booked on the charge of aiding an illegal abortion but would be released in the custody of his father and not held in jail. That night while Jackson and Walling lay on their hard cots in Central Station's basement cells, Will Wood slept on a featherbed in his father's room at the Grand Hotel.

At the end of another long day, three men were under arrest for murder and related crimes, and the police boasted of making great progress in the case. But none of the stories told that day rang true, and they all still provided more questions than answers. Walling said Jackson murdered Pearl in cold blood—just what the mayor wanted to hear—but what proof did he offer? He spoke of Jackson's gruesome comments before Pearl arrived, but when it came to actual events, he knew nothing. Jackson and Pearl were not even together the last time Walling saw her.

Walling said Pearl was pregnant, but neither Jackson nor Wood knew which was the father. Was that a motive for bloody murder? Jackson was clearly the smartest of the three and more likely to talk his way out of a paternity problem than resort to violence.

Jackson said that Wood alone was the author of Pearl's misfortune. As a favor to a friend, he enlisted Walling to procure the abortion, and there his involvement ended—he was nothing more than a go-between. But abortion was a serious crime, why would Walling put himself at risk to help Wood? Walling had no connection to Will Wood or to Pearl Bryan. Was his loyalty to Jackson that strong?

And the perfidious Will Wood, who arranged the abortion and stuck by Pearl, at least as far as the train station. Did he put himself at risk for the sake of his poor cousin who was violated by the evil Scott Jackson? Or was he counting on his friend Dusty to get him out of a bad scrape?

Three men knew that Pearl had come to Cincinnati for an abortion. What happened after she arrived was anyone's guess.

4 LEAVING GREENCASTLE

With Reverend Wood's promise to bring his son back to Cincinnati when his case was called, Will Wood was released to his father's custody. Father and son boarded the next train to Indiana, away from the sin and danger of the dirty city and back to the safety of Greencastle. Reverend Wood was still angry at the way the Cincinnati police had broken their promise, arresting his son after tricking him into incriminating himself. More than that, he was indignant that they could believe that Will had any but the most tangential connection to the awful tragedy. He took his son's word that all the trouble came from Scott Jackson, an outsider to Greencastle, who had devastated the Bryan family and now threatened his own. Reverend Wood was prepared to cooperate with Cincinnati but not at the expense of his son's freedom or his own reputation. When he was safely home, he would consider his options.

The train rolled through the seemingly endless expanse of Cincinnati, past the blighted neighborhoods that grew at the edge of the tracks, through railyards and stockyards, finally past the fringe of the city into Ohio farmland. As the train approached Indiana, the rolling hills of Ohio gave way to Indiana's flat fields. The Woods changed trains in Indianapolis and took the last leg of their journey through snow-covered fields so barren and lifeless in the February cold that they could have been traveling through a desert. Then in the evening twilight, the buildings of Greencastle appeared like a mirage in the wasteland.

Greencastle was just a fraction of the size of Newport, Kentucky, where Pearl Bryan's body was found, but even in the dead of winter, it felt more vibrant and alive. The town served as a marketplace for farmers and hosted thriving factories and foundries. Shops and offices lined the streets surrounding a courthouse and public square, a tranquil piece of greenery in better weather.

The greatest differences between Newport and Greencastle stemmed from the institutions that dominated the towns—Newport lived in the shadow of a military base, while Greencastle is the home of DePauw University. For the sake of the soldiers, Newport provided a prominent and well-lighted vice district; to benefit students, vice in Greencastle was dark and hidden.

Delos Wood and his son had barely walked through the door of their home when they were visited by a group of prominent Greencastle businessmen and civic leaders led by Marshall William Starr, head of Greencastle's police force. They told Reverend Wood, in no uncertain terms, that his son was not safe in Greencastle. The Bryan family said publicly that they held Scott Jackson and Will Wood equally responsible for Pearl's death, and the people of Greencastle would not welcome him back. They were angry about Pearl Bryan's murder and since the first day, hungered for revenge. The sentiment had not diminished; Marshall Starr told Reverend Wood that should the talk turn to action, he did not have the resources to stop a lynch mob. For the safety of his family and property, Wood should take his son away from Greencastle as soon as possible. Later that night Delos and Will Wood discreetly boarded a train back to Cincinnati.

Delos Wood was stunned by the animosity against his son in Greencastle. He was also shocked to learn that many in Greencastle and in Cincinnati believed that he was using the advantage of his high church office to shield his son from prosecution. The father and son returned to Cincinnati and stayed at the Grand Hotel until the preliminary hearing the following week, where Will Wood's trial date was set for February 23. This time, following the hearing, Reverend Wood did not attempt to secure bail for his son. He still believed that Will was innocent of any connection with the crime but was willing to let justice take its course without the hint of favoritism on his part. Following the preliminary hearing, Will Wood was locked in a cell in the Cincinnati jail.

Reverend Wood also agreed to allow Mayor Caldwell to intercept any mail addressed to Will in South Bend and have it forwarded to the Cincinnati police. The first batch of mail included a letter from Scott Jackson, which further indicated Will's complicity. Dated February 5, on Palace Hotel stationery, it appeared to be one of the letters Jackson had written just prior to his arrest.

The letter used a pre-arranged code where Pearl Bryan was referred to as "Bert" and "he" was used in place of "she." The letter was signed with a "D" for Jackson's nickname, Dusty. Especially incriminating was the ease with which Jackson assumed Will Wood's participation in covering up Pearl's death.

Palace Hotel, Cincinnati, O.
February 5, 1896

Hello Bill:

    Write a letter home signed by Bert's name telling the folks that he is somewhere and going to Chicago or some other place; has a position, etc., and that they will advise later about it. Say tired of living at home or anything you want. You know the way he writes. Send it to someone you can trust. How will Smith do at Lafayette? Tell the folks that he has not been at Indianapolis but at Lafayette and travelling about the country. Get the letter off without one second's delay and burn this at once. Stick by your old chum Bill. And I will help you out the same way or some other way some time. Am glad you are having a good time.

D.
Be careful what you write to me.

Prior to the murder, Reverend Delos Wood was held in high regard in Greencastle. He was the presiding elder of the Greencastle Division of the Methodist Episcopal Church, which includes the churches west of Indianapolis from Terre Haute to Layfette. Methodist ministers do not take a vow of poverty, and the Wood family was wealthy and well-connected throughout Indiana. They lived in a large, stately home on Washington Street in the city's finest neighborhood.

Respect for Delos Wood did not, however, extend to his son. Will Wood had been spoiled and precocious as a boy and became a holy terror in adolescence. A liar and a braggart obsessed with the prurient, he would speak endlessly of his romantic conquests and spread malicious rumors about girls he knew. The *Cincinnati Enquirer* summed up Will Wood's Greencastle reputation saying, "The youth is generally recognized as a cigarette fiend of unbalanced mind and of a totally depraved nature." Reverend Wood tried to straighten him out by sending him to college, and promised he would pay for medical school, including two years study in Europe, if Will would graduate from DePauw. He failed at two attempts.

The Woods were related to the Bryan family through Pearl's mother, and the two families were close, but even before the murder, the Bryans had a low opinion of Will and felt that he could not be trusted. When the circumstances of Pearl's death were made known, the Bryans stated without hesitation that even if Jackson wielded the knife, they held Will Wood equally responsible for Pearl's murder.

The Bryans owned a successful dairy farm outside of town and were among the wealthiest and most prominent residents of Putnam County. Alexander Bryan married Susan Farrow in 1848 and moved from Kentucky to Putnam County when central Indiana was still frontier. They settled outside of Greencastle and began farming the land and raising children. Alexander was an active Greenback Republican and with his wife attended the local Methodist Episcopal Church, living strictly by John Wesley's precept: "Earn all you can. Save all you can. Give all you can." They were young and strong and worked the land hard. By 1896, almost a half century later, they owned 275 acres of farmland and had built a spacious home of stone and timber that became known locally as the Bryan mansion. Here they raised their family—nine girls and three boys.

The older children had long since married and moved away. Their eldest son James, 44-years-old in 1896, had a large farm not far from his parents' and three children of his own; his daughter, Minnie, was born the same year as his own youngest brother, Frank. Two of his sisters were already young widows: Mary, who recently opened a dress shop in Greencastle, and Auta who had moved back to the mansion with her two children. Another sister, Jennie, just a year older than Pearl, had died of tuberculosis the previous autumn. Marion and Flora had also died young.

Alexander, now a bearded patriarch in his seventies, left most of the farm work to his son Fred, a husky, commanding and outspoken twenty-five-year-old, and nineteen-year-old Frank, who was as tall, lean, and strong as his brother, but less vocal. Pearl was the youngest daughter of the family, and although her brother Frank was four years younger, Pearl would always be the baby of the family, the one they all would pamper and protect.

Everyone in Greencastle spoke fondly of Pearl. She was petite, about five foot four with an attractive figure, a subtly embracing smile, and blonde hair that gave off red highlights in the sun. Her complexion was pale with a hint of freckles. While not a classic beauty, Pearl had a homespun prettiness and a winning personality that charmed everyone. She did not have the chiseled features and aquiline nose shared by most of Alexander Bryan's children. Pearl inherited her mother's soft, round face, the only one of Alexander and Susan Bryan's twelve children to have her mother's blue eyes.

Pearl had many suitors, but she seldom went out with the same boy twice, as if she were afraid to be tied to a small-town boy. Most of those in Pearl's high school class went to work or married after graduation, but Pearl had bigger dreams. She applied to study music at DePauw University and was accepted. It was a rare opportunity for an Indiana farm girl, but Pearl had the support of her teachers, and there was no question that her family could afford the tuition. She was smart, industrious, enthusiastic. Everyone believed she would make Greencastle proud.

Pearl Bryan and her second cousin Will Wood had been close since early childhood, and after the death of her sister Jennie the previous autumn, Will became Pearl's only confidant. Though Pearl was popular in Greencastle with many friends among her former classmates, she kept her secrets to herself. Pearl was aware of Will's reputation and had herself been the subject of some of his malicious rumors. She had been so angry that she snubbed him for a time, refusing to even acknowledge him on the street. But it did not last. Will Wood remained the person she trusted most. When Pearl became pregnant and was desperately looking for a way out, Will Wood was the only person in Greencastle who knew her secret.

Next door to the Woods' house on Washington Street was the home of Scott Jackson's family. The house was owned by Professor Edwin Post, husband of Scott Jackson's half-sister Mary. He was a classical scholar at DePauw, soon to become dean of the university. Scott Jackson's mother moved into the house several years earlier after retiring from a literary career in New York City. Scott followed soon after.

Will Wood was 17 years old when Scott Jackson moved in next door, and Wood was instantly drawn to the stranger from the east. Jackson was a sporting man, sophisticated and worldly with a natural way with women— exactly what young Will aspired to be. Though Jackson was seven years older, the two became close, and Wood went out of his way to impress his good friend. When the news came out that Will Wood had sent Pearl to Cincinnati for an abortion, speculation in Greencastle was divided over who was responsible—was Wood helping Jackson out of a jam or counting on his idol to save his own reputation.

The circumstances of Pearl's death interrupted life in Greencastle, and Will Wood was not the only resident forced to leave town as a result of the murder. Gus Early, the telegraph office manager who brought Pearl's name to the police, was fired by Western Union. Early had divulged the contents of telegrams sent and received by Fred Bryan, in violation of company policy. While everyone was glad that Pearl Bryan's body had been identified and her possible killer named, Western Union was not an arm of the police, and customers needed assurance that their messages would not be made public. Reportedly, after being dismissed by Western Union, Early moved to Richmond, Indiana, and went to work for another telegraph company.

Early was a high school classmate of Pearl Bryan and Will Wood and part of an elite circle of Greencastle young people who remained close after graduation. Though considerably older than the others, Scott Jackson was a part of this circle as well. During the parties and outings of the previous year, Pearl and Scott had apparently formed a relationship closer than their friends realized. No one in Greencastle was aware of a stronger bond between them than casual friendship. In fact, when the subject of Pearl's pregnancy was raised, many found it easier to believe that Will Wood was the father.

Wood had told his friends that he had "a soft snap" with Pearl Bryan, meaning he could get what he wanted from her with little effort. They did not believe him; before the murder Pearl's reputation was unblemished, and Wood was well-known for telling slanderous stories. Wood was insistent. He told his friend Homer Newhouse that he had gone to her house early one morning the previous summer when Pearl's parents had taken her sister Jennie to New Mexico to treat her tuberculosis. Frank and Fred were working in the field, and no one was home except Pearl who was still in bed. He let himself in, went up to Pearl's room, and got into bed with her as he had done when they were children. He told Newhouse he was intimate with Pearl on this occasion and several others.

Homer Newhouse was also present at the telegraph office when Wood told Gus Early about the prescription Jackson sent to end the pregnancy. William T. Grooms, another of their circle was present as well, and Wood said to him, "I am in tough luck. What would you do if you had a girl in trouble?" Grooms replied that it would depend on who she is. Wood told him to go to hell but would not say who the girl was. After the news came out, it was clear to his friends that Wood had been talking about Pearl Bryan and that he was the man responsible for her pregnancy.

Several of Pearl's female classmates who were interviewed together in Greencastle declared that they still held Pearl in the highest esteem. She was a girl of the most amiable disposition, they said. Too amiable, in fact, and inclined to yield to the requests or urgings of others. The young women were overcome with grief and indignation, anxious to have the killers pay for their crime. One woman declared that she would lead a lynching bee herself if those responsible could be brought back to Greencastle. The rest of the group loudly agreed to follow her.

No one in Greencastle seemed to know Scott Jackson very well, but everyone who spoke of him knew that he and Will Wood were close friends. After his arrest, Wood called Scott Jackson an evil man who had a bad influence over everyone he met, but at seventeen, he saw Jackson's life as a valid alternative to the dreary world of medical school that loomed in his future. Jackson came from a good family, but he had no trade, and in Wood's view, he lived a fast, carefree life without one.

Will Wood introduced Scott Jackson to two family members who would ultimately set Jackson's destiny. The first was Dr. Richard Gillespie, the son of another of Mrs. Bryan's cousins, and a recent graduate of the Indianapolis School of Dentistry. On Will Wood's recommendation, Scott took a job assisting Dr. Gillespie in his office, and there decided that dentistry would be a perfect career—respectable, not very demanding, and a good way to meet girls. It was later rumored in Greencastle that Dr. Gillespie's dental chair was where Jackson had seduced Pearl Bryan—the second of Wood's relatives to seal his fate.

Will introduced Pearl to Jackson at a Christmas party at the Bryans' home in 1894. According to Will, it was at Pearl's request. Many of their friends remembered that party. the Bryan home had a huge hearth, warm and welcoming, where they burned hickory logs. In the warm glow of the fire, Will introduced Jackson to all his friends that night and even introduced him to Pearl's parents. The Bryans remembered Jackson visiting the house several times after that, always in the company of their nephew. Jackson says he took Pearl riding once or twice that summer, but they were never romantically involved.

According to Jackson, that autumn, shortly before he left for Cincinnati, Wood told him that he and Pearl had been intimate, but he said he would not mind if Jackson called on her as well. "Why don't you go to see Pearl more than you do?" Wood asked, "It's a good thing." Jackson said that he did not take him up on the offer.

Whoever was responsible, Will Wood was the only person in town who knew that Pearl was pregnant. He had already admitted to giving Pearl the prescription from Scott Jackson and apparently had shown it to others. Whether it had been for Pearl's sake alone or out of self-interest, Wood had worked hard to arrange the end of Pearl's pregnancy. He and Pearl were both relieved when Jackson said she should come to Cincinnati for an abortion.

Despite what Will said in the mayor's office, Pearl's family verified that it was Will Wood who took Pearl to the train station the day she left Greencastle. She had told her parents that she was going to visit Lucy Fisher, a childhood friend who had moved from Greencastle to Indianapolis. Wood made all the arrangements with Jackson and may have told Pearl that he would accompany her to Cincinnati. But on the day they were to leave, family commitments prevented him from joining her—or so he said. Pearl, alone, would travel to Indianapolis, and there buy a ticket to Cincinnati. Will took her to the train station, but he had to pick up his father, who would be arriving on the same train Pearl would be taking out of Greencastle. As they waited at the station, he told her not to worry, Scott would be expecting her and would be there to meet her when the train arrived. But Wood's letter to Jackson had only said what day she was coming; he had not thought to include the time she would arrive or the train line she would be taking.

Pearl had been to Indianapolis only once before with her high school debating team, but she never traveled alone and never as far away as Cincinnati. It was not Pearl's nature to start any venture with so little preparation. If she had been expecting Will to guide her, this solitary journey would have caused her much anxiety.

Her fears welled up to near panic when she pulled into the Grand Central Depot in Cincinnati and saw no sign of Scott Jackson. She stood with her bags inside the terminal and watched as all her fellow passengers were met by friends and family and departed, until no one was left but a handful of railway personnel, and the great building was silent. Pearl picked up her bags and went outside to the dark and dirty city. Leaning in the doorway near a gaslight, she began to sob.

5 JACKSON AND WALLING

Through weeks of interrogation Jackson and Walling held fast to their stories—neither man saw Pearl after Wednesday, neither knew what happened to her, but each assumed the other was responsible for her death. Walling's story was weakening a bit. He backed away from saying Jackson intended from the first to kill Pearl in cold blood. He admitted that he and Jackson had discussed abortion before Pearl came to Cincinnati, and he said to Jackson, "Tell her to come up, and I will first take a peep at her."

On Jackson's instructions, Walling went to one of the railroad depots on Monday, trying to meet up with Pearl when they did not know what railroad line she would be taking. On Tuesday he went with Jackson to the Indiana House but remained outside and did not see Pearl. Jackson asked him again to perform the abortion, but Walling refused, saying it was too risky. He had no idea where Jackson took Pearl on Wednesday and could not say whether an abortion was attempted. On Saturday, Jackson told him that Pearl was dead and persuaded him to take a valise of her clothing to the college and keep it for a time in his locker. Later, Jackson took the valise and disposed of the clothes himself.

The police were inclined to believe Walling's story as far as it went but still thought he had much more to tell. Whether he was directly involved or not, they were sure he knew exactly what happened and could tell them where the head was. He was still protecting Scott Jackson, and it baffled everyone that Walling would risk prosecution for murder to protect a classmate that he had only known well for one semester.

Jackson and Walling were among the first Cincinnati prisoners to be processed using the Bertillon system. Recently introduced in America, the Bertillon system classified criminals using formal photographs along with precise and detailed measurements of the face and body to replace the haphazard "rogues' gallery" approach most police departments were using. While the methods of the Bertillon system are inherently scientific, the measurement process, particularly of the head, was strikingly similar to that of the more arcane study of phrenology, which used the size and shape of a person's head to determine his character. Phrenology, once all the rage, was out of fashion by the 1890s, but Cincinnati did have a practicing phrenologist, Dr. S. E. Hyndman, who performed his measurements on the heads of Jackson and Walling, and provided a detailed report of his findings, summarizing their characters:

> My analysis of Scott Jackson reveals a bold, fearless, intense organization, with a perverted amativeness, and unwise gratification of this faculty has changed his physical, intellectual and moral condition and debased his higher mental qualities. He readily and quickly reasons from cause to effect; is intensely selfish in whatever he does; would mislead anyone to assist himself and has strong perceptive powers. He is a good planner and a fearless executer; once his mind is made up to do a thing, neither God, nor man, nor the devil, would prevent the attempt, every faculty would be perverted.

> Alonzo Walling is easily led in the direction of friendship and in this, he would often do things which his better nature would revolt against. He would not go back on a friend until the very last, and then only to save his own life if he had promised to stand by him. He likes the society of the viscous better than that of the higher order. He would plunge into danger and calculate the chances afterward. His standard of morals is not of a higher order, his perceptive powers are small and if he were to be influenced, he would have to be managed through flattery.

Dr. Hyndman's assessment was probably influenced as much by public opinion as it was by the bumps on their heads. In Cincinnati, Scott Jackson was viewed as strong, self-centered, and fundamentally evil. Alonzo Walling was dull, weak-willed, and subservient to Jackson against his own best interest. Jackson was the master manipulator who seduced the farm girl, persuaded the preacher's son to send her to Cincinnati, and enlisted the country boy to help kill her. Some believed that Jackson had hypnotic power to impose his will on others and attributed that power to a property that even phrenology could not measure: his evil eye.

Every written description of Scott Jackson referred to the power of his eyes. They were steel blue, some said violet, and had a mesmerizing power that he used to beguile Pearl Bryan into an intimate affair that she kept secret from her friends and family. She was—referencing the most popular novel of the time—Trilby to his Svengali.

The intensity of Scott Jackson's eyes is clearly visible in his police photograph. Though photographs were still a rarity in newspapers in 1896, illustrations and line-drawn portraits were plentiful, and illustrators seemed to relish drawing the handsome Scott Jackson. His face appeared many times in the *Enquirer*, the *Tribune*, and the *Post* and was reproduced in newspapers across the country. Whether depicting him as dapper and refined or sallow and depraved, Jackson's portraits were always the focal point of the page, and those eyes were always the focus of the portrait.

As the story and the pictures spread from Cincinnati, they attracted the attention of women all over the country, some of whom felt compelled to write to Jackson and profess their love for him. They wrote to Cincinnati police as well, begging them to acknowledge what to them was so clear, that Scott Jackson was innocent.

In the city itself, the pictures had an even more profound effect, drawing crowds to the jail to see Jackson firsthand. While Jackson and Walling were being held in the Cincinnati jail, below Central Station, outsiders had almost unlimited access to them. Reporters would visit the cells at any time day or night. Ordinary citizens would stop by for the entertainment value or to satisfy some morbid curiosity as if the prison were a dime museum. A group of young girls started visiting Jackson's cell and brought him things the benevolent societies would not: candy, cigars, and fresh collars and cuffs for Court appearances. They had originally visited both Jackson and Walling, but Walling's attitude was unpredictable, and he was not always a gracious host. Jackson, on the other hand, was cordial to everyone, and even at his lowest moments, he was never too despondent to chat with a pretty girl.

Jackson and Walling made an odd pair. Scott Jackson, 26 years old, with a slender frame and delicate features, was an affable and confident speaker. Walling, seven years younger, was ruggedly built, relaxed, and taciturn. Each had lost his father at an early age, but beyond that, their backgrounds had little in common.

Scott Jackson's father, Commodore John Jackson, had moved the family from Maine to Jersey City, New Jersey, where he commanded several commercial vessels. He died, leaving the family financially sound. His mother, Sarah, was active in New York literary circles and at one time was president of Sorosis, an organization of professional women.

Alonzo Walling's father, a farmer, died when he was three years old. His mother, Sarah, moved with her three sons from Greenfield, Indiana to Oxford, Ohio. Like Sarah Jackson, she had raised her family alone.

It was purely by chance that Scott Jackson and Alonzo Walling became roommates in the fall of 1895. They were both new students at the Ohio College of Dental Surgery, but the previous year both attended the Indianapolis School of Dentistry. There they were classmates who knew each other just well enough to nod hello, but when they met again in Cincinnati, they greeted each other as old friends, both happy to see a familiar face in a strange city.

Sarah Walling had high hopes for her youngest son, Alonzo, and with the help of her wealthy brother, James Faucett, she was able to send him to college. Walling had enjoyed the schoolwork, but he found life in Indianapolis cold and lonely. He missed his friends and family in Ohio and wanted to return. Together, the family decided on a compromise. Alonzo would transfer to the Ohio College of Dental Surgery in Cincinnati, much closer to home.

Scott Jackson had a reputation as a good student in Indianapolis, but one who burned the candle at both ends. He spent as much time in barrooms as in classrooms. On New Year's Eve, he was arrested with a bunch of drunken revelers when the group turned rowdy in an Indianapolis brothel. His mother, a member of the Woman's Christian Temperance Union, withdrew him in shame from the Indianapolis School and took him back to Greencastle.

Dental college was supposed to be a fresh start for Scott Jackson, who had a serious run-in with the law back East. He was working as a shipping clerk for the Pennsylvania Railroad Company in Jersey City, New Jersey, and as he rose within the railroad company, his fortune became linked to that of his supervisor, Alexander Letts. Jackson's job included posting invoices and waybills and, as Jackson told it, Letts proposed that Jackson delay the postings temporarily, so they could use the money for their own purposes. As they began siphoning off money, they gained reputations as high-fliers at the racetrack, but they never put any money back.

Jackson was convinced that his good fortune was permanent, and he became engaged to marry a young woman he had recently met. Gradually, the embezzled sum reached $23,000, a small fortune at the time, and the Pennsylvania Railroad took notice. Pennsylvania Railroad filed charges against both Jackson and Letts, and as the company continued to amass evidence, they gave Jackson an ultimatum: turn state's evidence against Letts or stand trial. Jackson later admitted to testifying against Letts but claimed he had never, in fact, been arrested in New Jersey. Whatever the circumstance, Letts was sentenced to three years in a New Jersey penitentiary, and Scott Jackson walked free.

He may have avoided a prison term, but he lost his livelihood and, as a result, lost his fiancée as well. He left Jersey City for the brighter lights of Manhattan, where he tried his hand at sales, peddling patent medicine and corn cures. When this did not pay, he headed west to Greencastle to throw himself on the mercies of his mother. There he spent an idle year at her expense before eventually enrolling in the Indianapolis School of Dentistry in the fall of 1894.

Mrs. Jackson was pleased when Scott told her of his decision to become a dentist. She was happy to foot the bill for Indianapolis School of Dentistry if it meant that her son had found a direction in his life. But that venture failed on New Year's Eve, and she brooded while Scott spent another nine months idle in Greencastle. Finally, she agreed to let him try again, this time at the Ohio College of Dental Surgery.

After his reunion with Alonzo Walling in Cincinnati, Jackson found that he and Walling had more in common than dentistry; both liked to frequent saloons, and both enjoyed the company of loose women. While Jackson was in Greencastle that Christmas, Walling found the perfect rooming house at 222 West Ninth—a short walk to the Dental College and an even shorter walk to the dives and brothels on Longworth and George Streets. When Jackson returned, Walling agreed to share his room and the landlady, Miss Rose McNevin, was happy to have another roomer.

Fred Albion, a barber who lived in the same house, would often join Jackson and Walling when they went carousing. When money was scarce, the three would pool their cash to rush a growler and spend the night drinking beer and playing cards at Lawrence's Barber Shop where Albion worked. Fred Albion would later say that he was friends with both, but he liked Walling better because he was just a plain fellow. Jackson would sometimes put on airs.

Scott Jackson and Alonzo Walling grew to be closer to each other than they were to anyone else in the city. According to the other dental students, they were inseparable. In school or out, one was seldom seen without the other. Even when they went out with girls, they often went together. When Walling had a girlfriend, Jackson urged her to bring a friend for him, and the four would go out together.

They became true friends in a very short time, but that friendship seemed to end abruptly with their arrests. As the police had hoped, once in custody, they turned on each other, but not in a way that the police found helpful. Each accused the other of causing Pearl's death but offered no details to back up their accusations.

The Cincinnati Police were convinced that Scott Jackson was the murderer—he had a direct connection with Pearl Bryan in Greencastle, and he admitted that she had come to Cincinnati to see him. His motive for the murder was Pearl's pregnancy. With Pearl disposed of and her identity hidden, Jackson would avoid the consequences of fathering her child. The truth was so obvious to Mayor Caldwell and Colonel Deitsch that they never wavered in their conviction that they could sweat a confession from Scott Jackson.

But Jackson steadfastly refused to admit to any knowledge of Pearl's death. Yes, Pearl had come to Cincinnati for an abortion, but he had no idea how she died. He helped arrange the abortion for the sake of Will Wood, the true author of Pearl's misfortune. Walling was to handle the operation, but, by agreement, he had told Jackson none of the details. As hard as the interrogators pressed, Jackson would not yield. He would not confess.

Walling at first revealed his roommate's intention to murder Pearl Bryan, then later admitted that Jackson was trying to procure an abortion for her. But like Jackson, Walling could not say how Pearl died. He had no idea what happened to her after he saw her on Wednesday.

Neither man would admit to knowing what really happened in the three days leading up to Pearl's death. Clearly, one was lying, but which? What if both were lying? While each man put the blame on the other, both stories conveniently end on Wednesday, and neither could say what happened after. Whether intentionally or not, they had stymied the police with stories that could not be challenged or disproved. The authorities were sure of Scott Jackson's guilt and had hoped that Alonzo Walling would be a strong witness against him. That was not to be, and they had little choice but to build a murder case around both men.

6 FUGITIVES FROM JUSTICE

With questioning of Jackson and Walling at a stalemate, the police continued building a case on circumstantial evidence. It was not long before they turned up witnesses who had seen Pearl Bryan in Cincinnati, but at first, their stories tended to verify what the prisoners already said, adding little new information.

A hack driver told police that he picked up a pretty blonde girl at Grand Central Depot on the night of Monday, January 27. She was distressed that no one had been at the depot to meet her. Her friend had not shown up, and she did not know his address or how to get in touch with him. He was a student at the dental school, she told the driver, and he took her there, but the building was closed for the night. His letters to her were written on stationery from the Palace Hotel. Perhaps, he lived there. They stopped at the Palace Hotel, and the girl went inside, but she came back even more despondent. He was not there, and she had not brought enough money to stay there herself. The driver recommended the Indiana House, a moderately priced hotel near Fountain Square. He promised to pick her up the next morning so they could go to the college in the daylight. She agreed.

The girl was in better spirits when he picked her up the next morning. They went to the dental college, and she gave him a note to take in to Scott Jackson. Jackson relayed a message back to Pearl. He was in class at the moment but would meet her at her hotel that afternoon.

The night clerk at the Indiana House, remembered the blonde woman who arrived about 10:00 Monday night. She concealed her identity, registering as Mabel Stanley—Stanley being the married name of Pearl's sister Mary. He remembered her as modest and demure and somewhat timorous about sleeping alone in the strange room. A hotel employee escorted her to room 114, and she would not allow him to leave until he checked under the beds and assured her that no one else had a key to the room.

The next morning, she had breakfast in the dining room. The chief dining room girl, remembered her guest as someone who took great care in her appearance, wearing her hair in a well-coiffed Circe knot. She thought the woman's clothes were good quality but not fashionable by Cincinnati standards.

When the coach arrived, she left without finishing her breakfast. The woman returned late Tuesday night, accompanied to the door by an unidentified man. About 11:00 Wednesday morning, she checked out and was not seen again at the Indiana House.

As the police canvassed the neighborhood around Ninth Street, they learned that Jackson and Walling were regulars at Wallingford's saloon on the corner of George and Plum Streets, where they were known as Doc and Wally. Wallingford's had doors to the barroom on George and Plum and a separate ladies' entrance on George Street. The barroom was typical—dimly lit, sawdust on the floor, a scattering of tables, and a long bar with a brass rail where men stood drinking beer and whiskey. The ladies' entrance opened into a separate section they called the wine room, which had tables inside curtained booths or stalls lining two walls. Velvet portieres hanging in front of each booth could be closed to allow the occupants full privacy. A man could take a woman into a stall, and no one would know or care what went on behind the curtain. If he came in without a woman, one or two were always available.

The owner, Dave Wallingford, remembered that Scott Jackson had come into his saloon with a girl on Friday night, January 31, the night of the murder. Jackson took the girl to one of the booths, then stopped at the bar. He borrowed two dollars from Wallingford, promising to repay him on Sunday, had a shot of whiskey at the bar, and ordered a glass of beer and a sarsaparilla to be sent over to the wine room. Wallingford's porter, Allen Johnson, saw the girl when he delivered the drinks. He noticed her black cloak and black hat with pink flowers and came away with the impression that she was higher-classed than the girls they were used to.

Wallingford and Johnson both saw Alonzo Walling enter the saloon that evening. He stopped for a moment at the booth where Jackson and the girl sat, then left. Around 7:00 p.m., Allen Johnson was taking some trash to the alley, and he saw Walling return in a black curtained surrey—the newspapers usually referred to it as a cab, meaning a hired vehicle. Jackson and the girl left through the ladies' entrance and opened the surrey door and went inside. The driver, a white man Johnson did not recognize, was holding the reins when Walling climbed up onto the box beside him.

Jackson admitted that he had been to Wallingford's with Pearl, but it had been Tuesday night, not Friday. It could not have been Friday because Fred Albion had shaved him on Friday afternoon and Wallingford had said Jackson was wearing a full beard as usual when he saw him. They did not leave in a cab. He took Pearl by trolley to the elevated railway to see the lights of the city from Mt. Auburn. Walling also remembered being briefly at Wallingford's on Tuesday night. Scott and Pearl had asked him to stay, but he was afraid he would end up spending more money than he could afford.

The police questioned everyone regarding Jackson's beard. Fred Albion remembered shaving it off in his shop Friday afternoon, as did his boss Mr. Lawrence. The landlady, Rose McNevin, and her nieces remembered seeing Jackson Friday evening and commenting on how peculiar he looked without his beard. Wallingford and Johnson, however, did not remember it that way. The night they saw Jackson with a woman, he looked the same way they had always known him, with a full beard.

Jackson believed that this proved the day was not Friday, but the police ignored the discrepancy. Wallingford and Johnson saw Jackson, Walling, and Pearl together on Friday night, and that was exactly what they needed. Regardless of what may have transpired after Wednesday morning, the three were together again on Friday night. Jackson and Walling were both lying.

As the week progressed, more witnesses came forward who had seen and spoken to Pearl Bryan in Cincinnati. A salesman at Hockett Brothers Pianos on Fourth Street had incontrovertible proof that Pearl had been in the store on Wednesday afternoon. She had come in alone and played several of the pianos they had on display. He had enjoyed her playing and remembered having a pleasant exchange with her. She told him she was hoping to persuade her parents to buy a piano, and she left him her name and address, as well as her sister's address as she may be interested as well. This was information that could only have come from Pearl herself and was in her own handwriting.

When Walling was first questioned, he said that Jackson had considered poisoning Pearl with cocaine. H. C. Ulen, who had a drugstore on West Sixth Street, confirmed that Scott Jackson had purchased 17 grains (just over one gram) of cocaine on January 29, two days before the murder. Cocaine was used as an anesthetic by students at the dental college, and they were required to provide their own supplies, so Jackson's purchase was not unusual.

Sale of cocaine was not regulated, and the newspaper reported on "cocaine fiends" prowling the streets of Cincinnati after the saloons closed. But cocaine use by physicians was still relatively new, and there was some dispute as to the drug's effects and what would constitute an overdose. One physician told the *Enquirer* that an ordinary internal dose was one eighth to one quarter of a grain, but a hypodermic administration of one quarter grain had, in rare cases, resulted in convulsions and death.

A search of Jackson's room had uncovered a hypodermic syringe among his possessions. Jackson may have injected Pearl with cocaine, but more likely, he had put it in her sarsaparilla at Wallingford's. Dr. W.H. Crane, who analyzed the contents of Pearl's stomach for the Campbell County coroner, found one-quarter grain of cocaine and believed he would find more.

After each witness was interviewed by the police, they were taken to the jail to see if they could identify Jackson or Walling. Dave Wallingford and Allen Johnson, of course, easily identified their regular customers. The druggist identified Jackson as the man who bought cocaine.

The piano salesman saw Pearl meet a man on Fourth Street after leaving his store but did not get a look at his face. Tuesday night, when Pearl returned to the Indiana House, the night clerk noticed she was accompanied by a man not much taller than herself, but the man had stood in the shadows and the clerk could not say whether or not it was Jackson. Jackson and Walling both contradicted any witness who saw them with Pearl after Wednesday morning and flatly denied being in Wallingford's saloon on any night but Tuesday that week.

One afternoon Jackson was brought up from his cell to be identified by a plump woman dressed all in black. For an instant, their eyes met, and the ever-present reporters saw a flash of recognition cross Jackson's face. The woman then turned to Colonel Deitsch and said, clearly and firmly, "Yes."

She was Mrs. Plymouth Weeks, a spiritualistic medium, who lived and did business on Ninth Street, several blocks west of Miss McNevin's rooming house. Since the murder, there had been no shortage of witnesses ready to bring evidence from the spiritual world. Professional mediums claimed to communicate with Pearl; a Hindu mystic visited the murder site and had visions; a child in Chicago saw, in a dream, the location of the buried head and was taken seriously enough to initiate digging. Mrs. Weeks, however, was the only spiritualist to have seen Pearl Bryan and Scott Jackson in the physical world.

The young couple had come to her door on Thursday, January 30, and asked for a reading. "They were both blondes," Mrs. Weeks told reporters after her meeting with Colonel Deitsch. "Which struck me as peculiar, as from their action, I judged that they were lovers, and the choice is usually by contraries. Something in the woman's manner led me to believe that she was in trouble. She had a haunted expression about her eyes and was timid and apparently in mental agony."

Mrs. Weeks said that the woman asked if she and the man could have a sitting together, but the medium told her she never gave sittings to two people at once. After some hesitation, the woman agreed to sit alone. Weeks described the sitting:

> I took her across the hall to my séance room, and before putting out the light, I again scanned her closely. She was a pretty girl, only something in her make-up suggest to me that she was from the country. I thought I noticed signs of approaching maternity, but I said nothing. When she sank down on the chair I had placed for her, she appeared to be on the verge of hysteria, and I set the music box, which

sat on the table beside me, going. She gave a few convulsive sighs, and the séance began. I remember nothing further until I was awakened from my trance by the girl's sobs.

I questioned her about what had happened, and after some hesitancy, she said, "The spirit of my dead sister Jennie came to me, and I asked her what I should do. The spirit advised me to go home to my parents. But I told her that this was impossible, as my uncle and my parents would not permit me to stay home."

As she said this, the girl began to wring her hands and sob hysterically. I tried to comfort her when she suddenly broke out saying:

"Oh, won't you help me?"

I did not ask what her trouble was. I guessed at it. I asked if she was sure it was the spirit of her sister that had spoken to her, and she replied "Yes, I'm sure it was."

"Then," said I, "follow her advice and go home."

"Doc will never marry me, and I shall be disgraced," she exclaimed

I tried to comfort her and finally succeeded in some degree. During the conversation, I had broken up the circle and relit the gas. I was moved almost to tears myself at the sad plight of this poor girl and did not try to pry into her misery any further. The scene was not new to me, but somehow, I felt more than a passing interest in the helpless girl.

Finally, after she seemed to have regained control of herself, she viewed the situation in a more practical light and asked me whether I knew anyone who would take care of an erring creature like herself and help end her trouble. The question was asked too pointedly to be misunderstood, and I told her that I had never engaged in that kind of business, and even if I desired to do so, I would have no room for her. I also told her that I knew of no one who would undertake such a responsibility. She began to weep again, and once more, I had to comfort her.

"Why don't you go home and do as your sister tells you?" I repeated.

"I can't. I can't," was all she would answer.

Weeks led the girl back to the sitting room where her gentleman friend sat by the window reading the newspaper. She asked the man if he desired a sitting and he declined.

Weeks explained that the matter would have passed from her memory, and she would not have connected the couple with the murder if she hadn't read that the victim had a sister named Jennie. She also remembered that man called the woman Pearlie and she called him Doc. When Weeks saw Scott Jackson at the police station, she was convinced he was the man.

There were reasons to doubt this story. Spiritual apparitions aside, Mrs. Weeks offered no information that was not already printed in the newspapers. The fact that Pearl had a dead sister named Jennie, that Pearl was a country girl who was pregnant, even that both she and Jackson were blonde, had all been in news stories in several Cincinnati papers. The names she used are a problem too. Jackson was known as Doc in Cincinnati, but Pearl would use his Greencastle nickname, Dusty, and no one in Greencastle or Cincinnati had previously referred to her as Pearlie. But none of this mattered to the police, who were happy to find a witness that put Pearl in Jackson's company on Thursday.

Though pleased to have another eyewitness, the police did not want to delve too deeply into Mrs. Weeks's story. If it were true, then Pearl had likely come for more than a spiritual reading. In Cincinnati, as in other cities at the time, spiritual mediums often included abortion among their services. In her statement, Weeks had made veiled references to abortion and made sure to distance herself. Scott Jackson and Pearl Bryan may have been shopping for an operation in Cincinnati that Thursday. While all now admitted that Pearl had come to Cincinnati for an abortion, no one wanted to focus on any event that did not point to murder in Kentucky.

One theory of the murder speculated that Pearl had died as a result of an abortion in Cincinnati. Jackson and Walling had taken her body to Kentucky, and there removed her head to avoid identification. If true, it meant that Jackson and Walling could be charged with nothing greater than manslaughter. Everyone wanted these men to hang, and the only way that would happen legally would be on the charge of first-degree murder in Kentucky.

As the Cincinnati Police worked on tracking Pearl Bryan's movements while in their city, Sheriff Plummer was at work making sure that murderers would be tried and executed in Campbell County, Kentucky. From the beginning, Plummer had taken a personal interest in the case, appalled that such a gruesome murder had taken place in his jurisdiction. As details of the circumstances emerged, Plummer held a special hatred for Scott Jackson, the arrogant city boy from the East who had treated this innocent country girl so shabbily then brought her to the Highlands to finish her off. Jackson and his accomplice must hang in Kentucky under color of law, and Sheriff Plummer made that his personal crusade.

On February 11, Campbell County Coroner Tingley began an inquest into the murder on John Lock's farm on the morning of February 1. After two days of testimony from the autopsy physicians, Cincinnati witnesses, and lawmen from both sides of the river, the coroner's jury concluded that the murdered woman was Pearl Bryan of Greencastle, Indiana, that cocaine had been administered to her for reasons unknown, that she had been decapitated while alive, and that she was last seen in the company of Scott Jackson and

Alonzo Walling when she got into a cab with them in Cincinnati.

A Campbell County grand jury heard the same testimony and on February 14, issued the following indictment:

Indictment.
The Commonwealth of Kentucky Against Scott Jackson and Alonzo Walling:

The grand jury of Campbell County, in the name and by the authority of the Commonwealth of Kentucky, accuses Scott Jackson and Alonzo Walling of the crime of murder, committed as follow, viz.:

The said Scott Jackson and Alonzo Walling on February 1, 1896, before the finding of this indictment in the county aforesaid, did willfully, feloniously and with malice aforethought, kill and murder Pearl Bryan by the said Scott Jackson, with a knife or other sharp instrument, cutting off the head of the said Pearl Bryan so that the said Pearl Bryan did then and there die.

The said Alonzo Walling being then and there present, aiding and assisting the said Scott Jackson in the killing and murdering of the said Pearl Bryan, he holding the person of the said Pearl Bryan whilst the cutting as aforesaid was done by Scott Jackson.

Against the peace and dignity of the Commonwealth of Kentucky.

M.R. Lockhart
Attorney for Commonwealth

The indictment was remarkably explicit—Walling held her down while Jackson cut off her head—especially remarkable since there were no eyewitnesses to the crime and no evidence that either man had ever been in Kentucky.

The police in Cincinnati had agreed that the murder occurred in Kentucky, and after the Campbell County indictment, they dropped the Ohio murder charge against Jackson and Walling and charged them as fugitives from justice. They would remain in custody in Cincinnati until they could be extradited to Kentucky to stand trial there.

The task of implementing the extradition fell on Sheriff Plummer, who shuttled between Frankfort, Kentucky, and Columbus, Ohio, trying to convince two reluctant governors that Jackson and Walling needed to be transferred across state lines for trial. At issue was the safety of the prisoners; neither governor wanted to be responsible for turning them over to a lynch mob.

Even before the indictment, Jackson and Walling believed their extradition to Kentucky was inevitable and did not trust Plummer or Deitsch to wait for signed papers. Every time they were called from their cells, the jailers would taunt them, saying the time for the move had come. They had taken to wearing their coats and hats whenever they left their cells and stuffing their pockets with the few possessions they kept.

The prisoners prepared as usual on February 8, when two jailers came to escort them from their cells. Upstairs, the jailers handed over custody to Detectives Crim and McDermott and Sheriff Plummer. When they were loaded into a police wagon, Jackson and Walling felt sure their destination would be Newport, Kentucky, but it was just a short trip to Epply's Funeral Parlor.

They were led into a dimly lit viewing room with dark wood furnishings. A pure white coffin lay on stanchions in the center of the room, shining amid the gloom. Along one wall, the ubiquitous reporters were already gathered, and Jackson, looking around the room, immediately recognized Pearl's sister Mary and brother Fred standing behind the coffin. Leaning against the wall behind them was the coffin lid on which a silver plaque read "Pearl" etched on it in gothic letters.

The policemen and their charges entered the room silently, in a formal procession. Sheriff Plummer led the way, followed by the prisoners in handcuffs—Jackson cuffed to McDermott, Walling to Crim. Colonel Deitsch followed behind. Despite the solemn atmosphere of the funeral home, Walling wore a slight smirk. It seemed to amuse him that they would bring him here to scare a confession out of him. His brother Clinton was an undertaker. Walling was familiar with dead bodies, and they did not frighten him. His coolness prompted one reporter to observe, "This fellow is either one of the most cold-blooded villains in the country, or he is innocent of complicity in the crime."

Jackson, though, was trembling as his eyes darted around the room, taking in all the faces. The prisoners and lawmen approached the open coffin from the side opposite where the Bryans were standing. When Jackson looked down and saw the body lying inside, he gasped.

Pearl's small body was adorned in the white dress she had worn four years before at her high school graduation, but the high collar of the dress was sewn tight at the top. Above it, where her head would have been, lay a small white satin pillow. The only flesh visible, at the end of her long sleeves, were her tiny and delicate hands—as smooth as porcelain and nearly as white as the dress.

Colonel Deitsch broke the silence.

"Alonzo Walling. Do you recognize the corpse which lies in this casket?"

Walling responded clearly, "I have every reason to believe it is that of Miss Bryan."

"How do you know that?"

"From what Mr. Jackson has told me."

The Colonel turned to Scott Jackson.

"Jackson, do you recognize this corpse?"

"I suppose it is that of Miss Bryan," Jackson said, his voice trembling.

"What makes you think so?"

"I see her relatives here."

Colonel Deitsch paused for a moment, startling the hushed room, and said, "Alonzo Walling, did you kill this woman?"

"I did not."

"Who did then?"

"I have every reason to believe, from what Jackson told me, that he did."

Turning again to the other prisoner, Deitsch said, "Jackson, did you murder this girl?"

"I did not, sir."

"Can you look upon this corpse and deny that you committed the crime?"

"I can, and do, most emphatically," Jackson said, his eyes darting to and from the corpse as he spoke.

Across the coffin, Fred Bryan was seething, but held his tongue, as he had no doubt been cautioned to do.

"Who did kill her?" Deitsch asked.

"I have every reason to believe that Walling did," said Jackson.

Deitsch paused again, then more quietly said, "You say that you recognize the corpse?"

"I did not say that. I supposed it is because I see her relatives here."

This was no different from the interviews in the mayor's office. There would be no overflowing of emotion beside the coffin in the funeral home, no hysterical confessions.

Colonel Deitsch turned to Pearl's sister, Mary, and inquired if she had any questions for the prisoners. She looked in anguish from one prisoner to the other. There was a long pause.

"I do not, sir," she said at last.

"Mr. Bryan, is there anything you would like to ask?"

Fred Bryan tried to catch Jackson's eye, but the prisoner was staring fixedly at the floor. Fred declined also. Fred took his sister's arm and gently escorted her from the room.

When the Bryans had left, Sheriff Plummer went to the body and untied the neck of Pearl Bryan's dress. Exposed, the still ragged flesh and bone of her wounded neck shattered the image of Pearl as a China doll lying on white satin. Plummer angrily forced Jackson and Walling to look at the mangled neck, but once again, the sight produced no effect. Walling remained cool, Jackson nervous, but there was no show of remorse, no anguished confession. The men were silent.

Later that day, after the prisoners had been returned to their cells, Mary Stanley went with her brother to Central Station to see Colonel Deitsch., Mary, away from the unnatural scene at the undertaker's, regained the courage to finish what she had come to Cincinnati to do, and she asked Colonel Deitsch if she could, after all, speak with the prisoners. Deitsch agreed, and Jackson was brought in first.

"Mr. Jackson," she began, "I come to you and ask where is my sister's…" She broke down, unable to say the word. Jackson would later recall that she asked him for the location of "the intellectual part" of her sister.

After she regained composure, Mary continued, "For the sake of my poor mother and for my sisters and my brothers, I beg of you to tell us where my sister's head is. It is my last chance, and I want to send it home with her poor body. Won't you please tell me? I beg of you."

Jackson stood directly in front of her. He looked her straight in the eye. "Mrs. Stanley, I do not know."

She stood helplessly, staring at his retreating back as he was removed from the room.

Then Walling was brought in, and she nervously asked him the same question. While Jackson had clearly seen the gravity of the moment and gave at least the appearance of sincerity, Walling seemed to view it as just another annoyance in a day filled with annoyances.

"I do not know where it is."

Colonel Deitsch left the room, shaking his head. To the reporters waiting in the hall, he said, "I've been in many trying situations, but I never saw anything to equal that. How they could refuse to tell that poor woman where the head is I cannot understand."

That afternoon, Sheriff Plummer went down to Jackson's cell and told him to get ready; they would be going across the river. Jackson gathered his possessions and picked up his Bible. Plummer became incensed at the sight of Jackson holding the holy book.

"Put down that Bible, don't be a damned hypocrite." Plummer shouted, "I know my people. They are waiting for you with open arms."

Jackson and Walling were brought up from the cells once more and loaded into a waiting patrol wagon, where prison guards told them, law or no law, they were being taken to Campbell County, Kentucky, for a meeting with "Judge Lynch."

Inside the dark wagon, flanked by policemen, they sat on the hard bench, without exchanging a word during the ride. As prisoners awaiting an extradition trial, Jackson and Walling were no longer city business. The law said they could not be handed over to Kentucky, but they could at least be given to the county. The vehicle took a circuitous route to its destination, and it was not Newport, Kentucky, but the Hamilton County Jail on the east side of town. The prisoners were well ensconced in their new digs before they came to the realization that they were still in Ohio.

Reporters followed the wagon and watched as the prisoners were separated and checked into the prison. The men tersely responded to all questions put to them by their new jailers but were otherwise silent. Then when they were safely locked in their darkened cells, Walling in a brief, unguarded moment, gave a hint that he and Jackson, who had been accusing each other since their arrest, just may have been working in collusion.

They were brought in separately, down the same prison corridor, but the cells they were led to were a considerable distance apart. When Walling was situated in his cell, it was too dark to see who was in the cell across from him, but he thought it was Jackson.

"Is that you, Jackson?" Walling said in a loud whisper.

It was not Jackson, but another prisoner named Legner. Using a low voice to fool Walling, he said, "Yes."

"Keep quiet," Walling responded, "say nothing."

7 MISSING DAYS

Where Pearl Bryan slept Wednesday and Thursday nights was still unknown, and what she did between Wednesday afternoon and Friday evening was open to speculation. This did not matter to the police whose eyewitnesses, Wallingford and Johnson, saw Pearl enter a surrey with Jackson and Walling on Friday night. They focused their energy on finding the man who drove them away. Anything prior to that time was irrelevant.

From the time of the arrests, the police and the press had been swamped with unsolicited leads from private citizens who had seen Pearl Bryan in Cincinnati before the murder, alone or accompanied by Jackson or Walling. The night clerk at the Princeton Hotel believed that Pearl checked in on Wednesday night, registered as Mary Barr, and left, unobserved the next morning. A couple was seen quarreling on the corner of Race and Eighth Streets on Thursday afternoon— a well-dressed man and a blonde country girl. The witness was convinced they were Scott Jackson and Pearl Bryan. Another witness saw two men arguing with a blonde woman on Elm Street before entering the Lamar Hotel on Friday night. The Lamar Hotel did not keep a register, and the clerk had no recollection of the party. The police paid little attention to these stories, unwilling to follow evidence that did not advance the official narrative.

The newspapers were not so focused and continued to report everything that came their way. Dozens of letters poured into the newspapers— clairvoyants and spiritualists offered to reveal the identity of the murderer and people living miles away, with no connection to the case, presented detailed theories of what really happened. Most startling were the letters they received claiming that Pearl Bryan was still alive. From as far away as Virginia and Florida, Pearl had been seen after the body was found by people who recognized her from the newspaper illustrations and demanded an end to the injustice against those two poor boys. The papers published any letters they found interesting. The police rejected them all out of hand.

But three days after the arrest of Scott Jackson, William E. Starr, Marshal of Greencastle, Indiana, received a letter in the evening mail which he could not ignore. This letter stood out from the rest; it was concise and explicit and had a sense of urgency that caught Marshal Starr's attention. It was a short note, signed just with initials, mailed from Indianapolis, and addressed to the Chief of Police, Greencastle, Indiana:

> Sir – Some information of importance can be obtained concerning the murder of Miss Pearl Bryan if you will call on or arrest Miss Lulu Mae Hollingsworth, No. 1 Henry Street, Indianapolis, Indiana. She is afraid of being implicated, and that detectives will find out she knows of the causes of death and the medicines used.
>
> If she is used as a witness, I will testify what she has told me, an informant, who will watch her movements till you see her. She has been thinking of leaving the city, so see her at once, the sooner, the better.
>
> H. E. R.

Marshal Starr felt the letter had a ring of truth to it, and he took the next train to Indianapolis. There he met with Indianapolis Police Superintendent Thomas F. Colbert, who read the letter and agreed that the lead was worth following. He immediately detailed Detective Frank Wilson to accompany Starr on a visit to Miss Hollingsworth.

Number One Henry Street was a boarding house run by Mrs. Alice Shull, who reluctantly let the lawmen in and went to fetch Miss Hollingsworth. Lulu Hollingsworth was an attractive young woman, small in stature and somewhat disheveled, wearing a loose-fitting wrapper. Starr asked if she was acquainted with Pearl Bryan, Scott Jackson, Will Wood, or Alonzo Walling. She said she knew all of them except Walling. Starr told her of the letter he received, signed H. E. R., and asked if she knew the writer. It was Hal Radcliffe, she replied, she had seen him Friday night and had told him about meeting Miss Bryan at Union Station on Tuesday, January 28. She said she knew Pearl was going to Cincinnati to see Scott Jackson and said she had met Jackson herself when she visited a friend at DePauw University in Greencastle.

As Marshal Starr pressed her for more details, she hesitated, insisting that she would not say anything to implicate herself. Starr and Wilson decided to take her to police headquarters, and Miss Hollingsworth asked if she could go upstairs first and change her dress. She went up to her room and stayed quite a while. When she came downstairs, she was tearing a piece of paper to bits, and as she passed an open stove, she threw the pieces into the fire, saying she was glad to be rid of that letter. The men believed it was a damaging letter from Scott Jackson.

At police headquarters, Superintendent Colbert questioned Lulu Hollingsworth for two hours. She remained defensive the whole time, sitting with clenched hands, determined to reveal nothing. But the more she dodged his questions, the more Colbert was convinced that she had something to reveal, and he went after it harder.

Bit by bit, Colbert wrested a story from her that when pieced together was straightforward and consistent with what was already known about the murder but presented a completely different story. She said she was sitting in the ladies' waiting room at Union Station on January 28, the day Will Wood said he had seen Pearl off in Greencastle. After the train arrived in Indianapolis, a young woman entered the waiting room, unsure of where to go. Then she recognized Lulu, whom she had met previously in Greencastle, and approached her.

"Oh, I am Pearl Bryan, of Greencastle. Don't you remember me?" Bryan asked.

Lulu did remember her, and they sat together, chatting.

As they spoke, Lulu noticed that Pearl's face was somewhat swollen and asked what the matter. Pearl said she was in trouble, and Lulu said she could guess what the trouble was. Blushing, Pearl admitted it was true. Scott Jackson was the author of her misfortune, and she was going to Cincinnati to hide her disgrace—to perhaps have an abortion performed. Then, Pearl asked if Lulu knew of any drug that could help her.

"I had a similar experience and knew what to do," Lulu told Superintendent Colbert, "I told her what to get. The prescription was made up of three different articles, one of which was whiskey, and another was a deadly poison. The drugs were bought in this city, and the girl took them with her to Cincinnati. It cost 45 cents to get the prescription filled. I am positive that she killed herself."

"Did you buy the medicine?" asked the superintendent.

"I will not answer that question."

"Where was it bought?"

"It was bought at three different drug stores."

"You might as well tell me the truth," said Colbert, "Be honest now; didn't you buy that medicine?"

Lulu refused to answer, "You can't make me say anything to incriminate myself. You know that there is no court in the world that would require me to answer that question. Yes, you know more that; you know, no judge would allow me to answer it."

Colbert dropped the point and encouraged Lulu to continue the story her own way.

"I do know this," she said, "Pearl Bryan died by her own hand. Scott

Jackson is not guilty of her death. Before this murder occurred, there was an affair in which Pearl Bryan, Scott Jackson, and I were involved. I will never tell what that was until they are condemned to hang. If they are condemned to die, then I will tell the whole story, but not until then."

She went on to say she believed that Pearl had taken the drugs in Cincinnati, and, despite Lulu's warnings, she had taken too much. When the body was found, she was wearing only a light wrapper; Pearl would have dressed better if she intended to go out. She must have died in Scott Jackson's room. When Jackson saw she was dead, he took the body away and cut off her head to avoid identification. She didn't know for sure because she had not been in contact with Scott Jackson; the letter that she burned had not been from him.

The superintendent pressed her for more information, but Lulu became defensive again and would say no more. Colbert decided that a night in jail might loosen her tongue and left her in the custody of a police matron who took her to a cell in the women's side of the jail.

Lulu Hollingsworth had no prior police record, but the Indianapolis newspapers recalled that a girl named Louise Hollingsworth put half the state in turmoil when she disappeared from Coates College in Terre Haute three years earlier. She had inherited a large sum of money, at the time held in trust by her uncle, and foul play was suspected. Adding suspicion, her father had been treasurer of Knox County, and shortly before Louise's disappearance, the books had been audited and came up short. Accused of embezzlement, Hollingsworth was relieved of his duties and was under indictment at the time of his daughter's disappearance.

Louise Hollingsworth was eventually found in Indianapolis, employed as a servant by a prominent family, and living under the name of Ethel Gray. The reason she gave for leaving Coates College was her uncle's refusal to pay a rather large millinery bill she had run up at the school. More likely, she had been driven out by the taunts of her classmates over her father's criminal behavior. There was little doubt that Louise and Lulu Hollingsworth were one and the same.

Police detectives returned to Number One Henry Street and talked to Lulu's landlady. She kept to herself, they were told, and she very seldom had guests. Lulu did not have a regular occupation, living on the interest from several thousand dollars' worth of investments and on checks she received from her father. The detectives searched Lulu's room but found very little of value—a scrap of paper with the name "Scott" which suggested that she had been corresponding with Scott Jackson, and several empty boxes labeled morphine which may have accounted for Lulu's erratic behavior.

Detectives visited the drug stores on Washington Street, where Lulu said they purchased the drugs to precipitate a miscarriage, but none remembered the transactions. They had better luck at Union Station, where they showed the railway employees pictures of Lulu Hollingsworth, Pearl Bryan, and Will Wood. Several people recalled seeing Lulu at the station, and at least one man recognized Pearl Bryan and remembered seeing her with Lulu.

When Lulu was brought up from the cells the next morning, looking even more disheveled, she railed against conditions in the jail and her illegal detention. When she finally settled down, she agreed that her best course was to tell the whole truth. Then, she proceeded to tell Superintendent Colbert another tale, even more astounding than the last.

This time she told her story in a careless manner as if relating it to a friend, apparently unconcerned that she was offering evidence that may be used against her. She said that she told the truth about meeting Pearl at Union Station on Tuesday and repeated that they had purchased drugs, but added that before leaving for Cincinnati, Pearl had promised to return to Indianapolis on Thursday. Pearl arrived on Thursday, accompanied by Alonzo Walling, and the couple stayed at Fields Hotel on Georgia Street.

They arranged to meet Lulu at an early hour on Friday morning to divert suspicion. Pearl kept the appointment, but Walling had already returned to Cincinnati. Pearl had procured some medical instruments in Cincinnati, and Lulu was to use them to perform an abortion. They entered a hotel on the corner of Kentucky and Capitol Avenues. Lulu wanted to take a room, but Pearl declined, fearing detection. People from Greencastle were often in Indianapolis, and she did not want to be recognized. Instead, they went down a staircase and sat under a gaslight, where Lulu performed the abortion. Afterward, they went to Union Station, and Pearl took a train back to Cincinnati.

"She was very weak when we arrived at the depot," Lulu told Superintendent Colbert, "She complained of being sick."

Afterward, Lulu received a letter from Scott Jackson written two hours after Pearl arrived in Cincinnati. It said that Pearl was in his room and appeared to be dying as a result of the operation. She received a second letter from Jackson after Pearl died saying he had exhausted every means to save her life and was unsuccessful. Knowing he would be charged with murder if the body were found in his room, he rented a buggy and hired a black man to help him carry the body. On the Kentucky side of the river, they carried the corpse into the woods. They made the site appear as if a struggle had taken place, and the black man severed the head with a cleaver. The black man returned with the buggy, and Jackson took a streetcar with the head wrapped and bundled under his arm. He stopped on the old suspension bridge then threw the head into the Ohio River.

Jackson confided in her, Lulu said, because he felt she was implicated in Pearl's death. He knew the incidents of her death and the disposition of the body, while she alone knew the cause.

"Do you know what you have done?" Colbert asked when she had completed her story.

"I have told the whole truth," she responded.

"You have acknowledged yourself responsible for the death of this girl. You are little less than her murderer, and you have placed yourself in a very serious light."

"I have told all the truth, nevertheless."

As improbable as this story sounded to Colbert, it was not immediately refuted. No one knew for certain where Pearl Bryan was between Wednesday and Saturday, and Alonzo Walling had not slept at home on Thursday night. At Fields's Hotel, the police learned that a couple answering the description of Pearl Bryan and Alonzo Walling checked in on Thursday, registered as John Hanly and wife, and left a call to be awakened at 3:00 a.m.

Lulu Hollingsworth had been reluctant to talk and had not told her story voluntarily. When she did agree to talk after a night in jail, she was calm and well-spoken, giving every indication of being sane and better educated than the usual woman questioned at the police station. Superintendent Colbert's first inclination was to send Lulu, under guard, to Cincinnati.

But the story did not ring true, and the police in Cincinnati did not want her. Lulu Hollingsworth claimed that she had performed an abortion on Pearl, and two postmortem examinations had concluded that no operation had been attempted. Lulu had taken her story too far. Colbert had to conclude that Lulu Mae Hollingsworth was the kind of attention seeker that always gravitates around a crime like this.

He now believed that she had built her first story around newspaper accounts of the murder. While in custody she had no access to the facts, so her story went wild. Lulu Mae Hollingsworth had no direct connection to Pearl Bryan's murder. Either her mind was diseased by opiates, or her stories were the result of reading pernicious literature, giving her an unusual appetite for notoriety. While she was happy to finally be released, Lulu was still perturbed that the police had not believed her story.

"I will go to Cincinnati and be present at that trial," she told reporters after she was released from police custody. "I want to see the whole thing now, and I will furnish that letter when the time comes."

Though the story told by Lulu Hollingsworth could not have been true, it pointed out gaping holes in the story the Cincinnati Police were trying to sell. The police had maintained that it did not matter where Pearl was on Wednesday and Thursday because they had eyewitnesses for Friday night. But now it did matter. Lulu Hollingsworth had very nearly moved the focus of the crime to Indianapolis. Between the afternoon of Wednesday, January 29, and the morning of Saturday, February 1, when the body was found, Pearl Bryan, Alonzo Walling, and Scott Jackson could have been anywhere.

As the Lulu Hollingsworth affair was dying down, another woman came forward with her own shocking story, and this woman had direct ties to Jackson and Walling. When Alonzo Walling was first questioned, he was wearing a gold ring on his little finger. When asked where he got the ring, he said it was a gift from Miss Smith of Louisville. At the time, it seemed likely that "Miss Smith" was a name Walling made up on the spot, but it was significant that he named a woman from Kentucky. Colonel Deitsch confiscated the ring, believing it was Pearl's, and the story was reported in the newspapers.

Joe Carson of Covington, Kentucky, knew right away who had given Walling the ring. It was his sister, May Smith, and he took the next train to Louisville to bring her home. She had been married to Robert Smith and kept her husband's name, though they had been estranged for several years. Walling did not lie about the ring; it was given to him by May Smith of Louisville. Carson believed if she stayed in Louisville, the police or the newspapers would track her down. Better to bring her home to Covington and keep her hidden. May went back with her brother, but not to hide out; the next day, she was at Cincinnati Central Police Station requesting the return of her ring and the right to speak with her friends in jail.

May Smith had been a student at the Dixie School of Dress Cutting in Cincinnati in the fall of 1895 when Jackson and Walling were dental students. When May had a toothache, she went to the dental college to take advantage of the free services provided by the students there and was examined by Alonzo Walling. He determined that she had twelve teeth that needed filling and began a course of treatment. May was charmed by the strong young dentist with the gentle touch, and they were soon spending time together outside of the dental school. They remained in touch when May moved to Louisville to work as an instructor for the Dixie School there.

With Walling's consent, the Cincinnati Police returned the ring to May, and took her to the County Jail to visit him. She had a long conversation with Walling, and then asked if she could see Scott Jackson as well, and the police agreed. When her visits were through, she returned to her hotel—the Indiana House— where she was registered under the name Maria Swan.

At the jail, she told reporters that she had never seen or heard of Pearl Bryan, that Walling had never mentioned her name. One reporter from the *Enquirer* was not ready to accept that and followed her back to her hotel. He caught her before she could go up to her room, and she spoke freely about her friendship with Jackson and Walling. He asked whether Walling had ever, to her knowledge, performed a criminal operation on a woman.

She hesitated and said, "I would not like to answer that question."

"Do you know anything about the case which might throw any light on the mystery?"

"I could tell something that might be damaging to Walling and Jackson, but I am not ready to tell yet."

At that, the interview abruptly ended. The reporter returned the following day to see if a night's sleep had made her ready to tell but found that "Maria Swan" had checked out of the hotel.

May Smith's brief, tantalizing statements about the Pearl Bryan case printed in the *Enquirer* the next day, fed into the popular notion that Walling was an abortionist and added to the suspicion that May herself had been one of his patients. From the beginning, some had suggested that Jackson and Walling had an accomplice in preparation for the operation on Pearl, possibly a woman, probably from Kentucky. Even if the abortion was attempted in Cincinnati, Jackson and Walling would not have been familiar enough with the Kentucky Highlands to know of Lock's farm and were not likely to have found the place by accident. May Smith fit the bill as their Kentucky connection, and, by her own account, she had more to tell.

This was not May Smith's first involvement with murder. Four years earlier, she had an extramarital affair with a dockworker named James Crabtree. May's father, Thomas Carson, learned of the affair and put the blame on Crabtree for trying to break up his daughter's marriage to the reliable, hardworking Robert Smith. Carson went down to the Covington coal landing, sought out James Crabtree, and shot him dead. A Campbell County jury felt the action was justified and acquitted him of murder.

May Smith's background was revealed in an anonymous letter mailed to Mayor Caldwell, prompting a frantic search by police and reporters for Walling's girlfriend. Thinking she had most likely returned to Louisville, the police concentrated their search in Kentucky. May Smith had not left Cincinnati, and the *Enquirer* reporter eventually tracked her down for an interview. From statements that May later made, it appears that the reporter had taken her out drinking.

"Well, I might as well tell you the entire story from the beginning," she said after trying to evade the reporter's incessant questions.

She told him about meeting Alonzo Walling at the dental college and said she met Scott Jackson about two weeks later. Soon, all three had become very close and would go out together. Jackson suggested that May bring along a friend for him, and May would bring her brother's wife, Etta Carson, or more often, her school friend, Hattie Gans.

One night when Walling was away visiting his family in Oxford, Jackson went out with May and Hattie Gans. Hattie had to leave early, but May and Scott decided to keep drinking. According to May, Jackson drank heavily and spoke more freely than he would have otherwise. He said he thought Walling had left the city on account of some trouble he had with a woman.

"Jackson then went on to say that he himself had helped two girls out of trouble." May told the reporter about a girl Jackson had met on a ferry boat in Jersey City. She had tried to commit suicide, and he stopped her. She told him that she was pregnant, and he solved her problem by performing an abortion on her in his room.

"After telling these stories," May continued, "Jackson said: 'You remember me telling you about a girl named Pearl Bryan in Greencastle?' I said that if he had mentioned her, I had no recollection of it. Then he said: 'Well I and a friend of the named Will Wood have got her in trouble. I don't know which one of us is responsible. I have received a letter from Wood, in which he says he is going to send the girl down here. I told him that he could do so. If she comes, I will put her out of the way. I won't fool with her. I'll give her some stuff that will fix her.'"

The conversation had taken place on January 14, and the following day May took a steamboat to Louisville to begin her new job at the Dixie School there. On February 3, she received a letter from Scott Jackson which she related, from memory to the reporter:

> You remember I spoke to you about the girl Pearl Bryan and told you that Wood was going to send her to Cincinnati. Well, he sent her here. I told you I intended to put her out of the way if she came here. I really did not mean those words, but I gave her too much stuff, and I saw it was killing her. I thought she was dead. You can imagine where we were—at that woman's house. I knew I had to do something to keep from being caught. I got a vehicle and a colored man to drive it. I told Walling that he would have to help me, and he refused. I insisted and Walling finally helped me to put the girl in the vehicle. We drove to Fort Thomas, and I cut her head off. For God's sake, whatever you do, destroy this letter as soon as you read it.

May told the reporter she had followed Jackson's instructions and burned the letter. The reporter refused to believe it and continued to press her. Finally, she said, "Well, I concealed the letter between the mattress and springs of my bed in my room at Louisville. I came away in such a hurry that I forgot it."

"Is the letter still there?" the reporter asked.

"I suppose so."

"Can I get it if I go to Louisville?"

May backtracked, "No, I remember now that I wrote to the Listers, telling them to destroy my letters and this one in particular. I guess they did it."

The reporter was still skeptical, "Do you think they would destroy the direct evidence of such a murder?"

"I don't suppose they knew what that letter contained."

If the letter could be found, it would amount to a confession by Scott Jackson, but not of murder, of committing an illegal operation and concealing Pearl's death. Walling's role would be only as an unwilling accessory.

In Louisville, reporters spoke with Mr. and Mrs. Lister, May Smith's employers, who remembered May receiving letters written on Palace Hotel stationery, one from a man named Swan and one from Scott Jackson.

Mr. Lister said, "One day my wife was reading of the case in the paper, when May exclaimed, 'My God! I hope they will not get my letters.' At that time, she kept all her letters concealed in her room underneath the bed."

The Listers had rented a room to May in a house which they, in turn, had rented from a Mrs. Wells. Following May's departure, Mrs. Wells and her daughter had cleaned May's room and had found a bunch of letters and telegrams underneath her mattress. They said that they had read the letters and found their content of no consequence and destroyed them.

The day after May Smith had told her story to the reporter, Detectives Crim and McDermott tracked her down and brought her to the station for questioning. She told her story to Mayor Caldwell. It was virtually identical to what she had said the day before, except this time she knew for certain that she, herself, had burned the letter from Jackson.

But, by the end of the day, May recanted the entire story and admitted to the *Cincinnati Tribune* that the story had been told while under the influence of alcohol, and it was completely untrue. Her story was almost universally dismissed as an attempt to save her lover, Alonzo Walling. May Smith disappeared again, and this time no one looked for her.

The police felt no further need to investigate May Smith's role in Pearl Bryan's murder, but once again, the newspapers had underscored the fact that Pearl's whereabouts in the three days prior to her death were still unknown, and what transpired during that time could prove important. Both Lulu Mae Hollingsworth and May Smith had been discredited, but each case left lingering doubts in the public mind that each of these women knew more than the police were willing to admit. Confidence in the official story was eroding, and the police desperately needed to find the driver and complete the chain of evidence.

8 POLITICS

Mayor Caldwell became increasingly annoyed at reluctance of the daily newspapers to stick to the official story of the murder. The police remained doggedly committed to the one story they believed to be true, the story that would lead to the executions of Jackson and Walling in Kentucky, but the papers continued following leads that placed Jackson, Walling, or Pearl somewhere outside the police's prescribed path. Stories like Lulu Hollingsworth's and May Smith's were too large to ignore, but others were merely rumors and red herrings. The first and only priority of the Cincinnati Police was finding the mysterious horseman who drove the cab, and they wanted the press to share that priority.

The implied, and sometimes overt, criticism of the official investigation was straining the relationship between City Hall and press. Finally, Mayor John Caldwell lost all patience and barred reporters from meetings in Central Station, where to this point, they had free access. He ordered detectives to stop sharing information with newsmen.

The ban did not have the effect the mayor wanted. It only made the papers more critical. Under the headline, "The Investigation. It was Poorly Conducted from the Very Beginning," the *Cincinnati Tribune* succinctly outlined police failures, including failure to measure footprints at the scene, failure to question possible witnesses, and failure to discover where Pearl Bryan slept Thursday night.

The *Cincinnati Enquirer*, in an article titled "Was the Mayor Sarcastic?" said this of the mayor's ban; "Among the reporters, this is looked upon as unintentional sarcasm on His Honor's part. All information which has resulted in the solving of the mystery as far as it has been solved was handed over to the police, and the reporters have done about all the rest… As it is, everything has been done by outsiders and turned over to the police except the formal arrests. Walling had been kindly dismissed and might have disappeared but for the 'nerve' of an *Enquirer* reporter who put him under arrest and turned him over to the police."

The mayor's decree could not stop the newspapers from trying to beat the police at their own game, but eventually the editors, hindered by lack of official access, succumbed to political pressure. The *Tribune* stopped its investigation of alternative stories abruptly after February 12. That morning they led with a piece about a watchman at the Lamar House who had seen Jackson, Walling and Pearl Bryan on the corner of Sixth and Elm Street. This corner also happened to house the office of a Dr. E. L. Nichols, a dentist known to Jackson and Walling. The paper had also published a story from Richmond, Indiana, stating that Pearl was seen there in January, and a letter from a reader enumerating reasons to doubt that the body discovered was, in fact, that of Pearl Bryan. But the *Tribune's* lead story on February 13 was the paper's offer of $500—an amount equal to a Cincinnati factory worker's annual salary—for information leading to the discovery of the horseman who took Jackson, Walling, and Pearl Bryan to Kentucky the night of Friday, January 31. There was no follow-up of the Lamar House story or any new speculations, only news from Kentucky that the Campbell County Coroner had decided that the girl had been killed where the body was found.

The *Enquirer*, still heavily invested in the May Smith story, took longer to limit their coverage, but soon offered their own smaller reward, and no longer featured stories that strayed from the gospel according to Central Station.

Mayor Caldwell and the police were determined to keep the city focused on the one story that took Pearl Bryan, alive, out of Ohio, and for good reason. If Jackson and Walling were tried in Cincinnati, with only the current circumstantial evidence against them, first-degree murder would be difficult to prove. The defense would surely claim her death was due to a failed abortion, in which case, manslaughter was the most they could hope for. With the close national scrutiny the trial would inevitably attract, a verdict of guilty, could not be guaranteed, even for manslaughter. Jackson and Walling must hang, and this could only happen if they were tried for the simple, straightforward charge of murder in the Highlands of Kentucky.

Those who remembered a time when a public outrage over a murder verdict had driven the populace of Cincinnati into the streets felt a very real concern over botching this conviction. Twelve years earlier, the government of Cincinnati was a virtual feudalism of competing neighborhood gangs. Mayoral elections would often include half a dozen candidates with no one winning a majority and the winner too weak to govern. The gangs retailed every function of city government, and criminal verdicts were a big-ticket item.

Government anarchy was mirrored on the streets, and Cincinnati suffered a wave of murders. That spring, twenty-three indicted murderers awaited trial, including a man who murdered his wife with an ax and two men who killed an entire family to sell their corpses to a medical school. In March,

Joseph Palmer and William Berner were tried for robbing their boss, a livery stable owner, and beating him to death with a hammer. It was an open and shut case of murder in the first degree, but the fix was in, and on March 24, the jury handed a verdict for William Berner of manslaughter. The judge in the trial had called the verdict "a damned outrage," a cry echoed throughout the city.

The following Friday, the cry became "Hang Berner" as a torrent of angry men poured out of a community meeting bent on a lynching. Berner was already on a train bound for the penitentiary, so the mob spread throughout the city and began looting. The police, unable to quell the riot, telegraphed the governor for help from the state militia.

In the defining act of the uprising, the rioters set fire to the Courthouse and burned it to the ground. The militia mounted Gatling guns on sandbag barricades and overturned wagons. Sometime on Sunday night, the third night of the riot, the threat posed by the vicious guns combined with fatigue slowed, then ended, the mood of violence. But not before fifty-four men were killed and an estimated two hundred wounded.

The Courthouse was rebuilt, this time of stone and mortar. The state of Ohio rewrote Cincinnati's charter, attempting to check the city's corruption The effect it had was just the opposite. It provided George B. Cox the means to become the absolute boss of the entire city. The Courthouse Riot had in fact, been a revolution whose outcome no one could have predicted. Twelve years later, the memory of the riot and its aftermath was still fresh for Boss Cox, as it was for Mayor Caldwell, Colonel Deitsch, Cal Crim, and Jack McDermott, all of whom had been in public service at the time. In different ways, it was a lesson not lost on any of them: The people will live with graft and corruption. They will take exploitation by employers and politicians with nothing stronger than complaint, but when public safety is compromised by a legal system skewed in favor of murderers, they will rise up.

While not everyone in the police department endorsed Boss Cox's control of Cincinnati, none of them wanted another regime change from the street. They could not be weak or ineffective; Jackson and Walling had to hang, and preferably in Kentucky.

Sheriff Plummer also wanted Jackson and Walling hanged in Kentucky, but his reasons were deeply personal. The most heinous crime imaginable— the murder by decapitation of a young woman in the prime of life—had taken place in his county on his watch. He had done everything in his power to apprehend the murderers, but he was powerless to bring them to justice while they remained in Ohio.

Plummer had a special loathing for Scott Jackson, the arrogant, privileged outsider, who came to Campbell County to do his dirty work, thinking to escape the noose merely by denying the obvious. The Sheriff needed to see Jackson swing, and regardless of his taunts invoking Judge Lynch, he needed

Jackson to swing under the color of law. But Plummer had his own political hurdles to overcome. Boss Cox's influence ended abruptly at the Ohio River, and extradition is not a city matter or a county matter. Plummer needed the governors of two states to agree to hand him the prisoners, so he would now spend his time traveling between Frankfort, Kentucky, and Columbus, Ohio, pleading his case to two very stubborn men.

Sheriff Plummer would not expect a warm welcome in his state's capital. He was a Democrat and Governor William Bradley was a Republican. Though Kentucky tended to be a Democratic state, conflict between the old guard of Confederate sympathizers and a new group of populist reformers left the Democratic Party in a state of disarray that Bradley was able to exploit. Governor Bradley was hoping to ride the chaos to a seat in the U. S. Senate, and the last thing he needed was to be on the wrong side of a controversial and very visible criminal case.

The governor sent representatives to Cincinnati and Newport to follow the story and gather information to help determine Kentucky's interest. After weighing the evidence, he decided that Cincinnati was doing well enough, holding Jackson and Walling, and that it was best to let sleeping dogs lie. Sheriff Plummer was determined to change his mind and laid out a convincing case that Pearl Bryan was murdered in Kentucky by the two men being held in Ohio, and they must be brought to Newport to answer for their crimes.

Bradley still had reservations. The people of Kentucky had a long history of impatience with the wheels of justice and had become famous for defaulting to lynch law. Would the prisoners be safe in Newport? Sheriff Plummer told him he did not see any credible threat to their safety, but if one arose, he and his men could handle it. Finally, after warning that he would hold Sheriff Plummer responsible "both personally and officially" for the prisoners' safety, Governor Bradley signed the requisition papers requesting that the state of Ohio turn over custody of Scott Jackson and Alonzo Walling to the Commonwealth of Kentucky.

Sheriff Plummer found resistance in Columbus, Ohio as well. Governor Asa Bushnell, also Republican, followed the case and stated publicly that he was not convinced that Pearl Bryan was killed in Kentucky. Governor Bushnell was also worried about political blow-back from the wrong decision in such a high-profile murder case, especially while his predecessor, Ohio's favorite son, William McKinley, was running for President of the United States.

Governor Bushnell and Attorney General Frank Monnett met with Sheriff Plummer and had him recount every aspect of the case beginning with the identification of the body. Sheriff Plummer assured the still skeptical governor the death-wound had been inflicted in Kentucky.

Attorney General Monnett had a problem with the indictments.

Apparently, the court had backpedaled from the explicit indictments naming Jackson as the man wielding the knife and Walling the man who held her down. The indictments which accompanied the requisition papers were identical for both men saying one was the killer, the other the accomplice, without specifying which was which. Monnett referred to them as "alternative indictments" and was not sure they were legally sufficient for the state to honor a requisition.

But the real reservation was the same one Governor Bradley had.

"Do you apprehend any violence in the event that we allow the prisoners to be taken to Kentucky?" asked Governor Bushnell.

"None, whatever," replied the Sheriff.

"You think then that the people of Kentucky would not take such action as they so frequently do?" said His Excellency.

Sheriff Plummer took offense at this and could not hold his tongue, "I do not think your remarks are justified, Governor," he said. "And I do not like to hear the people of Kentucky spoken of in that manner."

The governor said he meant no offense, but he had a duty to perform, and he meant to perform it. "You will use all due vigilance to prevent anything in the nature of a lynching?"

"I most certainly will," the sheriff said. "I have never had a lynching during my services of 16 years in the Sheriff's office, and I don't want one at this time."

While Sheriff Plummer was correct that Campbell County saw no lynchings during his term of office, his predecessor could not say the same. In March 1879, a tramp named Peter Klein stopped to beg a meal at a farm in the Highlands. After eating, Klein turned on his hostess, raped her, ransacked the house, and fled. Klein was at large for five days before the Newport Police captured him. By nightfall, 5,000 citizens gathered outside the jail. The mob called for justice and did not trust the courtroom to give them satisfaction.

The standoff lasted twenty-four hours. On the evening of the second day, a troupe of armed horsemen rode from the south up Alexandria Pike into Newport. Vigilante justice had always been a fact of life in Kentucky, and following the Civil War, groups like the Ku Klux Klan, the Loyal Leaguers, and the Regulators kept order outside the law. It is unclear whether the horsemen in Newport were an organized group or an ad hoc vigilance committee, but they provided the spark to ignite the Newport mob.

They forced their way into the jail and pulled the prisoner from his cell. The mob took Klein to the Highlands and hung him from a sycamore tree. Anxious to see him die, they finished the job by shooting at the hanging man.

Seventeen years ago seemed like a lifetime away, and Sheriff Plummer assured the governor that citizens of Newport were no longer so prone to violence. But for those who had lived through the lynching, the memory was fresh, and the threat of recurrence was real.

After hearing Sheriff Plummer's plea, the governor and the attorney general met in private and came to the same conclusion that everyone else had. The only way to please the people of Ohio, Indiana, and Kentucky was the legal hanging of Jackson and Walling, and the only place that could successfully occur was in Newport, Kentucky. Governor Bushnell decided to trust Sheriff Plummer to make that peacefully happen and signed the requisition papers.

9 THE DRIVER

On Saturday afternoon, February 15, Patrolman Ed Swain walked his usual beat in a wealthy section on the north edge of Cincinnati called Mt. Auburn. As he passed the home of Major Winterfield, he saw George Jackson, the major's black coachman working in the stable, and the two exchanged waves as usual. The coachman put down his tools, walked over to Patrolman Swain, and asked him about the murder. He had the same questions everyone did: have they found the head? Have the men confessed? Any news on the driver?"

Then a question surprised the officer.

"I've been thinking a great deal about this case," said Jackson, "Suppose someone held a pistol up to this cab driver's head and scared him into driving the cab and keeping still afterward, would the police do anything to the driver?"

"No," replied Swain, "Under those circumstances, the driver would be all right."

With that, the coachman bid him a good day and went back to his work. But as the patrolman walked on, he pondered Jackson's question. It was just a bit too pointed, a bit too specific. Perhaps the man knew something he was not telling. Swain circled back to the major's house and confronted the coachman. If he had something to tell, he had better tell it now. Jackson admitted to having knowledge of the case but said he would only tell his story to the chief of police. Swain convinced Jackson to talk to his lieutenant first and let him determine whether his tale was worth the chief's time.

George Jackson was tall, strong, and very dark, an imposing figure, but visibly nervous as he entered the stationhouse. He took the seat offered and looked about him, assessing his surroundings and wondering if he had made the right decision to come. Jackson hesitated at first but once relaxed, he spoke freely; he had quite a story to tell.

The Friday night of the murder, Jackson said, he was commanding the Caldwell Guards, a black drill team that hoped to join the Ohio Militia. To that end, they practiced drills evenings around Smith Court, not far from City Hall. Just before they finished for the night, he left the First Sergeant in charge of the company and walked out to Elm Street to talk with some fellows who had been watching them drill.

A man in a white cap walked up to the men and asked if any of them wanted to make five dollars driving a cab to Newport. Jackson said he would do it and the man told him to wait while he made the arrangements. He returned about forty-five minutes later driving a surrey drawn by a spirited gray horse. Jackson took the reins and the man sat next to him.

"As I was driving along, I heard a funny noise in the back of the surrey," Jackson said, "a sort of a muffled sound. Something like a woman might make if she was suffering with a toothache."

"What did you think about it?" the lieutenant asked.

"Well, they had told me that they was two physicians taking a patient home, but I've read story papers and I thought something was wrong. I made a move like I was going to get out of the surrey, when the man on the seat pulled a revolver and put it to my head and said: 'You black son of a bitch, if you try to jump out of here, I'll send you to hell.'"

Jackson continued the journey, following the direction of the man with the revolver. When they stopped, the man got down from his seat and a man and woman got out of the back. The two men walked with the woman and one of them told Jackson to turn the surrey around and wait, he would whistle when they wanted him.

"How did the woman walk?" the lieutenant asked.

"She kind of stooped forward and leaned on the men." Jackson replied.

"Did she appear to be well?"

"No. She acted like a drunken person or one who was stupefied. They walked a short distance, and I heard a noise that sounded something like a groan. I got scared and took a piece of iron rail that was in the surrey and hitched the horse. I was scared, and I ran back."

Jackson said he ran all the way to the Newport bridge then walked the rest of the way home, returning some time after 3:00 that morning. Fearing retaliation from the men, he told no one about the trip. They said if he told, they had friends who would fix him.

The lieutenant felt Jackson's story was worth a hearing at Central Station. Colonel Deitsch was away in New Orleans on vacation, so George Jackson told his story to Night Chief Renkhart.

Renkhart knew this was big. He sent for Mayor Caldwell and had Jackson tell his story a third time. The mayor listened intently, then asked questions trying to throw him off, trip him up. But by the third telling, Jackson had smoothed out the rough parts; he had been consistent, telling essentially the same story each time.

Renkhart and detectives Crim and McDermott took George Jackson to Hamilton County jail to see if he recognized the men who had hired him to drive the surrey. Newspaper reporters, back in the good graces of the police, were present when Jackson told his story to Chief Renkhart and when they reached County Jail, a gang of reporters had already arrived. The policemen decided to take advantage of the crowd and enlist the press in an attempt to make the identification process as hard as possible for George Jackson. Portraits of Scott Jackson and Alonzo Walling had appeared in newspapers almost daily since the arrests. They feared he could be familiar with the prisoners' faces without ever having seen them.

They formed a circle of the men at the jail who were not in uniform, including jailers and reporters— forty men in total. Jackson, Walling, and Wood were added randomly to the circle. To further add confusion, all present were made to exchange hats and coats so the prisoners would not be dressed as described in the papers. Walling had on a stiff derby instead of his usual cloth cap. Scott Jackson wore a slouch hat.

George Jackson was led to the center of the circle and told to pick out the men he had driven to Newport. He had lost any sign of nervousness and seemed to enjoy the attention as he walked around the circle, looking each man in the face as he went. He knew right away they were not wearing their own hats and commented on it.

When he reached Walling, he stopped and said, "This is the man who sat behind me. I am almost certain, but he did not wear a stiff hat."

Renkhart then had Walling put on his own cloth cap, and George Jackson was positive Walling was the man.

Identification of Scott Jackson would not be as easy for someone who had only seen his face in the papers. Portraits of him had shown him with the full, well-trimmed beard he wore before the murder and with just a mustache as when arrested. He had shaved since his arrest, but not every day, and he now wore several days of scruffy growth on his face and neck.

James M. Allison, an *Enquirer* reporter from Covington, Kentucky, who was in the circle, would later testify to the identification of Scott Jackson. George Jackson said he never got a good look at the other man but could identify his voice, so he went around the circle asking questions of various men. He stopped at Allison, asked him to speak, scrutinized him closely, nose to nose, then said, "I think that is the man."

At this point, one of the policemen said, "Jackson, come over here."

Scott Jackson, who had been taking orders from policemen for the last ten days, thought he was being addressed and instinctively took a step out of the circle. He immediately realized his mistake and stepped back, but the motion was not lost on George Jackson, who shifted his attention to Scott Jackson.

George wanted to hear the man speak and had the prisoner say, "Go up, turn around and come back." After hearing several repetitions, George Jackson was certain of his identifications: Alonzo Walling was the man who sat next to him on the surrey, Scott Jackson was the man inside with the girl.

The Cincinnati police were ecstatic; they declared the murder solved. An unbroken chain of witnesses could trace Pearl Bryan, Scott Jackson, and Alonzo Walling from Wallingford's Saloon to Lock's farm. The circumstantial evidence they had been ready to take to trial, the hearsay and speculations, were now just side notes. The full weight of the case would be carried by the testimony of eyewitnesses.

The police could not be more pleased with George Jackson. He was well dressed and well-spoken, a public-minded workingman, employed by a prominent citizen of Mt. Auburn. His word was to be trusted. His integrity would not be impeached.

Lulu Hollingsworth and May Smith both said that Scott Jackson had hired a black man to take the body away. Though both of their stories had been discredited, they may have had some inside knowledge.

The story sent the investigation in new directions, and new witnesses emerged. One was Henry Underwood, a turnkey at the prison, who remembered seeing a mud-covered surrey on the Saturday the body had been found. An acquaintance of his had hired it from Mullen's stable to travel to a funeral and did not have time to wait for it to be cleaned. The description George Jackson gave of the vehicle was similar enough to prompt Underwood to call on Mr. Mullen.

The vehicle was a coupe-rockaway, a style often mistaken for a surrey. It had been rented to a young man with a dark complexion and mustache who paid Mullen $3 and left in a hurry. The rig was returned about four the next morning, with both horse and coupe covered with light colored mud. But Mullen could not positively state whether it had been the night of January 30 or January 31 and could not positively identify Walling at the jail as the man who rented the coupe.

George Jackson hesitated at first when asked to identify the coupe, but he was soon convinced that it was the rig he drove. When shown the two gray horses owned by Mullen, he identified the one rented that night. As Jackson became more sure of himself, he began pointing out details like the dent in the brass lamp. He said his boot made the indention as he climbed down in the dark.

The coupe was taken to Central Station for a thorough examination. There were bloodstains on the floor and on a lap rug in the back seat. Between the cushions, they found black beads that matched those on Pearl Bryan's hat. They also found a few strands of blonde hair inside the coupe.

But not everyone believed George Jackson to be the missing link. Why, after all, would the murderers hire a random stranger to drive them to the Highlands? By his own admission, George Jackson had no knowledge of Kentucky roads when he took the job. And according to George Jackson, Walling had hired him without knowing that he was a horseman. He was just looking for a warm body to drive the carriage. How would the killers possibly benefit by bringing a third party into their plan?

Scott Jackson called the story absurd without making reference to the crime. He commented to the *Tribune*, "Just look at it a moment. For the sake of argument, suppose Walling and I want to drive anywhere. Do you think we would hire anyone to do it for us? Walling was raised with horses, and I have driven behind some of the fastest in the state. Is it likely we would hire a strange Negro to drive us?"

The newspapers were now focused on the official story, but they were not compelled to rubberstamp it. While the police were congratulating themselves on having finally put in place the last link of the chain, the papers were digging deeper into George Jackson's history. By midafternoon, his story had lost much of its shine.

George Jackson was not the stable, well-established hostler he first appeared to be. He had come to Cincinnati in the fall of 1895, from Springfield, Ohio, where his reputation was somewhat shady. He was a high-ranking member of a lodge called the United Brothers of Fellowship, and he established a branch of the lodge in Springfield. From its members, he collected 27 dollars annually in dues, but these dues were never turned over to the organization. When the leader traveled to Springfield to collect, Jackson could not be found, and a warrant was sworn against him for the charge of embezzlement.

In Springfield, George Jackson worked as a hostler for a Dr. A. H. Vance. Both Vance and Springfield Chief of Police Van Tasse regarded George Jackson's story of the drive to Fort Thomas as a complete fabrication. He had a reputation in Springfield as a seeker of notoriety who was more than free with the truth. Most recently, he had accused lodge brother William Melvin of holding him up and stealing his watch. To substantiate his claim, he produced a handkerchief with Melvin's monogram, saying he pulled it from Melvin's pocket during a scuffle. As it turned out, William Melvin was not even in Springfield the day of the alleged holdup. It was believed that Jackson had pawned his watch and sewn the initials into the handkerchief himself.

A rumor reported by the Cincinnati press also said George Jackson, in cahoots with some white men, perpetrated an insurance swindle. These men had obtained the corpse of a black woman, declared it to be that of Jackson's wife, then claimed the money from a policy drawn on her life.

None of this mattered to the police. George Jackson's history, they said, had no bearing on the story he told. Whether he was a saint, or a sinner was not important. It did not alter the fact that he drove the vehicle carrying Pearl Bryan and her killers to Kentucky, or his willingness to testify to it.

The *Enquirer*, though, was not ready to let the matter rest. The paper suggested a practical experiment that, if successful, would conclusively prove the horseman's story. They would rent the same coupe-rockaway and the same gray horse that George Jackson allegedly drove that night. After dark, he would drive the carriage, duplicating his ride of the night of January 31, with an *Enquirer* reporter inside. If he could reconstruct it correctly and find, unprompted, the fence at Lock's farm, his story would be all but verified. It was not a destination easily found by someone who had never been there, and certainly it would not be found by someone who only knew the route from newspaper accounts.

At precisely 12:50 a.m., a strange procession departed Cincinnati City Hall bound for Kentucky. Mullen's coupe-rockaway was in the lead, rented by the *Enquirer*, driven by George Jackson, and carrying Night Chief Renkhart, Sheriff Plummer, and an *Enquirer* reporter. Detectives Crim and McDermott were behind them in Colonel Deitsch's horse and buggy. Next in line was another carriage of *Enquirer* reporters, and, behind them, representatives of other Cincinnati papers. In total, six vehicles.

Though George Jackson was explicit about the route he had taken to the bridge, no one cared about travel north of the river, and the procession took the fastest route to the Newport Bridge. Across the bridge, Jackson led them west then south down Licking Pike.

The rule, as stipulated by the *Enquirer*, was that passengers in George Jackson's vehicle could not speak. No one except for Jackson himself was to say a word, and Jackson filled the vacuum with a running commentary of his first drive down this road.

When they passed C. Robinson & Sons distillery, he pulled in the reins, peered into the darkness, and said, "This is the place where I tried to jump out. I had heard the girl's moanings long enough, and I was scared and wished myself shut of the job and determined to get away. Walling pulled a gun and began to swear at me. 'You black son of a bitch, if you try to jump out here, I'll send you to hell.' There wasn't much more said, but he made me get back, and we drove on."

Further down, they came to a farmhouse, and Jackson stopped again. "Walling was mad yet when we got here, and he continued his abuse of me. He said, 'We know your name and address, you black son of a bitch, and if you ever say a word about any of this to anyone, we will kill you.'"

By this time, though, no one was paying attention to Jackson's story. The reporter noticed around the same time as Sheriff Plummer that Jackson needed to turn east to get to the murder site on Alexandria Pike. He had already passed several crosscuts, if he did not take the next one, about a mile ahead, he would have to go all the way to Alexandria.

A little further on, he came to a farmhouse and pulled the carriage to a halt, saying, "Don't seem to me that I remember this house. I'm afraid we ain't on the right track."

Plummer could barely restrain himself. The next crosscut was three-quarters of a mile ahead, and the last, far enough back to put the whole venture in question. But, per the agreement, he held his tongue as George Jackson turned back the way he had come, north on Licking Pike. The rest of the carriages snaked along behind him. They came to a farmhouse on the right, and Jackson declared he had his bearings. He led the cavalcade down the road toward the barn. Late as it was, lights were still burning in the house, and a man came outside to see what the commotion was about. He was Henry Motz, who was spending the night with his neighbors, the Selbert family, who were mourning the death of their four-year-old child.

Sheriff Plummer explained the situation. Motz urged them to be quiet, so as not to disturb the grieving family, but yes, there was a crosscut to Alexandria Pike beyond the barn. He went back inside and fetched a lantern. It was a treacherous road, he said, and without the lantern, six carriages, on a moonless night, would never make it.

Motz held his lantern high, sometimes leading the parade, sometimes watching it, but he could not be everywhere he was needed. The horse pulling the second *Enquirer* coach took a turn toward Three Mile Creek, and the vehicle tumbled down the embankment, spilling four reporters into the mud. Progress stopped while everyone helped to right the fallen carriage.

Eventually, all were back in procession, and soon, to Sheriff Plummer's amazement, they struck Alexandria Pike. They were beyond Fort Thomas, and Jackson had to turn north. They came to the rail fence at Lock's property, and Jackson pulled the reins. This, he declared, was where they had taken the girl from the carriage into the woods.

Sheriff Plummer was satisfied that the experiment was a success. George Jackson proved he knew the route from Cincinnati to the murder site, following a road that even the Sheriff did not know. But the trip had been far from smooth and did little to quell skepticism among the reporters. Jackson had been following Walling's instruction; had Walling known this route?

Police and reporters now focused on finding the men who were with George Jackson when Walling hired him. Jackson had said that he was talking with four men, two members of the Guard, and two white men who had been watching them drill. Allegedly, Walling had addressed the group, offering any of them the job, and only George Jackson had accepted. Jackson had been unable to identify any of the men.

Reporters went to other members of the Caldwell Guards to see if they could help, and what they learned came as a complete surprise. The Caldwell Guards did not drill on the night of January 31. The first man they spoke to, Howard Scott, said the Caldwell Guards held a meeting at the home of Sam Ewing that night. It was serious business; they were court marshaling a recalcitrant member. As Captain of the Guards, George Jackson was there presiding and remained there until after 2:00 a.m. At Sam Ewing's home, reporters learned that his wife despaired at letting her husband join such a low organization but confirmed that George Jackson had been at a meeting in their house until well past midnight. At least eight members of the Guard concurred.

Jackson claimed it was the Guard members who were telling tall tales. They had the nights confused, and besides, they all had grudges against him. Howard Scott had been upset that his uniform had not been delivered when promised, and the others had their own reasons for wanting him discredited. They were jealous of him. The word of none of them could be trusted.

George Jackson's father, John S. Jackson, told reporters he believed his son's mind was deranged at times. When interviewed in Springfield, the elder Jackson explained his son had been a good-natured and obedient boy growing up but changed after a long illness. He began having epileptic fits, becoming rigid, and experiencing severe cramps. Only with prompt action and the utmost care was he revived.

"About this time," his father said, "he began laboring under the hallucination that he had innumerable enemies, some of whom were always seeking to do him injury."

On February 22, the headlines in the *Cincinnati Tribune* read, "The Evidence is Piling Up. No Doubt That George Jackson's Story Told to the Police is Utterly False." But the more the papers disparaged George Jackson and his story, the more the police supported it. Sheriff Plummer had been so impressed that George Jackson knew a road that even he, who made it his business to be familiar with the roads of Campbell County, did not, that he gave credence to the entire story. Night chief Renkhart admitted he was skeptical at first but was now a true believer. Others in the police department thought that maybe George Jackson had been wrong about some details, but his tale was essentially true. As for the rest of the Caldwell Guards, maybe attorneys for Jackson and Walling had visited them before the press did. The authorities had what they wanted, an unbroken chain of eyewitness accounts, and they were ready to take it to court.

Not long after George Jackson had told his story, two men arrived in Cincinnati by train from Illinois. One was middle-aged, gaunt, and wiry with whiskers that hung straight down like curtains from his cheekbones to six inches below his chin. His beard was grey at the roots, but the rest was a dull but pronounced black as if dipped in boot polish. The other man was in his mid-twenties, taller, with a raggedy mustache and three days' growth of beard. The older man was Captain John Seward, a private detective. The younger, William Frankly Trusty Jr., was an unemployed railroad brakeman, who claimed that he had driven Pearl Bryan's dead body from Cincinnati to Newport, Kentucky.

They had come from Urbana, Illinois, where Trusty had told his story to his father and John Seward. The detective saw an opportunity and brought the young man back to Cincinnati to pursue it. They kept their presence in the city a secret and stayed with a woman Trusty knew who lived on George Street.

Seward immediately went in search of those looking after the prisoners' interests. He contacted Walling's attorney, W.T. Shepherd, who was receptive to any story that contradicted evidence amassing against his client. Seward told him he had the man, a white man, who had driven Pearl Bryan's dead body across the river. His witness was willing to testify to that and to implicate others involved in Pearl Bryan's death in Cincinnati. If it were true that Pearl Bryan died in Cincinnati, Shepherd's client could not be tried in Kentucky.

Shepherd agreed to talk with Trusty who told the attorney that he had come to Cincinnati looking for work on the night of January 31, and he went to see the woman he knew on George Street. There was a lot of commotion in her rooming house that night. When he went into the hall to see what was the matter, a man who said he was a doctor offered Trusty $10 to drive a carriage over the river. He accepted, and at 10:00 p.m. they met back at the George Street house, where Trusty's lady friend made sure it was safe, and then helped the doctor and another man bring the body of a dead woman out of the house and load her, feet first, into the vehicle. The woman's mouth and eyes were open, but the body was cold and lifeless. There was no doubt in Trusty's mind that the woman was dead.

He drove alone with the corpse, he said, over the bridge into Newport. In downtown Newport, another man, joined him on the seat of the carriage and directed him down Alexandria Pike. When they reached their destination, the man paid Trusty the $10, threw the corpse over his shoulder, climbed the rail fence, and disappeared into the woods. Trusty drove back to the bridge, where he met one of the men from George Street who took the carriage back from him. He walked back across the bridge to Cincinnati, spent the night at Grand Central Depot, and the next day hopped a freight back home. After reading of the headless corpse found near Fort Thomas, Trusty was convinced it was the dead woman he drove from Cincinnati, and he knew he had to come forward.

Shepherd was impressed but skeptical. He knew it would take more than one man's testimony to overturn George Jackson's. Seward went into his sales pitch. He explained to Shepherd that investigation was his profession, and he had no doubt he could start from Trusty's story and locate other witnesses in the case. He had already met the woman involved, and he was sure he could find other witnesses, perhaps even the doctor.

Captain Seward convinced Shepherd to finance his continued investigations on George Street. Shepherd also hired him to investigate prosecution witnesses, trying to shake their stories and convince the Cincinnati witnesses not to give testimony in Kentucky. They agreed to keep Trusty's story a secret from the police and the press, hoping to ambush the prosecution in court with testimony that would, at very least, provide a reasonable doubt of the official story.

10 ACROSS THE RIVER

Scott Jackson was starting to feel the effects of incarceration and had lost the jocular nature he showed in earlier days. "I have no friends and no money," he told a *Tribune* reporter, "I wish I had the coin to hire a couple of good lawyers, and I'll bet that I would have no trouble in clearing myself."

In truth, Jackson's brother-in-law, Professor Edwin Post, provided him with excellent legal representation. Attorney D.D. Woodmansee, one of the best trial lawyers in Cincinnati, represented him at the arraignment, and former Police Court Judge James D. Ermston at the extradition hearing.

Walling was also well represented. His wealthy uncle, James Faucett, secured the Hamilton, Ohio, law firm of Morey, Andrews, and Shepherd. The firm would oversee his interests in both Ohio and Kentucky.

Will Wood's abortion hearing in Cincinnati resulted in a continuance. He was released on a $3,000 bond and left quickly to stay with relatives at an undisclosed location in Indiana. A grand jury convened in Greencastle, the seat of Putnam County, but it did not have enough evidence to bring charges against him. His Cincinnati case would be tried in April, roughly when Scott Jackson's murder trial was expected to begin, and he would likely broker a deal to turn state's evidence.

Jackson and Walling refused to go voluntarily to Kentucky, and their attorneys challenged the requisition order. The hearing, which began on March 7, was presided over by Judge Buchwalter, who limited attendance to those with a clear right to be there. The Bryans were there, Alexander and Fred with their entourage of prominent Hoosiers, and they had brought their attorney, Silas Hayes, to watch the proceedings and protect the family's interests.

When the hearing began, Walling's attorneys moved that the ruling for or against extradition be made for each man separately, opening the possibility that one prisoner would be sent to Kentucky and the other not. Jackson's attorney did not object. Since there were two requisition warrants, Judge

Buchwalter saw no problem with separating the cases, with the stipulation that both cases be heard that day.

Judge Ermston opened the case for Jackson, attacking the validity and sufficiency of the indictment. As the attorney general had, he argued that the indictment did not say which of the men did the killing or state conclusively how Pearl Bryan was killed. Ermston also asserted that the prisoners had the right to demand proof that they were in Kentucky at the time the murder was alleged to have been committed. Attorney Andrews, speaking for Walling, challenged the indictment on similar grounds.

Colonel Robert W. Nelson, a private attorney from Newport, voluntarily donated his time to the prosecution and led the Kentucky legal delegation, a role he would continue through the Kentucky trials. Nelson asserted that an Ohio court had no right to challenge the validity of a Kentucky indictment; it was enough that those who filed it believed it to be true. Any challenges must wait until the prisoners were in the jurisdiction of the indictment.

After hearing all the arguments, Judge Buchwalter retired to deliberate, promising to return by 2:00 that afternoon. Before leaving, he asked the defense attorneys if they planned to file habeas corpus suits. Both said yes, they had petitions prepared should he rule against them.

Standing on Court Street, on the south side of the courthouse, was a six-seat hack with a driver and two speedy horses, ready to take off at a moment's notice. Should Buchwalter rule in favor of extradition, Sheriff Plummer and Detectives Crim and McDermott would rush the prisoners to the waiting coach and, as fast as possible, cross the river and reach the Newport jail before the Ohio lawyers had time to file their papers and before a Kentucky lynch mob had time to gather.

When Judge Buchwalter returned to the bench, he ruled in favor of extradition, saying essentially that the fact that both governors had signed the warrant was enough to validate the indictment and was, in effect, the same as habeas corpus. However, he acknowledged that the laws concerning extradition were somewhat indistinct, and he would stay the extradition order for eight days to allow the defense time to appeal the case to Circuit Court.

The speedy hack would not be needed that day. The prisoners would remain in Cincinnati at least another eight days, but there was little doubt in anyone's mind that they would be going to Kentucky. Perhaps the most significant outcome of the hearing was when Judge Buchwalter ruled that the prisoners must be extradited; he ruled twice—once for Scott Jackson and once for Alonzo Walling. On that day, the Pearl Bryan murder officially became two cases, and that is how it would remain.

Jackson and Walling were returned to County Jail, where they would wait while their attorneys prepared their appeal to the circuit court. In Newport and Greencastle, the judge's delay fueled the fear that Jackson and Walling might escape punishment through some legal technicality. Threats of violence and violent demonstrations were increasing—some frivolous and easy to dismiss, others presenting serious danger. In Newport, a group of boys hung a stuffed dummy labeled "Jackson" to a telegraph line and threw rocks at it for an hour until chased away by police. A letter purporting to be from the "Moonshiners' Whiskey Organization" threatened to amass an army of 3,000 armed men to kill Jackson, Walling, and Wood. One threat taken seriously by Sheriff Plummer involved a man named Arthur Bryan, claiming to be Pearl Bryan's cousin, who had reserved 20 rooms at Betz's Hotel for a party of 40 Greencastle men traveling to Newport to lynch Jackson and Walling. In uncovering this plot, Plummer revealed that he had secretly engaged a large force of deputies to cope with potential mob violence.

On March 16, the circuit court upheld Judge Buchwalter's ruling, and the prisoners' attorneys said they would not take the case to a higher court—nothing now prevented the extradition. The following morning, Sheriff Plummer, with Detectives Crim and McDermott, took a patrol wagon to county jail to pick up Jackson and Walling. Their wrists were shackled, and they were led out of their cells to the waiting wagon. They wore the same clothes they had on when arrested, and after twenty-nine days in jail, both men now wore full beards, and their complexions had turned a sickly white.

As the wagon sped away from the jail, they were trailed by buggies and carriages carrying members of the press anxious to get a firsthand look at whatever transpired as the men were transferred to Kentucky. The reporters' plans were premature; this high-speed chase ended at city hall, and Jackson and Walling were unloaded and led to a room in the basement of the police station. It was a small, windowless room with two steel-barred cages in the center, separated by a partition made of sheet iron. Each man was placed in one of the cages.

This room, known as the sensitive cell or the "fly cell," had a hidden telephone transmitter pointed toward the cages. Wires led from the transmitter and battery to a room on the third floor where they were connected to telephone receivers allowing listeners to eavesdrop on conversations in the cell below. Unbeknownst to Jackson and Walling, everything they said in the cell would be overheard by the police. This would be the first time the fly cell was used in Cincinnati, and according to the *Cincinnati Enquirer*, the first time such an experiment had been attempted anywhere in the country.

Sheriff Plummer, Mayor Caldwell, Colonel Deitsch, Detective Crim, Detective McDermott, and a stenographer shared four telephone receivers to hear what they could of the conversation between Jackson and Walling. They assumed the prisoners would go to the front of the cage to speak to each other, putting them directly in front of the hidden transmitter. Jackson and Walling did not do as expected. Instead, they paced up and down in the cages as they spoke. They were able to hear each other, but the conversation was only picked up by the transmitter when they happened to be at the front of the cage. Consequently, the listeners could only hear portions of conversation and could not always tell who was speaking. Newspapers tried to reproduce what was transcribed by the stenographer, but it amounted to little more than gibberish punctuated by an occasional intelligible word.

The lawmen hoped to catch Jackson and Walling making incriminating statements regarding the murder, but even if they had heard the conversation clearly, they would have been disappointed. After nearly a month of separation, they spent most of the time laughing and joking with each other revealing just a hint of conspiracy. Detective Crim would later testify under oath to a bit of the conversation that he heard clearly:

> Jackson said to Walling: 'Lon, did you tell those newspaper reporters over at the county jail that someone had been furnishing me with whisky and cigars?'
> Walling answered, saying: 'No, I never made any such statement.'
> Jackson said: 'Then Fred is all right.'
> Walling says: 'How are they going to take us over the river and when?'
> Jackson says: 'I do not know.'
> Walling says: 'How will they do so? How would a carriage do?'
> Jackson says: 'If they would turn us out and let us go over from Fifth and Broadway, do you think we could find our way over there?'
> Jackson says: 'You are all right, old boy, stand pat. You have played your part well.'

The most surprising aspect of the encounter was how congenial it was, considering they had begun their custody angrily screaming accusations at each other.

"Just imagine," Sheriff Plummer told a reporter, "Two men who have accused each other of a foul murder meet for the first time and laugh and talk like the warmest of friends. Here are two men who apparently are trying to hang each other, greeting each other with the kindest remarks, and one tries to beg tobacco from the other. What do you think of that?"

Reporters waited in the dark corridor outside the basement cell until a message from Colonel Deitsch requested they leave the hall as their talking was thought to interfere with the transmission. They moved out of the hall but stayed inside, away from the large crowd that had gathered around City Hall. News had spread quickly that the prisoners were moved to Central Station and would likely move next to Kentucky. Men, women, and children thronged the sidewalks waiting for a glimpse of the prisoners.

After about two hours of listening, the lawmen were forced to admit they would not get what they wanted—no confessions, no incriminating remarks.

Sheriff Plummer came downstairs and called to reporters, saying he was ready to take the prisoners to Newport.

After the long delay, Detectives Crim and McDermott took Jackson and Walling to the courtyard of Central Station and into a waiting patrol wagon. Mayor Caldwell officially gave Sheriff Plummer charge of the prisoners, and Plummer took command of the wagon. Inside, Walling was handcuffed to Crim, and Jackson to McDermott. A sergeant held the reins as two gray horses stood ready to charge. Mayor Caldwell gave the order, and with a clang of the bell, the horses sprang forward. The wagon sped through city streets lined with crowds of people attracted by the clanging bell. Reporters, back in their own carriages, followed as rapidly as they could.

They crossed the Ohio River on the Newport Bridge, and as they neared the southern shore, Sheriff Plummer said to Walling, "We are now over the low water mark. We are now in Kentucky."

Walling said, "I'm glad of it."

Jackson said nothing. He had turned pale and appeared to be frightened of what would come next.

The horses had crossed the bridge at full speed but started to balk as they approached a large crowd that had gathered at the Kentucky end of the bridge. The mob was unexpected, and the lawmen were alarmed.

"If there is going to be trouble, I'm out of it," said Detective Crim. Now outside of his jurisdiction, he took his key and unlocked the cuff on Walling's wrist. McDermot unlocked Jackson's cuff, and now both prisoners were chalk white and trembling.

The horses pushed through the crowd and dashed up the street faster than the yelling crowd that followed. The courthouse was soon in sight, and the wagon turned into a side street where the Newport Jail stood at the foot of the grade. About ten officers were waiting there to protect the prisoners.

When the wagon stopped, Jackson and Walling wanted to run out of the wagon and into the jail, but Plummer said, "Wait until we see what the crowd is going to do."

The crowd did not follow them into the courtyard, and it became apparent that they were driven by curiosity, not anger. The prisoners were hurriedly taken from the wagon to the jail, and the door was locked. The officers then drove the crowd back and kept them a block away from the jail.

They made the run from Central Station in Cincinnati to the Newport Jail in eight minutes.

PART TWO

11 KENTUCKY

Soon after the body was discovered, even before she was identified, the Commonwealth of Kentucky offered a reward of $500 for the arrest and conviction of the murderer. A wide array of individuals who were involved with the investigation felt entitled to the reward. As the trials of Jackson and Walling approached, several staked their claim.

Louis Poock, the Newport shoe dealer whose independent investigation of the dead girl's shoes provided the clue that sent lawmen to Greencastle, Indiana, had already sent a formal claim to Governor Bradley. Poock was also working on a book on the murder, which stressed his role in the arrests.

A.W. "Gus" Early, the Greencastle Western Union manager who told lawmen about the telegrams sent and received by Pearl's brother, had filed his claim two days after the arrests of Jackson and Walling. Revealing the content of the telegrams had cost Early his job, and he now planned to travel to Kentucky and take to the stage telling his version of the story and playing his violin while awaiting the reward. The manager of the Grand Opera-house in Louisville received a letter from Early offering to perform on his stage.

George Jackson also had a claim to the Kentucky reward for completing the chain of evidence that linked Scott Jackson and Pearl Bryan to the murder scene. The $500 reward offered by The *Cincinnati Tribune* for the identity of the driver would surely be his, and why not the Kentucky prize money as well? Jackson also took to the stage and told his story at a Cincinnati dime museum.

Still in the shadows was William F. Trusty Jr., the Illinois brakeman, whose assertion that he drove Pearl's dead body to Kentucky threatened to split the state's case wide open. He and his "manager," Captain Seward returned to the Ohio Valley specifically to claim the rewards and were the only candidates actively working their claim. While their story was still unknown to the public, Seward and Trusty were working undercover in the pay of Walling's attorneys, accumulating evidence for an alternative version of Pearl Bryan's death, which, if proven, would uproot all other claims.

Cincinnati Detectives Crim and McDermott were certainly in the running for the reward; they had been on the case from the first day and were active in every stage of the investigation. But the odds-on favorite to win the Kentucky award was Campbell County Sheriff Jule Plummer, who had made the arrest and punishment of the killers his personal crusade. Like Crim and McDermott, he had worked every aspect of the investigation and additionally had informed Pearl's parents of her death and had met with two state governors to secure Jackson and Walling's extradition to Kentucky. Plummer did not publicly state his desire for the reward, but he expressed hope of being reimbursed for the money spent on travelling for the case.

Before any reward could be paid, Kentucky needed a conviction, and despite the overwhelming public belief in the guilt of Jackson and Walling, some reasonable people were saying that there was not enough evidence for an impartial jury to convict them of first-degree murder. Joseph Pugh, Police Chief of Covington, Kentucky, was one of the more vocal skeptics. He told the *Cincinnati Enquirer*, "In the shape in which the case now is, there is neither credible testimony nor reliable witnesses to present to a jury." He did not believe Jackson and Walling killed Pearl in cold blood. He did not find George Jackson's story of taking them in a cab in a circuitous route down deserted roads believable when they could have easily reached the spot by streetcar. And he questioned the character and credibility of the state's witnesses: George Jackson, who was "crazy about getting his name in the paper" and was wanted for embezzlement; Allen Johnson who, since coming forward as a witness was arrested for robbing his employer; and Dave Wallingford, who had since been arrested on a "delicate charge."

The biggest problem for the prosecution was raised by the defendants in their extradition hearing and by Governor Bushnell when he granted the requisition—outside of George Jackson's testimony, there was no evidence that Jackson and Walling were in Kentucky at the time of the murder. In fact, there was no evidence that either man had ever been in Kentucky. That situation would change as focus moved across the Ohio River.

Some witnesses from Bellevue, Kentucky—the town just east of Newport—came forward to say they saw Scott Jackson, Alonzo Walling, and Pearl Bryan in their town on the week of the murder. As with most of the revelations in this case, their stories did not fit neatly into anyone's pat explanation. On Thursday morning, January 30, a Mrs. Katie Holmes claimed to have seen two men and a woman talking with a neighbor, John Foster, from the window of her boarding house on Washington Street. One of the men was tall and dark, the other short and fair, and the woman wore a black cape and a black hat with pink flowers. John Foster, when questioned, confirmed the meeting. They had stopped to ask him if there was a ferry between Bellevue and Cincinnati. He told them there was no ferry in Bellevue. The nearest landed in Dayton.

Foster saw pictures of the prisoners in the newspapers, and he was convinced he had spoken with Scott Jackson that day. After seeing them first-hand in their jail cells, he was ready to swear that he had seen both Jackson and Walling that day. The woman kept her eyes on the river, and he did not get a good look at her face. He could not swear that she was Pearl Bryan, but he could tell she was a blonde. A girl from the country, he thought, not as finely dressed as a city girl.

They left him and walked south on Washington towards Foertmeyer's drug store. William L. Foertmeyer spoke slowly to the police in a thick German accent. Yes, he remembered seeing the two young men and the blonde girl but was less certain of the date than Mrs. Holmes and Mr. Foster were. It was the day his hired boy cleaned the windows, which was normally the last Friday of the month, however, sometimes circumstances, such as bad weather, would change that rule. He was sure it was either Thursday or Friday.

Foertmeyer went with John Foster to identify the prisoners, and he was able to say without a doubt that Jackson had been in his store. He was not sure about the other man. The young woman stayed outside, and the wind blowing from the east caused her to hold her hat in such a way that he could not see her face. She was blonde and wore a black cape. In the store, the taller man, Walling, did the talking, asking if there was a ferry or a skiff that docked at the end of Washington Street, and Foertmeyer told him what Foster had, that the nearest ferry was in Dayton. The taller man then purchased a cigar and offered one to the other man, who had declined. The two men rejoined the lady, and the three of them continued south.

Upon learning the man who was in his store was named Scott Jackson, Foertmeyer was reminded that the last week in January, he had received a telephone message from a Scott Jackson. His drug store had one of the few public telephones in Bellevue, and he had become a clearinghouse for messages. The message had been for Miss Maude Wagner and Miss Lida Rudy, to make an appointment to meet them at Maude Wagner's house. Maude Wagner was the daughter of Dr. George Wagner who lived in Bellevue.

A Mrs. Reardon, who lived on Van Vogt Avenue, which intersected Washington Street a block south of Foertmeyer's, had come across a photograph that must have blown into her backyard on Thursday morning, the day before the murder. It was the portrait of a young man, probably in his late teens, with his derby hat cocked at a rakish angle. She thought it must have been dropped by a sweetheart or mother. In attempt to find the owner, she showed the photograph to all the neighbors, but no one recognized the boy. She put it away without another thought until the following week, after the body had been identified and the papers began printing pictures of those involved. There was no doubt in Mrs. Reardon's mind that the subject of her photograph was William Wood, the boy from Greencastle.

Mrs. Reardon also told reporters of a curious occurrence on the night of January 31 she believed may have been connected to the photograph. She and her husband were in bed sleeping when they were awaked by a commotion outside the house. It sounded as though a large object had been dropped on their front porch. They listened and a bit later heard a horse and wagon stop in front of the house. It paused there for several minutes and took off at a gallop. It sounded as if someone had carried something through their backyard and left it on their porch while they waited for the wagon that then took it away in a hurry. When they checked the backyard gate in the morning, sure enough, it had been broken open.

Behind the Reardon's house was a vacant lot, which abutted the home and office of Dr. George Wagner, who lived there with his wife and daughters. According to the neighbors, the doctor was the nervous type, tightly wound, and eccentric. He could often be seen walking in his yard, talking to himself. Mrs. Reardon's opinion was that Pearl Bryan accidentally dropped the photograph on her way to Dr. Wagner's the day before he was to perform the abortion on her. She believed that Pearl died there and was carried in the night through the Reardon's yard and onto the waiting wagon.

Mrs. Reardon took the photograph to the Cincinnati Police and left it with Captain Hadley, who agreed that it bore a resemblance to Will Wood, but she was too frightened to tell the captain the whole story that she would later tell a *Tribune* reporter.

Maude Wagner denied receiving a telephone message from Scott Jackson or anyone else who called Foertmeyer's store. She also denied her father had any connection to Pearl Bryan. He had been unwell at the time, and shortly after Pearl Bryan's death, Dr. Wagner was voluntarily committed to the Eastern Kentucky Asylum for the Insane.

Sheriff Plummer and Detectives Crim and McDermott questioned all of the Bellevue witnesses and concluded that they proved Jackson, Walling, and Pearl had been in Kentucky the week before Pearl's death, but beyond that, the stories could not be substantiated. Mrs. Reardon's photograph and W.L. Foertmeyer's telephone messages were just two more crank theories in a case abounding in misdirection.

The lack of Kentucky witnesses was especially problematic for the defense, since they were not able to subpoena witnesses from Ohio and Indiana to testify in another state. Jackson's Kentucky attorney, Leonard Crawford, relied on depositions from the witnesses in Greencastle and Cincinnati. Friends of Pearl Bryan and Will Wood, in sworn testimony, blamed Pearl's ruin on Wood, and members of the Caldwell Guards in Cincinnati swore they did not train on January 31. Crawford read the depositions in court, but they did not have the impact of in-person testimony.

Of course, the prosecution could not subpoena out-of-state witnesses either, but the Cincinnati Police had little trouble convincing people to cross the river voluntarily to testify. George Jackson was anxious to testify in Kentucky, and reluctant witnesses like Dave Wallingford and Allen Johnson needed to stay in the good graces of the police. Without the persuasive power of the police, Crawford was left with the daunting job of persuading favorable witnesses to voluntarily cross the river and testify in Scott Jackson's defense.

Leonard Crawford was considered one of the most effective criminal lawyers in Campbell County, and Professor Post continued to spare no expense to secure topnotch representation for his brother-in-law. Crawford was prominent in Republican politics, having run unsuccessfully for Kentucky Attorney General in 1888.

Colonel Robert W. Nelson, a private attorney who had volunteered his services free of charge to the prosecution, was another of Campbell County's legal stars. Nelson was tall—in any setting, he would stand out as the tallest man in the crowd—and his presence commanding. Impeccably dressed, with a waxed mustache, he bore an air of smug intimidation. It was a rare match of two tenacious and unyielding defense attorneys.

Alonzo Walling, whose trial would follow Jackson's, continued to be represented by the Ohio firm of Morey, Andrews, and Shepherd. The Kentucky litigation was handled by another prominent Campbell County attorney, Colonel George Washington—a distant descendent of his famous namesake. W.T. Shepherd and Colonel Washington would be observing Scott Jackson's trial.

On April 21, the attorneys went before Judge Charles Helm to present preliminary motions prior to the beginning of Scott Jackson's trial. At 41, Charles Helm was young for a circuit judge, and younger than the attorneys appearing before him. On the bench, he was stern and humorless, and presided with unquestionable authority. He took pride in his reputation as tough and unyielding, and tolerated no nonsense in the courtroom, At the same time he prided himself on his fairness—a characterization that was not always shared by those who appeared before him.

Crawford and Helm came to blows during preliminary motions regarding the conduct of the trial. The defense disagreed with Sheriff Plummer's plan to limit attendance to spectators with tickets issued by his office. He argued that the Sheriff was biased against his client, and issued tickets to people hostile to Jackson while rejecting requests from his supporters. He was ready to speak at length on the matter, but Judge Helm stopped him.

"Your motion is entirely out of order, Mr. Crawford," said the judge, "and you hold yourself in grave contempt by making such a motion. What the

Sheriff is doing is under the direction of the court, and any exceptions to the action of the court will be held in contempt."

"But, Your Honor—" Crawford began, but was cut off again.

"No argument, sir, in a contempt matter. You cannot prescribe who shall be admitted to the courtroom."

"I do not desire to prescribe who shall be present." Crawford replied, "All I ask is a public trial, free of all restrictions."

"I insist, Mr. Crawford, that your motion and all remarks relative to it are in contempt, and I decline to hear any further argument. Have you any other motions?"

"None, sir, and nothing further to say, except that we file exceptions to the court's ruling."

"There can be no exceptions to a contempt matter, sir."

And that ended Crawford's first dispute with Judge Helm; it would not be his last.

After the proceedings, Crawford spoke to reporters in the hall outside the courtroom. He said that the defendant had a right to an open and public trial, but Judge Helm refused to hear any challenge to the existing plan. Crawford believed the Kentucky Court of Appeals would take a different view. Since he would be building the foundation for an appeal should the verdict be unsatisfactory, Judge Helm's ruling suited him perfectly.

Colonel Nelson watched Crawford address reporters and mocked his opponent. "That being the case, Mr. Crawford," he said. "I think we will be forced to have a rule issued against Judge Helm compelling him to vacate the bench if he continues to rule so much in favor of the defense."

The two attorneys then began to publicly taunt each other like two prizefighters weighing in before a championship bout.

"Never mind, Nelson," Crawford said to his opposing counsel, "you put George Jackson, the colored coachman, on the stand, and you will have all you can do to keep him out of jail."

"We'll have him on the stand sure," retorted Nelson.

"Just as sure as you do, I'll have him in jail," exclaimed Crawford.

"Well, say Crawford," Nelson responded sarcastically, "just give me the credit of originating the story that Jackson tells and all the details leading to his discovery. Do that for me, and my reputation as a criminal lawyer is made."

"No, I can't do that. Jackson told his story before you were in this case," Crawford shot as he left the room.

The stage was set. Everyone present could see animosities ran deep and disagreements in this case were beyond the merely legal. It would be an extraordinary trial.

12 THE TRIAL BEGINS

The square clock tower of the Campbell County Courthouse provided the first glimpse of Newport coming from Cincinnati over Central Bridge. The tower, stretching above three stories of red brick trimmed in white, was the tallest structure in Newport. Built in 1883, the impressive courthouse still felt new in 1896. Black and white tile on the lobby floor in geometric patterns led to a marble staircase with brass fittings. On a landing halfway up the stairs, a large stained-glass window stood on a landing halfway up the stairs and portrayed the art and industry of the Commonwealth. A mezzanine floor overlooked the lobby with hallways leading to courtrooms on each side. Above the second floor, a skylight with the Kentucky state seal in stained glass allowed light in through the roof.

The trial was held in one of the two courtrooms on the second floor of the courthouse. The room was large enough to accommodate three hundred spectators. A mahogany bar separated the gallery from the trial area, where Judge Helm would preside from the center, with the jury seated to his left and the witness box to his right, facing the jury. Next to the jury box, chairs were reserved for members of the press, members of the bar, and government officials.

As the proceedings opened on the morning of April 21, Sheriff Plummer, in his capacity as bailiff, had little control over the large crowd that overflowed into the yard surrounding the courthouse. Each day of the trial, Plummer issued spectator tickets, but on the first day priority was given to two large groups of non-ticket holders— one hundred prospective jurors summoned by the court and nearly a hundred prosecution and defense witnesses who would be sworn in together.

All eyes in the crowded room turned to watch as Scott Jackson was led in shackles to his seat at the front of the room. Neatly dressed in a black cutaway suit, he walked with a firm, rapid step and showed no signs of nervousness. His sandy beard had grown back but was somewhat ragged. His eyelids were tired and swollen, but the blue eyes behind them were as intense as ever as he scanned the sea of faces for anyone familiar. Very few in the courtroom could be counted as friends of Jackson, but he nodded hello to some reporters he recognized as he took his seat beside his lawyer.

Jury selection was the first order of business, and Sheriff Plummer took a roll of the hundred men summoned for jury duty. Any man not answering to his name was given a hefty fine of $100 to be collected by Sheriff Plummer. Prospective jurors could be excluded for a variety of reasons: not residents of Campbell County, not over 21, not householders; were members of the state militia or public officials; were physicians, surgeons, or attorneys; were druggists, undertakers, bank cashiers, telegraph operators, or agents of a railroad. Only one man, claiming suffrage in Cincinnati, was eliminated from the pool. The rest were called, one by one, to be questioned by Judge Helm.

When called, a prospective juror offered his personal reasons for exclusion from the trial: poor eyesight, hearing problems, age and infirmity, family hardships, etc. Judge Helm ruled on each case individually. Those remaining were questioned regarding their knowledge and opinions of the case. The most telling questions being, "Have you any conscientious scruples against capital punishment?" Very few answered in the affirmative. And "Have you formed an opinion on the case?" Nearly everyone had. Finally, "Can you fairly and impartially try this case from the evidence brought forward regardless of your opinion?" Some, in all honesty, felt they could not.

When Judge Helm had twelve men that satisfied him, he turned them over to the attorneys for preemptory challenge. Everyone—the press, the lawyers, and the general public— expected this process to take days. Leonard Crawford had signaled his intention to challenge this trial at every turn, in hope to enrich his case at appeal. He was already reluctantly, but realistically preparing for defeat in the trial at hand. Jury selection would be a perfect arena for technical challenges, sure to goad the judge into ruling against the defense. But to everyone's surprise, the jury selected by Judge Helm was accepted by both prosecution and defense.

They were a fair representation of eligible Campbell County men. Aged between 35 and 65, all were successful tradesmen or retailers all were married but for one widower, and all were active Democrats or Republicans. They were Baptists, Methodist Episcopalians, German Protestants, Roman Catholics; an Englishman, an Irishman, and the rest of German descent.

At 3 p.m., with the jury empaneled, Judge Helm, saw no reason to delay, and told Sheriff Plummer to swear in the witnesses. He called on the prosecution to give their opening statement and present as many witnesses as time would allow.

No one was prepared for this. Prosecutor Lockhart, like everyone else, expected the voir dire to take days. He gathered his notes and nervously scanned the room for his witnesses. Colonel Nelson, the de facto leader of the prosecution, had left the Courtroom already, his time too valuable for lengthy jury selection. Lockhart would have to open the case himself. While much of the gallery had also left, the crowd of reporters and observing attorneys was still thick inside the bar and had to pull their seats aside to clear a path for Lockhart to approach the jury, now seated to the right of Judge Helm.

Lockhart drew himself up and began. "It is part of my duty, gentlemen of the jury, as the Commonwealth's attorney in this action, to outline the evidence after you have heard the reading of the indictment. I shall state briefly the testimony and evidence which the Commonwealth will offer in support of this indictment."

He continued, "In the early part of 1895, Scott Jackson was at Greencastle, Indiana, where the unfortunate young lady, Pearl Bryan, lived, the youngest of a number of daughters of Mr. Alexander Bryan, an eminently respectable gentleman who had lived a number of years in the vicinity. The father of the unfortunate young woman was a native of Bourbon County, Kentucky, and removed in early years to the town of Greencastle, Indiana."

"I want to enter an objection," Crawford interrupted, speaking calmly but forcefully, "to the portion of the statement in which Mr. Bryan is said to have been a resident of Bourbon County, this state."

This breach of decorum in interrupting and objecting to the opening statement while it was still in progress was the sort of bold move expected by both the reporters and the Ohio Valley attorneys present. It explained why none had left the courtroom.

Judge Helm responded fairly to this early challenge. "You must confine yourself to what is in testimony, Mr. Lockhart," he said, addressing the prosecutor. Then he turned to the defense attorney. "However, Mr. Crawford, I cannot now decide as to the relevancy or irrelevancy of testimony, and I had rather you not interrupt the speaker again."

"And I shall not again interrupt him," Crawford said.

Lockhart fumbled a bit before fully regaining steam. He explained how the state would prove that Scott Jackson "by reason of his suave address and insinuating manner" had so engrossed the affections of this "unsophisticated country girl" that she yielded her virtue. He pointed his finger at Jackson and called him "a veritable Dr. Jekyll and Mr. Hyde. Up in Greencastle, he was a gentleman, but in Cincinnati, he was the consort of lewd women of both colors."

Lockhart said the commonwealth would show, by multiple witnesses, that the defendant persuaded Pearl Bryan to come to Cincinnati, that he was seen with her that week on both sides of the river, and "that there could be no human being save this man who was with the unfortunate girl, Pearl Bryan, at these times."

Lockhart worked himself into a frenzy as he described the murder scene, the headless corpse, and the quantity of blood that had soaked into the ground and dripped from the privet leaves above.

"The Commonwealth will show," he said, "that the condition of the body and the neck showed beyond a reasonable doubt that it was right there, at that place, that the decapitation was done, and …" Lockhart turned quickly, again pointing his finger straight at Jackson and raising his voice to thunderous, "that this is the man who performed that horrible deed."

Jackson looked back at Lockhart without flinching, but with a cool fascination, as if he were watching a theatrical production.

"If that should be the testimony of the Commonwealth, gentlemen," Lockhart said, addressing the jury, "beginning with the arrival of Scott Jackson in Greencastle in 1895, detailing his acquaintance with the unsophisticated girl, proving that she yielded to him her person and her chastity; that she was ruined by him; that by him she was brought to Cincinnati … if this story is told, link by link … if it is shown that he is extremely skilled in the use of the knife with which the crime was committed, we think this jury will have no difficulty in believing him guilty as charged."

When Lockhart finished his opening statement and took his seat, it was still early enough in the day for Judge Helm to call for witnesses. The prosecution called John Huling, the teenaged farmhand who found the body on his employer's property on the morning of February 1. Huling gave terse, straightforward answers to questions regarding what he saw and did that morning, verifying when and where the body was found but offering no new information. Crawford objected to some of the questions but did not cross-examine Huling.

The next witness, Coroner Tingley, gave a much more vivid description of the scene. He provided the first detailed account of the condition of the body and the first opinion as to cause of death.

"On viewing the stump of the neck, I found an irregular cut on the back, and upon turning it over found a smooth cut," Tingley testified, "The incision was as though a clean disarticulation had been attempted."

"Did you notice any other cuts?" asked Lockhart.

"Across the fingers of the left hand were cuts. The first finger just slightly cut. The other fingers were cut deeply."

Lockhart went to the meat of the coroner's testimony. "In your opinion, doctor, was the head cut off at that place?"

"I think it was cut off at that place."

"Was the head cut off after death, or did death result from cutting off the head?"

"I think the artery was severed while the heart was still beating, judging by the amount of blood on the privet leaves overhead."

"How much blood was there about the place?"

"It is hard to say, but judging from the size of the clots and amount in the ground and that which had been washed away by the rain I should say about a quart and a pint in volume."

"Can you state whether the head was severed by an expert or not?"

"It must have been severed by someone having knowledge of anatomy and surgery."

"What sort of instrument made the cuts on the hand?"

"It must have been some sharp instrument."

"Could the cuts have been made by the hand grasping the knife?"

"Yes, sir. They could have been, as though the knife had been drawn through the hand as it was being closed."

Crawford objected to this speculation but was overruled by Judge Helm, who said the witness was giving expert testimony. Crawford filed an exception to the ruling.

The coroner described the autopsy. The physicians removed the stomach and sent it to a chemist for analysis. They preserved the other organs in embalming fluid and sent them along with the body to be buried in Greencastle. They also found a fetus of about five months' gestation.

"Was there any evidence that here had been any attempt at a criminal operation?" Lockhart asked.

"Not with instruments." Tingley replied, "There was no sign of violence at all."

"What was the condition of the fetus?

"It was in a healthy condition."

Crawford objected to the question. Once again, he was overruled, and again, he filed an exception.

"Was the fetus alive at the time when the woman was killed?"

"Objection."

"Overruled, Mr. Crawford."

"Exception."

When Judge Helm took issue with the frequency of defense objections, Crawford promised, going forward, to raise as few objections as possible.

Lockhart finished with the witness, Leonard Crawford rose to cross-examine and went straight into one of the central questions in the case: was Pearl Bryan murdered where the body was found?

Tingley was unable to precisely pinpoint the time of death, but said it was between eight and fifteen hours before he examined it at 9:00 a.m. He believed the head had been cut off during life because there had been "a free and complete hemorrhage," which would have been impossible after death. Under Crawford's questioning, the coroner conceded that there were conditions under which the blood would stay liquid for some time after death. When asked how much blood he found on the ground, Tingley repeated that there were two large clots amounting to a quart and a pint of blood. Crawford asked what proportion of a body's weight was blood, and Tingley responded about one-thirteenth—in Pearl Bryan's case it would be ten pounds, or in volume, ten pints. That means that Pearl Bryan lost thirty percent of her blood, somewhat less than a complete hemorrhage.

There were no witnesses after Tingley It was 5:00 when Crawford finished his cross-examination, and Judge Helm ended the session. It was a busy day in the courtroom. A jury was selected days ahead of expectations. Through Coroner Tingley, the prosecution made its central argument, that Pearl Bryan was decapitated alive where her body was found.

The brief questioning also revealed the direction the defense would take. Crawford would object as much as possible on technical grounds, and he would challenge the prosecution's assertion regarding the decapitation. He had already begun to sow seeds of doubt.

13 BLOODY CLOTHES

Judge Helm entered the courtroom at 9:35 on the second day of testimony, and Sheriff Plummer called the room to order. As soon as the Judge took his seat, prosecuting attorney Lockhart stepped forward to consult him, and for several minutes they held a whispered conversation as the spectators sat down to wait.

While the judge and prosecutor conversed, Sheriff Plummer emerged from the witness room carrying a dressmaker's dummy attired in Pearl Bryan's clothing, still streaked with the dirt of John Lock's farm and saturated from the neck to the breast with the stain of dried blood. He set the dummy between the judge's bench and the witness stand, in full view of everyone in the courtroom. To the spectators, it was almost as if the headless girl had risen to give testimony in her own murder trial.

Crawford was immediately on his feet, loudly protesting.

"May it please the court," he said, "I stated yesterday afternoon that I wished to make as few objections in this case as possible, but I must make one now. The sheriff has just brought into court a figure for exhibition, a highly objectionable figure. I wish it removed from the courtroom. I think it highly objectionable."

Colonel Nelson rose for the prosecution. "This is part of our testimony. Of course, the gentleman would object to the testimony."

"I do not object to any testimony, but I do object to this." Crawford shot his hand back toward the hideous display. "I decidedly object to any dummy figure being brought into the court, and I ask the court to remove it."

Judge Helm looked up from his conversation and was as startled as everyone else by the bloodstained figure.

"I think Mr. Crawford is right," he said.

"If the court so desires," said Nelson, "of course, we are willing to remove it, but we have a right to put the clothing upon any receptacle so that the jury may examine it. It is as valid to put it on the figure as in any other

93

place. I want to know what objection he has, except that the gentleman wishes to exclude all the evidence in the case. In the Durant case, a dummy was permitted."

Nelson was referring to the 1895 San Francisco murder trial of Theo Durant, in which the torn dress of the victim Blanch Lamont was displayed in the courtroom on a dummy for the extent of the trial. But a California precedent had little value in a Kentucky court.

"Colonel Nelson, I have sustained the objection." said the judge, "The sheriff will remove the figure and return the clothing separately."

The sheriff carried the dummy back to the witness room and returned with an armful of clothing, which, at Colonel Nelson's request, he draped over the railings surrounding the witness box, where they would remain for several days.

Pearl's sister, Mary Stanley, was the first witness to sit in amidst the dead girl's bloody clothes. Still in deep mourning, she wore a black dress, black gloves, a black hat, and veil. She kept the veil over her face as she testified to the frustration of those in the crowd who hoped a look at Mary's face would help them visualize Pearl's. But Mary did not resemble her sister. She had her father's angular features. Pearl had been soft and fair like her mother. What came through the veil as Mary spoke was the tremendous sadness of this woman, who was here to do her duty but wanted nothing more than to be home alone with her sorrow.

Nelson began gently, and asked Mrs. Stanley about identifying the body. She told of childhood scars and marks that would only be known by someone as close as an older sister.

He asked about the fleshy stretch of skin extending between the victim's toes. Mrs. Stanley acknowledged that Pearl's feet had this feature.

"It would be termed a web foot?" Nelson asked.

"Probably would be so called."

At Nelson's request, Mrs. Stanley gave an inventory of the clothes she knew Pearl had taken, articles that had become familiar to those following the case—the plum dress, the fur-trimmed cape, the black hat with black beads and pink roses. Many of the items were hanging beside her on the rail of the witness box as she spoke.

Mrs. Stanley testified that Pearl took the clothing in two grips, one of brown alligator skin and a larger one of light brown leather.

Nelson showed her two valises, and without hesitation, she identified both as belonging to the Bryan family.

He then held up each of the articles hanging on the witness box. The corset and union suit Mary identified as the type and quality her sister wore. Nelson held up the bloody, green-checked dress.

"That dress, I know is hers." Her voice choked. "I helped to make it."

On hearing this, one of the jurymen, John Boehmer, tried vainly to stifle a sob, and tears filled the eyes of several other jurors.

Nelson held up the tiny pair of boots and said, "Look at these shoes, Mrs. Stanley, and say whose they are, or were if you can."

"I am sure they were Pearl's shoes."

At this, Boehmer began to cry in earnest, and tears spilled silently down Mrs. Stanley's cheeks. The courtroom was silent, but for the sounds of muffled sobbing.

Judge Helm turned to Mary Stanley and quietly offered to let her leave the witness stand until she recovered her composure. She declined, saying she would stay until the questioning was finished.

Nelson waited a few moments then had her identify the black hat found in Newport, a brown kid glove, and a piece of gold chain found near the body. He then showed her a pillbox containing a few strands of blonde hair found in the coupe-rockaway and asked if they looked like Pearl's.

"They look like her hair.," she said. "There is so little of it; I cannot say positively."

Finally, he showed her three handkerchiefs found in Scott Jackson's room, and she identified two of them.

"Do you know Scott Jackson?" Nelson asked.

"I have only seen him on the street in Greencastle."

"Is that he?" Nelson pointed at the defendant.

She wheeled slowly in the revolving chair until she faced Scott Jackson. Their eyes met, neither flinched. She turned and faced the jury. "Yes, sir." Crawford did not cross-examine.

Nelson called two Greencastle merchants, Joseph Piercy, a druggist, and Isaiah Vermilion, owner of a dry goods store to also identify Peral's clothing. Vermilion remembered selling Pearl some of the clothing on display. Piercy was not personally acquainted with Pearl Bryan but knew her by sight. He positively identified the pocketbook he had sold to her. Neither shopkeeper was cross-examined.

Nelson would unfold the story slowly, with agonizing detail, displaying the bloody clothes as much as possible, and showing the emotional effect they had on Pearl's family. His aim was to establish the dead girl's identity, remove any doubt that she was beheaded alive, and drive home the true horror of the crime before bringing Scott Jackson into the picture. But the Indiana witnesses had their own timetables. Those who came from Greencastle traveled together and would leave together whether Nelson was ready or not. Nelson took a break from the bloody clothes to examine Dr. Robert G. Gillespie, who would be returning soon to Greencastle.

Dr. Gillespie, the young Greencastle dentist who hired and advised Scott Jackson, was a nervous and soft-spoken witness. Even questioned by Silas Hayes, a hometown attorney, his testimony was hesitant. After establishing that Gillespie knew and employed Jackson, Hayes produced a letter Gillespie received from Jackson, asking him to identify it. This prompted a round of objections by Crawford, all overruled by Judge Helm.

Hayes showed the witness a stack of letters, some addressed to Pearl Bryan, some to Will Wood, and asked him to identify the handwriting. With some reservation, he identified the writing as Scott Jackson's.

Crawford jumped to his feet in objection to the introduction of the letters. Judge Helm overruled, allowing the letters to be entered as evidence. The prosecution reserved the right to read them in court later. Crawford made sure the stenographer noted his exception to the ruling.

Hayes asked Gillespie about conversations he had with Scott Jackson when Jackson was home for the Christmas holiday. Gillespie said Jackson was sitting in his office, deep in thought. When he asked him what the matter was, Jackson told him that Pearl Bryan was in the family way. Gillespie asked if he had illicit intercourse with Pearl Bryan. Jackson first said no, but in a later conversation, after Jackson had been to see Pearl that Christmas, he admitted to having intimate relations with Pearl. Jackson asked Dr. Gillespie for advice, and Gillespie told him to marry the girl. Jackson told him he could not do that under any circumstances.

Crawford's cross-examination of Dr. Gillespie concisely summarized the Christmas conversations.

"You asked him when you first saw him whether he had illicit relations with Pearl Bryan?" Crawford asked.

"He denied. Yes, sir."

"After that, he went out to see her, you say?"

"Yes, sir."

"Then he confessed that such relations existed?"

"Yes, sir."

The cross-examination ended.

When he returned to the clothes, Nelson called Pearl's mother, Mrs. Susan Bryan to the stand. She was also in deep mourning, dressed in black with a black veil, holding a black lace fan, and a handkerchief edged in black. She took the stand surrounded by the dirty, bloody clothing taken from her daughter's body.

Before the testimony began, Crawford rose. "If it is not expecting too much, I would like to know what the state expects to prove by this witness."

"We don't ask the defense what it expects to prove by every witness. What do you expect to prove by your witnesses?" Nelson asked Crawford directly.

"We expect to prove this man's innocence."

"I've no doubt that is your great desire," said Nelson.

"Now, if the court will permit me," said Crawford. He spoke to the judge but addressed the whole courtroom. "I desire to say that I admit that every article of clothing identified by Mrs. Stanley as the property of her sister was in the possession of Pearl Bryan in Cincinnati."

But that would not do for the court or the prosecution. They did not care whether Crawford admitted they were Pearl's clothes. Mrs. Bryan would also identify her daughter's clothing.

Under questioning, Mrs. Bryan explained in detail the identification she made of her daughter's body at the undertakers. Nelson raised each bloody garment for the grieving mother to identify.

In a wavering but determined voice, Susan Bryan verified the items she knew were Pearl's. When she was uncertain, she said it was the style Pearl wore.

She said, of the checked cotton dress, "This dress was made by my daughter and myself. She made the sleeves and yoke, and I made the skirt. It was made for the daughter who died while we were in Mexico. She was thin, and the dress was large for her. When daughter Pearl started away, I told her to use it as a dressing gown to keep from catching cold while she was dressing or combing her hair. It was not intended to be worn at any other time."

Crawford rose and again announced that he would save the court's time and admit that all the clothing belonged to Pearl Bryan. Again, Judge Helm refused, and allowed the prosecution to present their case in their own way.

Nelson continued to hold up items of clothing for Mrs. Bryan to identify until Crawford could not contain himself. "I insist that, as I have already admitted, that the clothes belonged to Pearl Bryan. The introduction of these witnesses is simply for the purpose of producing an effect on the jury. And I object to it."

Nelson, with an air of righteous indignation, said, "As I am representing without fee the Commonwealth in this case, I object to that sort of reflection. It is without precedent and an injustice to the Commonwealth and the dead girl. It is the first time in my experience in the practice of criminal law that an attempt has been made by counsel for the defense to prevent the introduction of the testimony by the Commonwealth."

Judge Helm interceded firmly. "The gentlemen will not indulge in personal reflections." He had already ruled on this matter. Nelson would continue holding up items of clothing.

Mrs. Bryan went on to identify the handkerchiefs, the shoes, the hat, the skirt, the stockings, and the dress. Whether or not it was the express purpose, her testimony absolutely produced an effect on the jury.

In his brief cross-examination, Crawford veered away from the bloody clothing and asked how many times Scott Jackson was at the Bryans' house.

"Well, I don't know exactly," said Mrs. Bryan. "I know he was invited there to spend the afternoon twice, and those were about the only times I shook hands with him. He was introduced to Pearl in the dining room by another young man."

"Mention the name of the other young man, if you would," said Crawford.

"Will Wood."

"And who introduced Jackson at your house?"

"Will Wood."

"When?" Crawford fired his questions quickly, barely giving the witness time to answer.

"Last Christmas, a year ago."

"Was Will Wood a habitual visitor at your house?"

"Yes, sir. He visited us frequently."

 "How long had he been visiting?"

"Well, if you'll allow me to tell you, his mother was a niece of mine, and he used to visit us often."

Colonel Nelson called Mrs. Bryan twice more in the course of the prosecution to speak in detail about Pearl's appearance and demeanor, and the circumstances, as she had understood them, of Pearl's trip from Greencastle. Each time she wore her black mourning clothes and spoke softly through her black veil Mrs. Bryan evoked the deepest sympathy of everyone in the courtroom.

The testimony of Pearl Bryan's mourning family members was a visceral reminder of the devastating impact of her violent death. Nelson succeeded in eliciting the sympathy and anger of everyone in the courtroom including the jury. Next, he would need to focus that anger onto Scott Jackson.

14 EYEWITNESSES

By the fourth day of testimony, jurors began to show signs of strain. They had been sequestered since the first day and slept together in another courtroom outfitted with a row of cots. The twelve jurymen appeared each morning fatigued and disheveled, looking no better than Scott Jackson when Plummer's men led him into the courtroom each day.

Jackson, though, would come to life as he sat down next to his attorney. Before each session began, he would speak softly with Leonard Crawford and scan the crowd for people he knew and took comfort from familiar faces.

When he saw his brother-in-law, Edwin Post, for the first time, he asked, "How is mother?"

Professor Post told him his mother was quite ill. Mrs. Jackson had been bedridden since her son's arrest and would not be attending the trial.

Jackson tried to explain to Post the positive aspect of the trial so far, in attempt to convince him that his money had been well spent. The professor nodded, impassive; the money would be spent regardless of his opinion.

Despite three days of damning testimony, the position of the defense was not hopeless. Nelson scored some emotional blows with the bloody clothing and the somber, heartrending testimony of Pearl's sister and mother. Still Nelson had proved little more than the identity of the headless girl. That she was Pearl Bryan was never seriously in question. When Crawford asked undertaker White in cross-examination how many times the body had been incorrectly identified while she lay in his establishment, the speed and vehemence of Nelson's objection was exceeded only by Judge Helm's sustaining ruling. The dead girl was Pearl Bryan—this could not be challenged.

Crawford had better luck with Nelson's parade of medical witnesses. The coroner and the prominent Campbell County and Cincinnati physicians all testified that the cause of death was decapitation while the victim was still alive. Dr. Gilbert I. Cullen, a Cincinnati physician who saw the body at Lock's farm, testified that someone with a sharp knife could decapitate a body in a matter of seconds. But the quantities of blood inside and outside the body were still raising doubts. The drops of blood found on the underside of privet bushes above the body were consistent with a severed artery, but there appeared to be too much blood remaining in the body for death by exsanguination. Decapitation of a live body should have left more blood on the ground. Crawford hammered this fact in every case.

The other questions that tripped up each medical expert were the effects of cocaine and chloroform on blood coagulation. Cocaine was used medically as an anesthetic to assist in childbirth and to increase heartbeat, but with unpredictable results.

Dr. W.H. Crane, the Cincinnati chemist who analyzed the content of Pearl's stomach, testified to finding about two and a half grains of cocaine—probably ingested, possibly injected with a hypodermic needle. When asked what a lethal dose of cocaine would be, Dr. Crane said records of cocaine deaths showed amounts between six-tenths of a grain and 22 grains had proven fatal. None of the other physicians could be any more precise. When asked about chloroform, some of the experts concluded that it could delay coagulation, but none would speculate on the effect of both drugs in combination.

Though less than conclusive, the medical testimony had successfully underscored the horror of the crime. It was time for Nelson to tie Scott Jackson to that horror.

The spiritualist, Mrs. Plymouth Weeks, testified that a young couple came to her house for a psychic reading between 11 a.m. and 1 p.m. on Thursday, January 30. She testified that the woman said her name was Pearl Bryan. The man she learned later was Scott Jackson. Jackson whispered to his attorney throughout her testimony and chuckled out loud when she pointed him out in court. In response to Leonard Crawford's only cross-examination question, Mrs. Weeks admitted that due to the private nature of their conversations, her clients very seldom gave their names.

Witnesses from Bellevue, Kentucky, testified to seeing two men and a woman on Washington Street the week before the murder. Katie Holmes timidly recalled the trio walking down her street and stopping to talk to her neighbor, John Foster. One man was short and fair, the other tall and dark. The girl with them appeared to be from the country, not dressed stylishly, wearing a black cape, and a hat with roses. Mrs. Holmes could not positively identify Scott Jackson, and she could not say for sure if the day was Thursday or Friday. An extremely nervous witness, Katie Holmes fainted upon leaving the stand.

John Foster, on the other hand, was a strong and confident witness who distinctly remembered seeing them around noon on Thursday, January 30. He was positive that the two men were Scott Jackson and Alonzo Walling.

The woman bore a resemblance to the various portraits of Pearl Bryan saw seen in newspapers. Foster testified that he had positively identified both men when they were held in the Cincinnati jail.

The elderly druggist William L. Foertmeyer recalled identifying the men, first at the Cincinnati Jail when he went with John Foster and learned that their names were Jackson and Walling, then again, at Sheriff Plummer's request, at the Newport jail. Foertmeyer testified that Walling bought a cigar from him and asked about ferries to Cincinnati. He did not get a good look at the woman who remained outside and kept her face turned away. She wore a black cloak and a black hat with red roses, and when a gust of wind caught her hair, he saw that she was blonde.

Foertmeyer's testimony was a disappointment to anyone who had followed the Bellevue rumors before the trial. He was still unable to recall if the day he saw Jackson and Walling with a woman was Thursday or Friday. He remembered receiving telephone messages from Scott Jackson, but at the time, did not connect the two events. He also did not state who was to receive the messages.

The facts in the testimony of these witnesses were vague and somewhat contradictory. Pearl could not have been seen by Mrs. Weeks in Cincinnati between 11:00 and 1:00 on January 30, and also by John Foster in Bellevue at noon the same day. Surprisingly, this discrepancy did not come up in cross-examination, but it was not lost on the *Enquirer* whose headline the following day read "Testimony That Will Not Stand." Despite the patina of doubt around each of these eyewitnesses, Nelson had made his point. Jackson, Walling and Pearl Bryan were seen together after the time both men said they had last seen her.

The eyewitnesses who really mattered were the ones who saw Pearl Bryan enter the cab with Jackson and Walling in Cincinnati on Friday night and later walk into the woods after leaving the cab in Newport. The drive began at Wallingford's saloon in Cincinnati.

Dave Wallingford described his saloon to the court, including the wine room or sitting room with its curtained stalls. When asked what kind of people frequented the place, Wallingford said, "All kinds. Some are nice people, and some aren't so nice."

Wallingford testified to meeting Jackson and Walling around August of 1895, and since then, they had come in nearly every night. Walling came in on Thursday night with Fred Albion. Jackson came in on Friday night accompanied by a young lady, about 5 feet, 2 or 3 inches tall with a light complexion. Wallingford identified the hat and dress as the ones the young lady was wearing. Jackson left her in one of the stalls and went to the bar where he ordered sarsaparilla for the girl and "the usual," a shot of whiskey, for himself. Jackson borrowed two dollars from Wallingford, which he paid back the following day.

He said that Walling came in later through the George Street door and asked for Doc. Wallingford directed him to the sitting room stall where Jackson was sitting with the girl. Walling stayed about 15 minutes. Then they all left by the George Street door. A cab was standing on the street outside the door, but he did not see them enter.

Allen Johnson, a porter at Wallingford's, gave a more succinct characterization of the saloon's clientele: "Laboring men and ladies of ill repute." He told the Court that he worked there for four months prior to that night and knew Jackson and Walling that whole time. Doc and Wally, as they were known at Wallingford's, were in the saloon nearly every night. He had never known either man to bring a woman there prior to Friday night, January 31. Jackson left her in one of the stalls and went to the bar to talk to Dave Wallingford. While Jackson was borrowing money from Wallingford, Johnson took the girl a glass of sarsaparilla.

Nelson showed him the black hat with pink roses, and Johnson identified it as the hat worn by the woman with Jackson. Nelson then pointed to the bloody housedress, and Johnson identified that as well.

Johnson went on to testify that some fifteen minutes later, Alonzo Walling arrived at Wallingford's, greeted Johnson, and stayed just long enough to make his presence known to Scott Jackson and the woman. Then the three of them left by the "ladies' entrance" on George Street. They all got into a cab and left.

On cross-examination, Crawford tried to shake Johnson's certainty. He phrased the question a variety of ways, suggesting that the day Jackson borrowed the money from Wallingford was Monday or Tuesday, before Jackson shaved his beard. Johnson could not be swayed, the night was Friday, January 31.

Crawford turned away from Johnson and prepared for another line of questioning. He asked about a meeting Johnson had with Walling's attorneys, Andrews and Shephard, in a Cincinnati saloon.

"Mr. Shepherd told me he did not want me to come over to Newport." Said Johnson, "I told him that the people on this side would make it unpleasant for me if I did not go over and testify in Newport."

The cross-examination of Allen Johnson continued to a second day, but Crawford did not get much more from him. On redirect examination, Colonel Nelson revisited Johnson's meeting with Walling's lawyers. Nelson had Johnson say again who Andrews and Shepherd were and had him point out Mr. Shepherd, who was sitting in the courtroom. Johnson explained that he was tending the bar at Billy Ford's saloon and the attorneys were there talking to Dave Wallingford. They bought Johnson a drink, then asked him where Clara Bates's place was.

"Who is Clara Bates?" Nelson asked.

"She keeps a house of ill fame." Johnson responded.

"Did you take them there?"

"Yes, sir."

Nelson paused, this was the significant question, "What did he say about your coming to Kentucky to testify?"

"He told me no law on earth could compel me to go to Kentucky to testify against Jackson, that I was beyond the jurisdiction of the Court. He said he would be in town on the 14th and prepared to pay me more money than the witness fees I would get."

Nelson finished his questioning, and Johnson moved to leave the witness stand when Crawford rose and asked Johnson a few more questions.

"Do you know a man by the name of John Seward?" Crawford asked.

The question startled Johnson. He sat back down, eyeing Crawford warily.

"No, sir," he said.

"I want to ask you if you stated to John Seward, or, if you don't know him by that name, to anyone, at the corner of George and John Streets in Cincinnati, some time in this month of April, that if there was money in it, say $25, that you could say the woman that Jackson had at Wallingford's was not Miss Pearl Bryan?"

"No, sir, I did not."

Crawford let it go. He had no more questions for Allen Johnson, and Johnson stepped down.

It was the first mention in court of Captain John Seward, who was scheduled to testify for the defense. He would no doubt contradict Johnson's denial and tell how the bartender tried to sell his story. At the time, Seward was an operative of Andrews and Shepherd, and if such a bargain was indeed proposed it was likely initiated by Seward. While Crawford was not able to trip Johnson up during his testimony, he was able to question Johnson's motive for testifying. Johnson balanced his fear of the police with his desire for personal gain, and the law won.

W.T. Shepherd sat behind the defense table and occasionally leaned forward to give Crawford advice on Cincinnati witnesses he interviewed and police and government officials he knew by reputation. His Kentucky associate, Colonel Washington, usually sat at the clerk's table by the wall opposite the witness stand. The two viewed the trial from different perspectives as if by this triangulation, they could build a strategy. But during the testimony of Allen Johnson, Colonel Washington sat with Shepherd, and both men listened intently.

Shepherd was a particularly unattractive man – weak chinned, balding, with bulging eyes and arched eyebrows that gave him a look of perpetual astonishment. This became a look of indignation when he and Colonel

Washington approached Judge Helm during the lunch hour to protest the testimony of Allen Johnson. They were upset that Johnson had given the impression they attempted to buy his testimony. In fact, they said they met with Mr. Johnson to learn, firsthand, what he knew in this case and to make sure he was aware that Cincinnati police had no jurisdiction to compel his testimony in Kentucky. If money was mentioned at all, it was by Allen Johnson and not the attorneys.

More importantly for the attorneys, they wished to clarify Allen Johnson's statement regarding Clara Bates. The witness left the impression that Shepherd and Andrews left Billy Ford's saloon to visit a brothel. While they did not deny they paid a call on the house of Miss Bates, it was purely professional, on behalf of their client to interview the women there. They investigated the claim that Walling had gone to Clara Bates's following the murder and left his bloody rubbers there.

The attorneys wanted their actions to be clarified to the court and for Allen Johnson's testimony to be disallowed. Judge Helm agreed that the evidence given by Allen Johnson concerning attorneys Andrews and Shepherd's visit to Clara Bates's house was detrimental to their reputation and had no relevance in the case. When the afternoon session began, he duly instructed the jury to disregard this testimony.

Colonel Nelson did not agree. "If it please the Court," he said, "I wish to say that until the conclusion of the testimony, the relevancy of this testimony, together with any other testimony yet to be introduced, will depend upon the testimony finally introduced. Now, I don't wish to have a discussion on this point. I don't care whether the testimony is admitted or excluded, but I respectfully suggest that the final discussion in the matter of the relevancy or irrelevancy of testimony be rendered by Your Honor after all the testimony is in."

Judge Helm agreed in principle with Colonel Nelson's argument, but in this case, it was implied that two gentlemen of the bar had visited a house of ill-fame, which was entirely foreign to the case. Nelson and Crawford briefly sparred over whose questioning had elicited this accusation, but Judge Helm was determined to keep the focus of the trial on the defendant and not on any attorneys in the case. His ruling on Allen Johnson would stand.

15 A RAPID YOUNG MAN

A buzz of excitement spread through the courtroom when the prosecution called William Wood to the stand. He was the first of the star witnesses, the man who would pin Pearl Bryan's downfall on Scott Jackson and directly tie him to Pearl's trip to Cincinnati. It would be testimony guaranteed to turn Crawford's defense from reaction to outright attack.

Will Wood emerged from the witness room and walked slowly to the stand with the same smug half-smile of his newspaper portraits. In marked contrast to his father's gray beard and clerical dress, the beardless 19-year-old wore a new suit with jacket and collar cut in collegiate style. The *Cincinnati Enquirer* described Wood in Court as "…the youth who, by his manner, seems to desire people to think him a rapid young man."

Will Wood had the distinction of being the only person with fewer friends in the courtroom than Scott Jackson. He was, of course, despised by Jackson and his supporters, but he was equally hated by the victim's family, who made it clear that, cousin or not, they wished he were on trial as well.

Trying to avoid the Bryans, Wood chose to travel to Cincinnati via the Vandalia railroad line after learning they would be taking the CH&D. It did not help. While he rode the crowded trolley car from Cincinnati to Newport, Wood was subjected to a vicious kick to the shin. He looked up to find that his attacker was Fred Bryan, who ordered Wood to stand on the platform outside the rear of the car for the rest of the trip. Wood complied, and considered himself lucky not to have been killed on the spot.

Will Wood took a relaxed, rather less-than-respectful posture on the witness stand. It was all a huge misunderstanding, he testified. He never any but the best intentions for his cousin. In fact, he never engaged in any evil thoughts or deeds before Scott Jackson moved in next door. It was Jackson who ruined Pearl Bryan and persuaded her to go to Cincinnati for the abortion. Wood's involvement began and ended with his introduction of Scott to Pearl. When he learned of Pearl's condition, he passed along Jackson's prescriptions to end it, but he had no hand in filling them. He listened when Jackson talked of abortion, but he did not participate in its arrangement. He did not comply when Jackson asked him to perpetrate a deception, and when Jackson pleaded, "Stand by me," Wood did not.

Wood tried to portray himself as an innocent boy who resisted corruption by the evil man from the East. Censoring his usual speech patterns, he often paused in his testimony to find inoffensive words to make his points. Silas Hayes, the Greencastle attorney, did the questioning for the prosecution, but any comfort Wood may have gained from examination by a hometown lawyer was dashed by a barrage of defense objections. Though most were overruled, they were a dark reminder that Leonard Crawford would also have a turn at the witness.

Crawford did succeed in suppressing some of Wood's testimony. Hayes tried to have him summarize the letters Jackson had sent to him to relay to Pearl, including instructions for terminating her pregnancy. There was no evidence that these letters had been destroyed, and the physical letter, Judge Helm said in support of Crawford, is the proper way to introduce such evidence.

The prosecution did get one summarized letter into evidence— the letter handed to Wood by his uncle on the train from South Bend to Cincinnati when in the informal custody of detectives Crim, McDermott, and Plummer. Wood told of reading the letter then tearing it up and disposing of the pieces on the train. Judge Helm took his word that the letter was no longer extant, and despite Crawford's objections, allowed Wood to reconstruct its content from memory.

Wood stated, "It was dated Cincinnati and began 'Hello, Bill. I have made a great mistake and am in trouble. I want you to stand by me. I wonder if Doc will stand by me.' It went on in that kind of raving manner. I read it only once."

Crawford objected again, "I move the court to exclude from the answer that 'it went on in a raving manner;' if he knows what the other words were, he can state them to the jury, if he does not, he cannot state his opinion."

The objection was sustained.

"Who was the 'Doc" he referred to in the letter?' Hayes asked.

"I suppose he referred to Dr. Gillespie."

Crawford got up again, and this response was excluded as well.

Hayes continued, "State to the court and jury how often, if more than once, the expression or inquiry, whether you would stand by him, was used in that letter."

"Three times."

Attorney Hayes now produced an actual letter in an envelope and handed it to Wood. "State whether you recognize this letter and the handwriting as being that of the defendant, Jackson."

"It is. It was written in the same hand as all my letters from him were written."

"I will ask you to state to the court and jury what name the defendant, Jackson, if any other than her own name was used in speaking of Pearl Bryan."

"Bert," said Wood.

"How frequently have you heard him speak of her as Bert?"

"Frequently in his letters."

Hayes read to the court the letter Jackson sent to Wood after the murder asking him to forge a letter from Pearl to her family saying she had left home- -in every case referring to Pearl as Bert. Hayes then returned his attention to the witness.

"I will ask you, Mr. Wood, to state to the court and jury whether or not there were ever any improper relations between yourself and Pearl Bryan."

"There never were."

"State what your relations to her were."

"Purely social."

"State whether or not you have ever visited her as a suitor, courted her, or anything of that kind."

"I never did."

Mr. Hayes concluded. Leonard Crawford rose and walked slowly to the witness stand. Wood paled. This would not be the gentle questioning of the gentleman from Greencastle, anxious to take his side against Scott Jackson. Crawford intended to blame Will Wood for Pearl's ruin.

Referring to sworn depositions, Crawford questioned Wood on conversations he had with his friends prior to the murder. William J. Grooms recalled that two weeks before Pearl left, Wood told him he had a girl in trouble. Wood denied having the conversation.

Ed Hunt in Indianapolis said Wood told him he had "something nice in Greencastle." After some hesitation he said it was Pearl Bryan and he could resume relations at any time. Hunt called him a liar.

Wood denied making these statements saying, "No, sir. If I should have had that conversation and he called me a liar, I'd have knocked him down."

Homer Newsome testified that Wood told him he went to Pearl Bryan's house and finding her alone and in bed, occupied the bed with her.

"I never said anything of the kind because there is no truth in it." Said Wood.

Crawford continued to relate stories from the depositions, including an occasion when went to Pearl Bryan's house to repair her piano, and when he learned no one else was in the house, he continued his improper relations with her. The questioning, at this point, became so explicit that neither the *Enquirer* nor the *Tribune* deemed it fit for publication. Wood denied each case.

Crawford questioned Wood on the fact the charges against him in Cincinnati for assisting procurement of an abortion were dropped after he agreed to come to Kentucky and testify against Scott Jackson. Wood testified that he came voluntarily, and his decision was not tied in any way to the charges against him.

After briefly questioning Wood about the letter he tore up on the train, Crawford told the Court that several other letters from Will Wood were among the effects in Jackson's room, which were taken by the police. He demanded that the letters be turned over to the defense, after which he would continue his cross-examination of Wood.

The prosecution first denied any knowledge of the missing letters, but eventually, they were located and given to the defense. Three days later Crawford recalled Will Wood to the stand to continue his cross-examination and to read the letters in Court.

"Where were you on February 1st of this year?" Crawford asked the witness.

"Plymouth, Indiana, John Wiltfong's, a clerk of the District Court."

"Do you remember writing a letter to Scott Jackson from Plymouth?" Crawford took a stack of papers from the table and walked back toward Wood.

"Yes, sir." Wood answered, "I think it was on Sunday. It may have been Saturday."

"Was it in type, or was it handwritten?"

"On a typewriter."

"How did you sign it?"

"I signed it with a 'B,' I think."

"Look at this letter. Is that the one?" Crawford handed Wood three typewritten pages.

"Yes, sir," he responded. "That is the letter."

"Look at the interlineations of pencil. Are they in your hand?"

"Yes, sir."

Crawford took the papers back from him.

"Where were you about February 3?" Crawford asked.

"South Bend, Indiana, the Oliver House." Wood responded.

"Did you write a letter to Scott Jackson from there?"

"I did."

"Look at this letter. Is this the one?" He handed wood another letter.

"Yes, sir, it is."

Crawford requested the letter be put in evidence, and he prepared to read them in Court, but Judge Helm was uncomfortable with what he already heard from Will Wood. He asked to see them, and after perusing them briefly, decided that they were not fit for mixed company. The judge requested that all ladies present leave the courtroom, and looked to Sheriff Plummer to make sure they complied. Reluctantly, and with much protest, the female spectators were escorted out. When the room was quiet and devoid of delicate ears, Crawford read them. The letters were reproduced in the Cincinnati newspapers, once again omitting the passages deemed too offensive.

Circuit Court of Marshal County
Plymouth, Ind.
February 1, 1896

Dr. Scott Jackson
Corner Court and Central Avenue
Cincinnati, Ohio

My Dear Dusty:

Surprised, eh? Well, here I am away here, this is one hell of a town, you know that I used to live here? I have saw or seen, Ha! Ha! Lots of my old friends, several old girls, one or two of my old "girls" you know what I mean, they were awful glad to see me, somewhat surprised, but nevertheless I had a hell of a time last night, was up till three o'c this morning, I have been up so late here of late that I feel like – well you may know what.

Well, how is Dusty? I suppose he has come back by this time, that he is well and enjoying himself etc. How are you anyway? Has anything happened yet to you or anybody else? If not, why not? I had one hell of a dream last night, I thought that somebody I knew, I don't remember who, came from your place, and was going to make trouble. I thought I owed them something I don't know what, of course, but then it was that way. I thought I – well no use to put it to paper, or any place else. I want to know the latest, all the news, if you have let a chance go by without improving it I am going to raise hell with you and then some.

If you have grown chicken hearted you ought to be shot, that is all I have to say about it, but I want you to write me all you know and if you don't know anything write me what you don't know if that suits you any better.

I go to S. B. Monday morning, I want to be here three nights, one night won't do me any good. Say, God damn it, what do you know? I don't want you to know anything that I don't know, you know that I am very jealous hearted, and few other kinds of hearted to boot.

Well, I went around to see Cora last afternoon that I was home. I think she is the dearest girl in town. I was going to call on Stella, but I couldn't find the nerve and I guess it is just as well that I did not, for I don't think that she was very anxious to see my blooming face anyway. Although I think well of her she hardly recognizes me on the street, I am going to give her a chance very soon I hope, if everything goes well.

I am staying at John Wiltfong's he has a son that is a hell of a sport. There is nothing that he won't do. He is onto all the sporty people in town, they all think there is nobody like Charley, he always thought well of me. He was awful glad to see me when I came he is a hell of a good-looking fellow. He took me around to see my old people, when I lived here we always ran together. He used to be as slow as I was but he has changed somewhat since I saw him last. He is alright.

I guess my folks wouldn't do a thing to me if they knew that I was up here in this town. They think that I learned all my meanness the year that we lived here, well now, I don't know as to that do you? If there is anything that I haven't run across yet, is that so?

I hope you have seen your Kentucky people since you wrote, give Blanche my very best.

Well write me to my "office" next time you write, and write all the news.

My best to Wally and all the rest,

Yours,

B.

Will Wood sat calmly on the witness stand as Crawford read and did not seem to realize the utter contempt his letters inspired in those still in the courtroom. "He was profane and sacrilegious to a degree," wrote the *Cincinnati Tribune*, "and exhibited a condition of total depravity little expected of the son of a minister of the Gospel."

The second letter offered more of the same. Wood maintained a quiet expression, but he apparently enjoyed the sensation his letters were causing.

Oliver House
South Bend, Ind.,
February 3, 1896

Dr. Scott Jackson
Corner Court and Central Avenue

Cincinnati, Ohio

My Dear Dusty:

Yours of last week, not received, damn it. I wanted to hear from you so bad. Here I am way up here by my lonesome, raising hell. If I had rye whiskey into my carcass I might write an interesting letter. Doc is simply a twin Jesus. I have to be so careful what I say that I am just about crazy. Somebody's "A Cold Day" is at the Oliver Opera House tonight. I have gotten acquainted with one of the girls, and have a "comp." You see, I am hot stuff: "Got lots of money?" "No, damn it, but I have one hell of a good face."

This girl's name is Nellie Disher, a brunette about Stella's size, only not quite so well made. She has the mon, she buys my rye whiskey and helps me drink it. Whoop! Hell, I feel good; shake, old man, here's to you. Get Willie one.

You better stay away from here, at least till I'm gone. I told Nellie about you and showed her the photograph of you and me in Greencastle. She is dead stuck on your picture.

I am so glad to be rid of Greencastle. God damn that old place anyway. I never intend to go back there again except for a visit. When the old Gent says come home, you are spending too much money, I am going to skip. C? Whenever you want to C me just send me the price, and I am there, C?

I have a girl on the go here by the name of Daisy Hoham, she is a bird.

I will tell you what happens next if you do the same.

B.

When the reading was finished, Crawford indicated he was through with the witness. Colonel Nelson rose for redirect questioning, anxious to mitigate the damage the letters had done.

"How old did you say you were?" Nelson asked.

"Nineteen." Wood responded.

"How old were you when you first met Scott Jackson?"

"About seventeen."

"State what influence Scott Jackson used over you."

"He had great influence over me and everybody else he associated with. It was an influence I cannot explain. I did about whatever he wanted me to. I was always trying to keep up my end of the string with him."

16 DEAR FRIEND PEARL

Before calling their most damaging eyewitness, George Jackson, Nelson had one more sidetrack to take. Crawford scored a blow when he read Will Wood's letters to the court. Wood was damned by his own words, and his testimony reduced to indecent boasting and self-serving excuses. The prosecution had its own stack of incriminating correspondence to read in court.

Mr. Hayes had letters, provided by the Bryans, sent from Scott Jackson to Pearl Bryan, he revealed not only Jackson's intimacy with Pearl but also the duplicity of his character. The letters had the opposite effect, so much so that the *Enquirer* observed that Hayes appeared to be addressing the jury in Scott Jackson's defense.

The first letter was sent to Pearl from Indianapolis in 1894 when Jackson was a new dental student there. It was the letter of a lonely man without much to say, apologizing for poor penmanship, asking after news from home, and sending condolences over the illness of Pearl's sister Jennie. Beyond showing that he and Pearl were close enough to correspond, there was nothing incriminating about the letter.

The next letter went a step further. It was just a short note, during that memorable summer in Greencastle, apologizing for missing a social event at Pearl's home.

Greencastle
June 13, 1895

Dear Pearl:

I had hoped to see you before this, but, as I have not had the pleasure, I feel as though I ought to let you know why we were not at your house on Friday evening last. The trouble was Bro. Wood could not go, and I did not know where to get anyone to go with me. I assure you that I am very sorry I could not have had the jolly time intended, but could not. I hope that we will be able to get out when Minnie comes again.

Very truly yours, in friendship

Scott

The next letter, from July of the same year, seemed to suggest some shared secret in the matter of Pearl's health.

Greencastle
July 13, 1895

Dear Friend Pearl:

I received your very kind letter and would have answered it before this but I intended to call at your home yesterday. I will try and get out to see you some time soon. I ought to have done so in this last week. Somehow one thing or another has kept me from it.

I trust you are feeling much stronger. Be sure and take good care of yourself. Plenty of rest and no worry, eat well and pleasant thought will help you wonderfully.

My very best and kindest regards to your mother and hoping to have the favor of seeing you soon, I am your friend,

Scott

Hayes read a letter Jackson wrote to Pearl a week later after receiving word of her sister Jennie's death in New Mexico. After being excluded from the courtroom for Wood's letters, women were back in force for these. After the letter of condolence was read, many were audibly sobbing. The jurors glanced at each other in amazement. This was the first positive view they had of Scott Jackson. Maybe he was not the cold-hearted monster they were led to believe.

Greencastle, Ind.
July 20, 1895

To My Dear Friend Pearl:

I learn this morning of the sad bereavement that has visited you. Believe me, I extend to you my sincere sympathy in this time of trouble. I only wish I might find a way of showing you my real friendship.

The great God and Father has seen fit to call unto Himself the dear sister who has left us not only beloved by the family, but respected and loved by all who has ever known her. The pure and upright life has fulfilled its mission here and has been called to receive her reward - to wear the crown of everlasting life and glory in her Father's home.

There are many, many causes for rejoices. Her arrival home, to the dear ones and being among friends. Her relief from the cares, trial, hardships and suffering of this land of ours. She has only left us for a short time. Just gone to meet the Giver of all pure and loving gifts and prepare herself for the coming of those she loves best and dearest.

I would call and see you, but knowing that so many of your friends are with you, that, perhaps, you may not desire so many others about. But I assure you I think of you. If I can be of any service, you have but to command.

With heartfelt condolence to your mother and yourself, I am, very truly yours, in friendship,

Scott Jackson

The last letter to Pearl was written from Cincinnati when Jackson found himself, once again, a student in a strange city.

Palace Hotel
Vine, Sixth and College Streets
Cincinnati, Ohio
October 24, 1895

My Dear Friend Pearl:

Here I am in old Cincinnati, and I do not know as I enjoy it as much as I expected. I do not have the time to run about as much as I would like. They keep us very busy at the college all the time. Three lectures in the morning is the rule, and work every afternoon in the laboratory or infirmary. At night we have to write up our lectures and get ready for work to-morrow. So we have no time to run about. I see this pen is of little account. Hope you will be able to read this scribble.

I think as a letter writer I am somewhat of a failure.

I do not know of any news to write you, and cannot think of anything of interest to tell you. This is a horrid dirty place. They use a great quantity of soft coal here, and there is a thick cloud of smoke hanging over the city all of the time. Clean linen is out of the question unless you change every hour or so.

I have not yet met any of the young people here excepting a few of my classmates. I am rooming with one of the boys who was at Indianapolis last year, and take my meals here at this hotel. It is awfully lonely for me here. True, there are crowds of people and all kinds of amusements to be indulged in, but at night I am usually so weary that I retire early.

Oh, how I do miss the young ladies of Greencastle. You all made it so pleasant for me this summer. I am sorry circumstances forbid my making any just returns, but when a poor fellow is busted what can he do? I shall always remember the summer of '95 as the most enjoyable I have ever had.

I trust you will not think me forward in writing to you. I do not want to forget any of the friends who were so kind to me and hope I may have the pleasure of hearing from you once in a while.

I hope that this finds you enjoying the very best of health, and that you are having a good time. Kindly give my very best regards to Miss Hibbitt when you see her and also to Minnie. I hope all are well at your house, and, trusting I may have the pleasure of hearing from you in the near future, I am, very truly yours in friendship,

Scott Jackson.

While Scott Jackson was considered a good student by his professors, even they knew he found plenty of time to "run about" in Cincinnati and did so at every opportunity. But it was clear to everyone in court that this man, accused of seducing and ruining this poor girl, is now worried that he is too forward in simply writing her.

The last letter read was not to Pearl but to Dr. Gillespie, and was perhaps, the most remarkable. It was dated January 31, 1896, the day Pearl Bryan died, but it did not have the tone of a man who was about to commit murder. Jackson's letter asks Gillespie to stick by him, and the prosecution presumed he was asking Gillespie to stand by him in his denial of murder. In general, though, the letter had the sound of a harmless missive to a friend and mentor.

Palace Hotel

Vine, Sixth and College Streets
Cincinnati, Ohio
January 31, 1896

Hello Doc:

Well, well! At last here goes that long-promised note. Have just come from a lecture, and am en route to grub. I have thought many times of sending you a letter, but somehow time seems very short, and I have not had the time this term for corresponding that I had last term. They are poking it at us thick and fast and are keeping us hard at work. Am plugging away at chemistry and anatomy, getting in shape, if I can, for exams. Have not done very much work in the infirmary this term but have to get at it at once.

We received notice on Wed. that we each had to make a full solder upper case, and it must fit the model when finished. Have to grind all teeth separately, and a lot of other trash. Am almost sick of it now and haven't hardly begun. All of the boys are kicking and none of us are anxious to tackle the job, but in this case, it must be done.

Well, old man, how are you and how is business? Oh, say, did that plate fit our friend Hughes O.K.? Had a letter from mother the other day, and she tells me your janitor is going to quit you and go to South Bend. Well, I hope it will be a good thing for the boy.

Now, old man, I do not know any news to write about, and that is one of the reasons I have put off writing until this time. Everything is moving along first-class, so far as I know. We have had some very nice warm weather here, and I am glad to say it has helped me to partly get rid of my cold, but it is very bad yet.

How is everybody? Give all my friends my very best regards, and let me know all the news, and stick by me without fail. Be sure and keep track of all the dear girls. And next summer I am hoping we will be able to make some good coin in and round about old Greencastle. I am expecting a piece of bridge work next week – seven teeth, anchor on L central, R, cusped and r, second molar. It will be a daisy, if the patient comes back.

Well, I am getting hungry, so will quit. My best regards to your wife, and don't forget to stick to your old college chum.

Jack

Let me hear from you when you can.

The letter reading had backfired — where the prosecution heard innuendo and conspiracy, the jury and most in the courtroom heard kind words from a lonely student to his close friends. Maybe if Nelson read them rather than Hayes and added his own inflection and commentary, they would have come closer to the mark he intended. Instead, they showed the jury a softer side of Scott Jackson than they had yet seen.

None were so surprised at this move by the prosecution as the lawyers who had come to observe the trial. Attorneys who spoke to the press after the day's session agreed that the letters had seriously damaged the prosecution's case, and some went so far as to say with these letters in evidence, the jury would never agree upon the death penalty.

17 THE LAST LINK

The afternoon of April 28 saw the largest crowd at Scott Jackson's trial and the largest gathering of women spectators. Judge Helm's censorship made the proceedings even more appealing. At least fifty women were in attendance, and the scene in the gallery before the hearing resembled a theatre before the rising of the curtain. George Jackson was to testify, the lynchpin of the state's case, the last link in the "unbroken chain," the only person who could tie Jackson, Walling, and Pearl Bryan to the scene of the murder.

Doubts concerning George Jackson's veracity and character grew since the day he walked into the police station. Though everyone wanted to believe him, no one was sure how he would hold up under Crawford's harsh questioning. Outside of court, the prosecution downplayed his value to their case, but he was still the link that held their story together, and if he broke, it would set them tumbling.

George Jackson was calm and composed as he took the stand. He answered the questions put to him loudly, with deliberation but without hesitation. Nelson asked his name and occupation, then about the Caldwell Guards, the black drill team which he captained, specifically about their drill on the night of January 31.

"How late did you stay there?" Nelson asked.

"Until 12:20," Jackson responded.

"Where did you go then?"

"Over Smith to George, and there I left the Quartermaster; when he left, I went with two white men who said they belonged to company K, of the First Regiment."

Jackson explained that he first met Alonzo Walling after the company drilled, the night of January 31. Walling approached the men and asked if any of them wanted to earn $5 driving two students with a sick patient to Newport. Jackson said he would do it, and Walling went to get the cab. About 45 minutes later, Walling returned with the coupe-rockaway, drawn by a

118

spirited gray horse. Jackson drove over the bridge down to Alexandria Pike with Walling sitting next to him in the box.

He heard the sound of a woman moaning as if suffering from a toothache coming from inside. Then he heard the crash of glass. Frightened, Jackson started to jump off the cab. Walling pulled out a gun and said, "You black son of a bitch, if you don't drive on, I'll drive you to hell."

Jackson drove on, turned left down a mud road to Licking Pike, and stopped where Walling told him. The man inside got out first then helped the lady out. Walling got down, and the two men helped the lady over the fence.

"Tell the jury who the man was who pulled the gun." Nelson, driving home the killer's names.

"Alonzo Walling."

"Who was the man on the inside of the cab?"

"I heard the name since. It was Scott Jackson."

It was an abbreviated and more concise version of the story George Jackson had been telling since coming to the police. The story was familiar to nearly everyone in the courtroom but was not universally believed. Crawford would put it to the test.

He began his cross-examination by referring to depositions from Springfield, Ohio, regarding George Jackson's reputation. He then went to work on the troublesome details of Jackson's story. Jackson didn't know if the toll was paid going over the bridge, couldn't remember if there was a toll gate on the Pike, didn't know how many people were in the carriage until they got out, and couldn't describe landmarks he would have seen on his trip there and back.

The toughest questions, the ones Crawford pressed relentlessly, where the attempt to determine the route Jackson took and duration of the trip. The ride began when Walling handed George Jackson the reins at around 1:00 a.m. They crossed the Ohio River and followed a roundabout and unfamiliar route down a dirt road to the crime scene. After Jackson and Walling led the young woman into the woods, George Jackson became frightened. He left the scene on foot after he tied the horse to a piece of railroad iron he found in the carriage.

"You could not have been very much frightened when you tied the horse," said Crawford.

"Oh, I was pretty badly frightened," said Jackson.

"You were frightened enough to run away?"

"I didn't stay there."

"Did you run or walk?"

"Yes, sir. I ran."

As Crawford questioned him regarding the trip back to Cincinnati, Jackson seemed to have trouble with the details.

"How far did you run? Crawford asked.

"I ran until I got to the Newport River." Said Jackson.

"All the way? Up and down?" Crawford pressed.

"Yes, sir. Up and down through the fields and anything else."

"You followed the Pike?"

"I didn't run all the way on the Pike," Jackson hesitated, "I followed the lights, what I concluded was the way to Cincinnati."

"Then, you went back on the pike the way you came?" Crawford asked, trying to picture the location.

"Yes, sir, and the dirt road."

"Then how soon did you leave it;" Crawford asked, "could you see the lights?"

"Yes, sir. I could see the lights shining in the lamps."

"When you went down the mud road, could you see the lights?"

"Yes sir, at the end of it."

Jackson had retraced his steps, following the treacherous muddy road back to Licking Pike.

"Then what did you do?" Crawford asked.

"Then I kept what I thought was the lights in Cincinnati and came right on," said Jackson.

Except for the lights of Cincinnati, Jackson had trouble describing his return trip. He could not tell where he was in Newport when he reached the Ohio River or seeing the Licking River. He was also imprecise as to the time it took him to return home.

"What time was it when you got back to Major Widdifield's?" Crawford asked.

"I can't say about the time."

"As late as two o'clock in the morning?"

"It was later than that."

Crawford continued to press him, "Was it quarter after 2?"

"I can't say." Jackson thought for a moment, "As near as I can recollect, I got home and made the furnace fire, made the fire in my room, and just sat down when the electric lights went out."

Jackson could not say what time he returned home. Crawford took another tack, "Is it not a fact that when you first told your story, you said you got home at 3 o'clock?

"When I first told it, I said it was after 3 o'clock."

"Did you not afterward say it was five?"

"I did not say it was."

"Are you ready to say it was five now?"

"I am not ready to say what time it was."

"George, was it daylight when you got to Widdifields's?"

"No, sir, it was not."

Crawford had him retrace his journey home once again. Jackson explained that he did not stick to the road because if the fellows he drove found he had left, they might try to follow him. The route became confusing, and when Crawford tried to reconstruct what Jackson had said regarding the road and the lights, Jackson said Crawford misunderstood him.

"I said I went back up to the new road," Jackson corrected, "and after I found the road, I got off the road to follow the lights to Cincinnati."

Crawford tried to follow, "After getting to the Pike, leaving the dirt road, you came this way?"

"No, I did not say that. I went back the way I came to the dirt road and started down the dirt road and got off the dirt road and went through the field."

Crawford continued to question him on his return route, but with no resolution. He switched the questioning to the drilling of the Caldwell Guards, then to the circumstances of Jackson bringing his story to the police and why he waited nearly two weeks before coming forward.

"Why did you not tell it sooner?" Crawford asked.

"Because I was threatened." He said.

"Who threatened you?"

"Alonzo Walling, he said if he ever heard of my saying anything about this drive, he would blow my damned brains out," said Jackson.

"Before you told your story, did you hear anything about any reward?"

"No, sir, I never heard anything about any reward."

"Did you not read in the *Tribune* about $500 reward?"

"I do not take the *Tribune*."

"You had not seen the *Tribune* or the *Enquirer* before you told your story?"

"No, sir; I had not. I was not reading much of any paper at that time."

Jackson said he did not come forward after Jackson and Walling were arrested because they had told him they had friends who would tend to him if he said anything. They had his address and knew where he could be found. But after the arrest, he also feared that they might say he was connected. He brought the story to the police before they could come looking for him.

Crawford returned to the beginning of the drive to the murder site and how long took in each direction.

"How far do you think it is from George and Elm in Cincinnati, over the route you took to the bridge, then zigzagging out the Licking Pike, up the dirt road and back on Alexandria Pike where the wagon stopped?"

"I could not say how far," Jackson responded.

"You have been over the road since?"

"Yes, sir, once since."

"Well, how far do you think it is?" Crawford pressed, "Three miles?"

"Further."

"Three and a half?"

"I could not say," Jackson sat up, looked around the room, "I would not like to say, I might make a mistake."

"You want to be careful about making mistakes?"

"I always have been, yes, sir."

Crawford did not relent, "How far is it from the Cincinnati end of the bridge up to where you live?"

"I guess about two miles, and maybe more than that."

From the start of the trip to the Newport Bridge was about a mile and a quarter. On the Kentucky side of the bridge, using the circuitous route down Licking Pike through the mud road, striking Alexandria Pike south of the murder scene, then heading north to the point where Jackson, Walling, and Pearl Bryan got out was about five miles. After tying the horse, George Jackson retraced his steps to the bridge on foot, then walked another two miles. While not impossible, it was unlikely that George Jackson could have left after 1:00 a.m. and completed the journey before dawn. Crawford returned to this in his closing arguments.

Crawford did what he could to discredit George Jackson's testimony, but neither Nelson's questioning nor Crawford's cross-examination changed anyone's mind. Those who believed him found Jackson to be a credible witness who told a consistent story and held up well under cross-examination. Those who believed Jackson's story was a complete fabrication found nothing in his testimony to make it more credible. But unless it could be proven false, George Jackson's eye-witness testimony was still the most damaging evidence against Scott Jackson.

18 SCOTT JACKSON TESTIFIES

Sleeping away from home and family took a toll on the wellbeing of the jury. By the second week of trial, they entered the courtroom with eyes bleary and bloodshot, their demeanor fatigued and careworn. White's Funeral Parlor donated the use of a pump organ to the jury room to brighten their off-hours, and Sheriff Plummer did what he could to make their ordeal bearable. On Sunday, he hired an omnibus to give them a tour of the Highlands, finishing with a stop at the YMCA where they could bathe. But on Monday, it was the same monotony. Normally active tradesmen and men of business were forced to sit still for hours paying attention to testimony, while trying not to worry about what was happening to the business in their absence.

Colonel Deitsch and Mayor Caldwell both testified regarding the questioning of Jackson and Walling when they were first arrested. Crawford objected to their testimony, saying that it was invalid because the prisoners had been coerced. He also wanted the court to disallow anything Walling said against his client.

Judge Helm thought the questioning was proper but disallowed testimony to anything said by Walling unless Jackson had also been in the room and did not disagree. The judge also had problems with testimony regarding the conversation between Jackson and Walling in the fly cell, introduced by Detective Crim. He questioned the listeners' ability to distinguish, through the telephone line, who was speaking and even questioned their first-hand knowledge of who was in the cell, since the listeners were out of eyeshot. In the end, he wisely ruled to exclude all testimony regarding the conversation overheard in the fly cell.

Following the testimony of Colonel Deitsch, the prosecution rested their case.

Leonard Crawford opened the defense with two controversial decisions—he chose to forgo an opening statement going directly to testimony, and called, as his first witness, the defendant, Scott Jackson.

The room was electric on April 30 when Scott Jackson strode to the witness stand. This was the highlight of the show. The spectators, who had been straining to see even the back of his head, would now see his face, and would hear him speak in his own defense.

Jackson was less nervous than the witnesses who testified against him and appeared as cool and collected as anyone in the courtroom. His sandy beard was full once again and recently trimmed. The day he testified, he wore fresh linen and looked as dapper as the young lawyers who had come in to watch the proceedings.

Jackson stood with his right hand raised, his face flushed as the oath was administered, to which he responded soundly, "I do."

Crawford began.

"Mr. Jackson, tell the Court and jury how old you are."

"I was 27 years old last month."

The questioning began with Jackson's early life in Wiscasset, Maine and Jersey City, New Jersey. He spoke of the seven round trips across the Atlantic that he had taken with his father as a boy.

After his father's death, Jackson went to work as a messenger boy for the Pennsylvania Railroad Company in Jersey City. After a year or so he was promoted to an inside position, making manifests for freight bills and waybills. Eventually he took charge of the billing department.

"What was the cause of your leaving the railroad?" Crawford asked.

"I was discharged for being an associate of the chief clerk." Said Jackson.

"Tell the circumstances connected with your discharge."

Jackson paused before answering, "It is rather a long story, Mr. Crawford."

"Well, tell it. This is your trial."

Jackson told his version of the embezzlement at the Pennsylvania Railroad Company, placing all the blame on the assistant cashier, Alexander Letts. As Letts rose in the company, Jackson was promoted as well and the two became friends outside the company. During the period when Letts was Assistant Cashier and Jackson Chief Clerk, the monthly statements showed a shortage of $23,000. Among the freight bills upon which no cash return had been made were several signed with the initials S. J. When questioned by the company what he did with the money, Jackson said he signed the bills according to Letts's direction and turned the money over to him. Letts left the company prior to the investigation and soon after, Jackson was discharged along with other clerks who signed fraudulent bills.

"Were you arrested as a result of this?"

"I was not."

"Did you testify at the trial of Letts?"

"I did, sir."

"Where is he now?"

"In prison at Trenton, New Jersey, the last I heard of him."

The prosecution did not directly bring out Jackson's New Jersey career, but the story had been in circulation since February and was much more damaging than Jackson portrayed on the stand. Coming from Jackson's lips, the tale of a young man brought down by his own innocence softened the impact, but would it stand up to cross-examination?

Crawford paced as he questioned Jackson on his move to Greencastle. He lived in his mother's house and found work in a dental office. After deciding to make a career of dentistry, he enrolled in the Indiana Dental College in Indianapolis.

Crawford walked across the room, turned and said loudly, "Mr. Jackson, did you get in any trouble in Indianapolis?"

Jackson sat up straight. "Once," he said.

"Tell what that was, fully."

Jackson took a breath and began another damning story. "New Year's Eve. A crowd of college boys came up to me as I was standing in front of a hotel. They were talking, laughing and joking very loudly. Someone suggested that we take a drink and we adjourned to a saloon in the vicinity. We had three or four cocktails there, and then we went out. One of the party proposed a trip about the town and we agreed."

"Tell where you went and all that happened."

"On West Washington Street. I don't know the number or the name. While there, a fuss started between two of the college boys and a great deal of noise was made. I don't know how it started or by whom. I was in another part of the room at the time. We were all arrested."

"What sort of house?"

"House of ill fame."

There was murmuring in the gallery. It seemed as though Jackson was trying to slip the noose over his own head.

"What was done with you?"

"Taken to the police station."

Jackson explained that he was charged with visitation and fined ten dollars. Following his arrest, Jackson left school and returned to Greencastle where he lived with his mother and worked in the dental office of Dr. Gillespie.

Crawford questioned Jackson about life in Greencastle and his employment with Dr. Gillespie then jumped to the heart of the matter.

"Mr. Jackson, when did you first meet Miss Pearl Bryan?"

Jackson responded without hesitation, "During the Christmas holidays of 1894 and 1895, at her home."

"Who introduced you to her?"

"William Wood."

Crawford asked the extent of Jackson's relationship with Pearl Bryan and how often he saw her. Jackson said when he worked for Dr. Gillespie, he would see here pass the office as often as every other day. That summer he visited her six or seven times.

"Did Will Wood talk with you about the intimacy between him and Pearl Bryan?" Crawford asked.

"He did." Said Jackson.

"When did he first speak of it?"

"Along about the latter part of September 1895. One day Wood said to me 'Why don't you go out to see Pearl more than you do?' I asked him why, and with a great deal of implied significance he said, 'It's a good thing.' I told him I thought he was lying. I cautioned him against talking that way about his cousin. He said, 'All right, but I know what I am talking about, and I don't care if you go out to see her at all.' He intimated a good deal on that occasion and several times afterward."

The questioning turned to Jackson's enrollment in the Ohio College of Dental Surgery. He arrived in Cincinnati in October, and at the time was living alone in a rooming house, taking his meals at various restaurants and hotels. He returned to Greencastle for the 1895 Christmas holidays.

Then Crawford asked the most damning question, "Jackson, did you have criminal intercourse with Pearl Bryan?"

The crowd stirred. Jackson seemed as startled as anyone in the room at the suddenness of the question, but he must have known it was coming. He flushed but had a ready answer.

"Yes, sir."

Crawford asked when. Jackson said during the holidays, Christmas 1895, but never before that. It was after Wood had told him Pearl was already pregnant.

"How many times did you have intercourse with Pearl Bryan?" Crawford asked.

"Twice." Jackson responded.

"Where?"

"At her house. In the parlor."

Crawford paced slowly, back and forth, as if lost in thought, trying to solve a puzzle. Everyone sat very still. No one wanted to miss a word.

"Now, Jackson, had you received any letters from Wood from the middle of October through the holidays upon that subject?"

"Yes, sir."

Crawford asked when he had received them, what they said, and how he had replied. Jackson said he received them in November or December.

Nelson objected, demanding to see the letters.

"Have you those letters?" Crawford asked Jackson.

"No, sir. I destroyed the letters. They were so vulgar and obscene."

"Did you destroy all of them?"

"I am sorry to say I did not destroy two of the letters." Said Jackson.

"Were those the two I read the other day?" Crawford asked.

"Yes, sir."

"How many were there, what did they contain, and what did you reply."

Before Jackson could answer, Nelson objected to the question and his objection was sustained. Crawford tried to rephrase the question and Nelson objected again with a lengthy argument against the competency of the question. Crawford countered, arguing that the testimony was necessary to prove a motive for the crime by another, and that the defendant did not seduce the girl in August or September as alleged by the Commonwealth.

"I expect to prove," Crawford said, glancing around the room, that Will Wood seduced the girl."

To which Judge Helm said, "Jackson's admission of having had carnal knowledge of the girl was a confession of seduction."

"I would not call that a confession of seduction." Crawford said.

"Well, do you expect to prove that William Wood had a motive in this girl's death?" asked the judge.

"Yes, sir, I do, and I think that the letter from the witness to Wood will lay plainly a motive before the Court."

"I think such testimony would be nothing but hearsay in nature." Said Judge Helm, "If you had asked Will Wood whether he had seduced the girl and he had admitted it, such admission would be competent testimony. He only can know. Any further information must needs be of a hearsay character. I sustain the objection."

Colonel Nelson surprised everyone by abruptly withdrawing his objection. Crawford proceeded cautiously, asking about Jackson's letters to Will Wood.

"Did you, prior to the holidays, send a prescription to Wood?"

"Yes, sir." Said Jackson.

"Have you that prescription now?"

"I have not."

"What became of it?"

"The last time I saw it was when I placed it in an envelope and mailed it to Will Wood, with a letter I had written him." Said Jackson.

"Did you receive it back again from Pearl Bryan?"

"I did not."

Crawford asked him to describe the prescriptions he sent. One was a mixture of Holland gin and cloves another was a prescription including ergot of rye. None of them worked and Wood was desperate.

"When you went to Greencastle on the holidays did you talk to Wood about it?" Crawford asked.

"Yes, sir. He said something would have to be done soon or he would have to leave town and stay away forever. He watched for me and at every opportunity talked to me on the subject of his trouble. He went everywhere

I did and came to Dr. Gillespie's two or three times a day to see me, asking me to help him out of his trouble."

"Did you have any other conversation with Wood before you left for Cincinnati?"

"Yes, sir. I had two conversations that forcibly impressed me. On Saturday he walked up to me and asked me about the operation for an abortion. He tried to find out all he could, and asked me how they were performed, how much money was necessary to have one performed, the risk the subject would have to take, and all about it. I told him I knew nothing of abortions except what I had read and had never heard a lecture or seen a demonstration of an abortion. He asked me if I knew anybody who might be willing to commit an abortion for him, and if he did not get out of his trouble, he would have to leave town."

"What did you tell him?"

"I told him I did not know anybody then but would take the matter up for him."

Crawford asked about the content of several letters and postal cards he had received from Will Wood after returning to Cincinnati. He wrote that Pearl was still in trouble and was desperate enough to resort to anything. Wood asked again about abortion.

"Did you write him a letter in regard to her coming here?"

"He wrote that she was coming, and for me to get someone to care for her in her trouble. I wrote him that I had someone to consent to assist her out of trouble, a fellow student."

"Who was it?"

"Alonzo M. Walling."

Jackson was questioned about his association with Walling, how they had been acquainted in Indianapolis, and after meeting again in Cincinnati, became roommates at Miss McNevin's rooming house. He said he showed Walling the letters received from Will Wood after Christmas asking about abortion.

"I said to Walling: 'Can we help Billy out?'

"And he replied, 'Yes, but it must be on the q.t. I tell you, I'll get a room all right, but it must be understood that nobody is to know where the room is. I'm not looking for newspaper notoriety.' He said he had a friend who would furnish him with the necessary remedies."

Jackson relayed this information to Will Wood, who wrote back, asking when he should send Pearl down.

"Did you tell him when to send her to Cincinnati?" Crawford asked.

"I did not."

"Did she come?"

"She did."

Jackson explained that he and Walling failed to meet Pearl the night she arrived and received a note the next morning saying that she was staying at the Indiana House under the name Mabel Stanley. He and Walling went to see her that afternoon.

"What conversation passed between you?"

"She said…"

"One moment," Colonel Nelson said. "We object."

Crawford turned to the judge. "Cannot the prisoner tell what he did and said about the vital point at issue? Is not this part of the res gestae?"

"I can't go into a lecture of criminal law, gentlemen," said the judge, "but he cannot go on and say what was said prior to the commission of this crime."

"Why cannot the prisoner show details covering this space of time?"

"I sustain the objection, Mr. Crawford."

"Then, I reserve an exception." Crawford turned back to his witness.

"Don't tell the conversation. Tell what you did."

"I stayed six or seven minutes, not longer than ten minutes, and then took her valise and went downstairs and out of the door."

Crawford looked at his opposing counsel as he said to Jackson, "I will ask you what Walling said."

"Go ahead," said Nelson.

Jackson responded, "Walling asked what made Wood send her so soon. He wanted time to make certain arrangements. I told him that she was here and wanted to know what he was going to do. He said, 'Hustle and get a place for her.'"

Crawford asked Jackson when he next saw Pearl Bryan. He said he met her on Tuesday at Fourth and Race. Walling was not with them, and he and Pearl spent the afternoon walking around Cincinnati.

"We went into various large stores like a country girl would like to see in a large city. I showed her Fountain Square, the Post Office, and the theaters in that vicinity," Jackson said.

They parted around 4:30 p.m. and agreed to meet again at Fourth and Race at 6:00. They went to Wallingford's saloon, where they were to meet Walling. They sat at a table in one of the curtained stalls, and he asked if she wanted a drink.

"What did she say she wanted?" Crawford asked

"Beer." Jackson replied, contradicting Allen Johnson's testimony that Pearl ordered sarsaparilla. "I went to the front saloon and found Walling waiting for me there. There was an Italian behind the bar, and I told him I wanted beer for myself and lady. Walling and I talked a little while, and I asked him to walk back into the room where Pearl was. He said, 'No; I am broke, and it takes money to associate with ladies in a saloon.'"

"How long did you stay there?" Crawford asked.

"Not more than 10 or 15 minutes."

"Had you ever been there with Pearl before?"

"I had not."

"On Tuesday, you and Pearl left Wallingford's," said Crawford, stressing the day, "where did you go?"

"I walked up and down, showing her the city by gaslight," Jackson said. "Thinking she would like to see the suburbs and view the city from the heights, we boarded a Norwood car and took a ride to Walnut Hills, to the end of the road."

"What time did you get back?" Crawford asked.

"I don't know. It might have been 10 o'clock," Jackson said.

"What became of her?"

"She went to the Indiana House."

"Where did you next see Pearl?" Crawford asked.

"Saw Miss Bryan at 11:30 or 11:15 that morning at Fourth and Race streets."

Jackson said at that meeting he told her that Walling would meet her that evening at the same place. He left her on her own, went to have dinner then studied in his room.

"When did you next see Pearl?"

"I never saw her again in life. I saw the body of Miss Bryan at an undertaking establishment across from City Hall. I think it was Epply's."

"Why do you say you saw Pearl Bryan's body there?"

"Objection, Your Honor," Nelson said. "Is this cross-examination or direct?"

The objection was overruled; Jackson continued. "The reason I say I saw Pearl Bryan's body was that I saw her sister and brother there, and they had been weeping."

"Did you go Wednesday afternoon with Miss Bryan to Hockett's piano store on Fourth Street?" Crawford asked.

"I did not."

"I will ask you if you were out on Licking Pike Thursday morning?" Crawford began rapidly firing his questions.

"I was not."

"Was Walling there?"

"I do not know, sir."

"Did you go to Bellevue?"

"I did not."

"Did Pearl go to Bellevue?"

"Not to my knowledge."

"Did Walling?"

"He never told me so."

Crawford paused, then asked, "Have you been to Fort Thomas?"

"I have. It was the latter part of October 1895." Said Jackson.

"Who with?"

"Alonzo Walling," Jackson keeping his composure, spoke of an innocent outing, "We walked to Newport and asked someone to direct us to a Fort Thomas car. We got aboard and rode out and spent some time looking at the sights there."

"Were you in Fort Thomas since that day?"

"I certainly was not at Fort Thomas; I might have been in Newport."

"When had you been in Newport?"

"No, I never was in Newport." Jackson corrected himself, "I remember it was Covington."

"When in Covington?"

"Walling and I met two ladies and walked home with them to Covington."

"Do you know who the ladies were?" Crawford asked.

"Yes, sir. Mrs. Smith and a Mrs. Somebody. I forget her name." It was May Smith, and very likely, her sister-in-law, Etta Carson.

Crawford asked Jackson about his daily activities on Thursday and Friday. It was just his regular routine: lectures at the college, meals at Heider's, drinks at Wallingford's, wrote letters at the Palace Hotel, spent some time with Hattie Gans. Friday morning, Fred Albion shaved Jackson's beard, and that evening it was the talk of Rose McNevin's rooming house. His first intimation that anything may have been wrong with Pearl came with Saturday's paper.

Jackson said, "After buying the paper and reading part of the account of the finding of the body, I said to Walling: 'Great heavens, what's this?'"

They were having dinner at Heider's. Jackson asked Walling if the body was Pearl Bryan. Walling denied any knowledge of the matter. But back at their room, Walling had several wrapped bundles that Jackson realized contained Pearl's clothes. Walling said they had to get rid of them quickly.

Jackson described how he and Walling disposed of Pearl's clothing. One package, containing a skirt, a box of face powder, and a chamois, he took to the bridge and threw in the river. Walling told him to take a valise and another bundle and put them under the seat of an outbound train. Instead, Jackson threw the bundle down an open sewer. He intended to throw the valise off the bridge, but there were too many people around, so he left it at Kugel's saloon.

On Wednesday, he was walking past the barbershop where Albion worked, and Walling came out to talk with him. He asked Jackson if Will Wood could be trusted. Walling wanted Jackson to have Wood write a decoy letter to Pearl's parents, purporting to be from Pearl, saying she had gone somewhere else. Jackson, panic stricken, complied with the request.

"Was it the one read to the jury?" Crawford asked.

"It was." Jackson responded.

Jackson testified about his arrest and questioning by the police and Mayor Caldwell, first in a room crowded with reporters and later, more harshly, away from reporters. It was the same story told by Mayor Crawford and Colonel Deitsch, but this time from the point of view of a man badgered to confess to a crime he did not commit. He told how Deitsch and Plummer had convinced him he was going to Kentucky when he was actually taken to Epply's to see Pearl in her coffin.

He challenged some of the evidence found in his room. Jackson claimed he had never before seen a pair of stockings and some ladies' handkerchiefs allegedly found behind his trunk. A pair of white gloves identified as ladies' gloves were his own. Crawford had him put the gloves on to prove it. The gloves had never been worn, and Jackson had some difficulty putting them on, but they did fit.

Crawford questioned Jackson on his arrest and treatment by the police, about his identification by George Jackson and other witnesses, and various other minor points. When the examination was finished, Crawford walked back to the defense table and said to Nelson, "Take the witness."

All eyes were turned to Colonel Nelson as he rose from his chair. "The Commonwealth has no questions to ask this witness," he said.

The crowd was stunned. They expected Nelson to skewer Jackson. He voluntarily brought up all his sins: his embezzlement in New Jersey, his New Year's arrest in an Indianapolis brothel, even his criminal intercourse with Pearl Bryan in her family's parlor, and he tried to explain them all away. The spectators were counting on Nelson to turn it back on Jackson, to chastise and browbeat as they knew he could until Jackson added murder to his admissions.

Perhaps Nelson was afraid that Jackson was too persuasive, or too calm and rehearsed to guard against being tripped up. He admitted to all but the murder, and he would never go any further. It would have the same effect as the letters, making Jackson appear more victim than victimizer. No sense giving him further opportunity to charm the jury; better to treat his words as insignificant.

The room broke into a storm of raised voices. Judge Helm banged the gavel and had to keep banging until all were silent again. Helm was taken by surprise as well. Scott Jackson testified for six and a half hours, spinning every aspect of the case in his favor, and Nelson let his testimony stand unchallenged. Before Jackson left the stand, Judge Helm asked him to clarify a few minor points regarding Pearl's valise and about his identification by George Jackson. Then he ended the day's session.

19 THE INSULT

The animosity between Crawford and Nelson in the courtroom grew palpable as the trial progressed. It was beyond that of two legal opponents—they appeared to have a genuine personal dislike of each other. Each objection, whether sustained or overruled, included a nasty dig or sarcastic remark.

Nelson, stung by criticism outside of court for his failure to cross-examine Scott Jackson, became especially harsh in challenging defense witnesses. Though seldom sustained, Crawford continued his frequent objections through Nelson's cross-examinations.

With Jackson's testimony finished, Crawford turned to witnesses who would challenge the prosecution's case, beginning with their assertion that Pearl was killed by decapitation where the body was found. W.E. Abbot, embalmer for White's Funeral Parlor, testified that more than a quart of blood was drained from the body before it was turned over to the post-mortem physicians, more than would have remained if she had bled to death. Abbot did not believe the cuts on the fingers were fresh, and he noticed a mark below the left breast that appeared to be from a hypodermic syringe.

District Physician Dr. Fredrick K. Clark, who was present during the embalming, also saw the mark and agreed it was from a needle. Dr. Clark thought the finger wounds looked like they were received after death.

In his cross-examination, Colonel Nelson accused Mr. Abbot of drunkenness, suggested he was terminated from his prior job for drunkenness, that he had come to court drunk and was, in fact, on a three-day drunk right now. Abbot denied it vociferously, but Nelson persisted until Judge Helm admonished him. Nelson then belittled Dr. Clark by informing the court that he had been a sign painter prior to practicing medicine.

Nelson had no such criticism for Crawford's next witness, Dr. J.A. Jeancon. Jeancon was a London-trained professor of medicine at the Cincinnati Eclectic Institute and published author who served as a surgeon during the Civil War. Dr. Jeancon estimated it would take ten minutes to do a clean disarticulation of a human head, and if performed on a live person, the intensity of blood flow when the artery was cut would make it impossible to continue.

As he did with the state's medical witnesses, Crawford asked Dr. Jeancon and his other expert witnesses about the effect of drugs on the coagulation of blood after death. The consensus was that asphyxiation by chloroform would tend to leave the blood liquid, but cocaine's effect was unknown. Cocaine would counteract the depressing effect of chloroform, but none of the doctors could agree on the lethal dosage of cocaine, or its effects in combination with chloroform.

J. M. Allison, a reporter for the Cincinnati *Enquirer* and a resident of Covington, Kentucky, was subpoenaed to testify for the defense. Allison was at the Hamilton County Jail the night George Jackson identified Alonzo Walling and Scott Jackson and was in the circle of men gathered to make identification more difficult. He told how George Jackson was having trouble identifying the man inside the coach he drove to the Highlands. When George Jackson was nose-to-nose with Allison, one of the policemen said, "Jackson, come over here." At this, Scott Jackson instinctively took a step out of the circle, and a moment later was identified by George Jackson.

Henry Motz, of Covington, testified about the night George Jackson reenacted his trip to Lock's farm. Mr. Motz had to show him the entrance to Three Mile Creek Road and lead the procession by lantern light, with one buggy falling over the embankment.

David Lock, former Newport Police Chief, was one of the first witnesses at the murder scene. He saw one set of men's footprints leading from the fence and mud on the fence rail where he climbed over. David Lock saw no women's footprints and no sign of struggle. He was convinced that the body was carried over the fence already dead. When challenged by Nelson, Lock became even more specific, saying he saw an indent in the ground where the man dropped the body to finish his climb.

Ruth Gottlieb, a reporter for the Covington Record, also saw only a man's footprints. She was at the scene early and feared that the woman's footprints others saw were her own.

Scott Jackson's landlady, Rose McNevin, and her two sisters were the only Cincinnati witnesses to voluntarily cross the Ohio River to testify on his behalf. Rose McNevin appeared in court on Saturday, May 2, and told essentially the same story she told reporters in February, but more simply and with more certainty. She said Walling came in on Thursday night with a bag of apples he shared with the family. She sat with Walling that evening, and they could hear Jackson in a rocking chair upstairs. The following evening, January 31, Scott Jackson's freshly shaved face was the talk of the house. She swore Jackson was in his room on Friday night, and if anyone left the house before midnight, she would have known it. She further testified she saw him the next morning and that two persons slept in the room Jackson and Walling shared.

The *Cincinnati Tribune* called Rose McNevin "without a doubt the brightest witness of the trial." She was a very proper and precise woman who expected the same from her questioners, and she quickly locked horns with Colonel Nelson when he rose to cross-examine.

"Now, Miss McNevin, could you tell all about the goings and comings of your boarders every…"

"Roomers, sir."

"O, yes, your roomers, Miss McNevin."

"Yes, I could tell…"

"Excuse me, Miss McNevin, I have not finished my question."

Nelson asked if she knew when each of her 12 roomers entered and left the house, and McNevin asserted without hesitation that she did. Nelson went on to posit a dozen or more situations, real, hypothetical, or fantastic, where someone living in the house could have entered or left without McNevin's knowledge. More often than not, he referred to them as boarders and each time she corrected him—they were roomers, she provided room but not board. And in each case, she denied the possibility of her roomers entering or leaving unnoticed. No one could have gone either in or out by the hall door at any hour before 11:00 p.m.

This continued for more than an hour. Nelson showed no sign of stopping, but Judge Helm had heard enough. He told Nelson to conclude his cross-examination. The witness had given her testimony. Nelson protested. Miss McNevin testified positively that if Jackson and Walling had gone out, she would have heard them, and he felt he could shake that statement if he were allowed to continue.

"Your Honor," Nelson said, "there is no portion of humanity which can be as positive as a woman."

"And they are usually right, Colonel," Crawford called out.

Nelson turned quickly and shot back, "Mr. Crawford has not associated with respectable people enough to know."

Crawford jumped up, livid, flushed, searching for words to express his anger without offending the court. "Mr. Nelson has not associated with me enough to know."

The judge pounded for order.

"Gentlemen, you cannot expect me to permit this."

"Oh, it's all right, Your Honor," said Colonel Nelson, with a dismissive wave of his hand. "Mr. Crawford knows what I said was a pleasantry."

But Crawford did not take Nelson's statement as a pleasantry. Judge Helm finally ruled that Nelson could continue his cross-examination of Miss McNevin, but all eyes were on Crawford, who was in no way placated by

Nelson's flip remarks and was incensed all the more by Judge Helm's acquiescence.

He rose to his feet. "Now, I am an officer of this court," Crawford said, "performing my duties to the best of my ability. I desire to make an inquiry, which I hope the court will appreciate and permit. Colonel Nelson has just made a remark, under protection of this court, reflecting upon me, and in the same breath, he has said that he did not intend it as a reflection. I want to know what he means by such contradictory statements made with such rapidity," Crawford's voice rose with his fury. "And I wish to say that I intend to hold him personally responsible outside of court."

The Judge rapped violently for order.

Colonel Nelson sprang to his feet and shouted, "I am personally responsible at any time, for anything I say."

Judge Helm continued pounding until both men were quiet. He turned to his clerk and said, "Enter an order finding Mr. Crawford guilty of contempt and fining him $25."

Nelson sat down and said to Mr. Hayes, loudly enough for the room to hear, "I'll go out and meet him now, right now, goddamn him."

Crawford turned his indignation to the court and, as professionally as possible for a man blind with rage, said, "Mr. Clerk, have you a check?"

Judge Helm said, "Mr. Crawford, you can settle that privately."

"I prefer to settle it now." Crawford strode up to the clerk's desk, and the trial paused while Crawford paid his fine.

For the remainder of the afternoon, Crawford ignored Colonel Nelson, addressing Mr. Hayes of the prosecution instead when necessary.

Rose McNevin's sisters, Jenny and Millie, testified. They both corroborated their sister's evidence, but neither gave as detailed testimony, and neither was pressed as hard as Rose. No one in the court was listening to the testimony anyway. All were watching Crawford, waiting for a continuation of the fight.

There was no continuation that day, but there was no reconciliation either. The burning question was how seriously Crawford planned to hold Nelson "personally accountable outside of Court." A challenge like that was not taken lightly in Kentucky. The *Daily Leader*, Lexington Kentucky, ended their account of the incident by assuring their readers, "Neither attorney was armed."

By 1896, the notion of a duel to the death between two prominent attorneys active in local politics seemed like a remnant of another era. But the people of Northern Kentucky had reason to believe the feud between Crawford and Nelson could end in bloodshed. Just a year before, two local politicians —both as distinguished as Crawford and Nelson— had a gunfight on the steps of the First National Bank of Covington leaving one man dead.

It was the end of a longstanding feud between John Ludford Sanford and

William Justus Goebel, two prominent Democrats who agreed on absolutely nothing but party affiliation. Goebel was a reformer, Sanford, a Confederate veteran who stood with the old-time party men. For years they fought it out in the press.

They met by chance in front of First National Bank and had an argument that ended when Sanford pulled out his revolver and fired. The bullet missed when Goebel jerked aside reaching for his own pistol. Goebel fired, hitting Sanford between the eyes. John Sanford received an elaborate Confederate funeral with hundreds of mourners. Goebel was acquitted on the grounds of self-defense.

The shooting of John Sanford was still fresh in people's minds, and they knew Crawford and Nelson were fully capable of repeating it. When Judge Helm ended the session Saturday, May 2, the people of Newport feared only one of the adversaries would be in Court Monday morning.

20 WILLIAM FRANKLY TRUSTY, JR.

Court convened late Monday morning, but there were no surprises. When Sheriff Plummer called the room to order, both attorneys were in their usual places. Crawford apparently did not seek out Colonel Nelson to hold him responsible, but he did not forgive him either. The bad blood did not subside. Nelson did not look in his opponent's direction, and Crawford's disdain for Nelson was obvious from across the room, but he was calm and was determined to seek satisfaction in the courtroom rather than the field of honor.

Since the trial began, Crawford had been implying without details that he had new witnesses that would turn the case upside down. A reporter for the *Louisville Courier-Journal* confronted him directly saying, "There seems to be an impression from the way you are conducting the case that the defense has something up their sleeves."

"Well, maybe we have," Crawford replied.

"Will you tell us what that sensation is to be?"

"I am afraid to tell myself," said Crawford with a smile. When pressed, he elaborated, "We propose to show that Pearl Bryan was killed outside the jurisdiction of the Campbell County Circuit Court."

Rumors abounded over what Crawford planned to reveal. One said that at the proper time, he would produce the long-missing head of Pearl Bryan. Another predicted that among the unrecognized names on the witness list was a woman who would claim that Pearl Bryan died in her Cincinnati apartment. Captain Seward's name came up in Court connected to an alleged attempt to suborn Allen Johnson's testimony, but beyond that, Seward, Trusty, and others on the list were still unknown to the press. The time came for Crawford to stop being coy. It was time to spring his sensational testimony.

Crawford called the first of Seward's witnesses, a 27-year-old Cincinnati bartender named George Dayton, who would set the scene for the events on George Street. Dayton was pale and shaking as he took the stand.

After confirming Dayton's identity, Crawford asked, "Where were you on January 31?"

"I don't know where I was," Dayton said quietly.

"Do you know where you were upon that evening?" Crawford asked.

"No, sir."

The answer seemed to surprise Crawford. He walked over to the witness stand.

"Well, were you near the corner of Plum and George Streets anytime during the week ending February 1 of this year?"

"No, sir."

Crawford took a step back and looked over to his associates. He attempted to hide his disappointment when he turned to the judge and said, "If it please the court, I have evidently been misinformed as to what this witness knew about this case, and I ask that he be discharged."

As Dayton moved to step down, Colonel Nelson expressed a desire to cross-examine Mr. Dayton. Crawford objected. His witness had testified to nothing but his name. What was there to cross-examine? Crawford was overruled. Nelson approached the witness, holding a sheet of paper which he handed to Dayton, saying, "In whose handwriting is this letter?"

George Dayton looked at the letter. "John Seward's."

Dayton did not recall when or where Seward gave him the letter, but he testified to having several conversations with him, both in Cincinnati and Newport.

"State what he gave you the letter for and what he said to you at the time," Nelson said.

Crawford objected to the question, and Judge Helm sustained the objection. The ruling brought Nelson to action. He asked that the jury be removed from the courtroom so he could argue the proposition to the court. The judge agreed, the jury was removed, and Colonel Nelson addressed the court in his usual loud and fervent manner:

> If it please the Court, the record, in this case, discloses the fact that John Seward is a witness in this case and has been employed by the defense to hunt up testimony. The witness is the product of this John Seward. I want to show that Dayton has been coached on just what to say, that he has been in consultation with counsel for the defense, and before I get through, I expect to prove that John Seward, the detective, has been guilty of subornation of witnesses. I want to read this paper, showing what, just how and what has been done. I want to know if counsel for the defense will object to the reading of a paper that will

show this and assist to perpetuate a fraud upon the Commonwealth of Kentucky, a fraud upon the jury, and a fraud upon this honorable court. I am putting it on the high moral proposition. This witness, Seward, is a scorn to humanity, who ought to be in the penitentiary, and I contend the court owes it to the Commonwealth that the examination may be rigid, and before we get through, I propose to show that the witness, Dayton, was coached to lie.

This witness was a disappointment to the defense, and, in all fairness to counsel on the other side, I don't think that they would purposely introduce a perjured witness. I am firmly convinced that the counsel for the defense is not a party to this conspiracy. We will prove that John Seward is not only deserving of the scorn of humanity but that he has committed an offense of such seriousness as will warrant his being confined within the walls of the penitentiary. This Court, in the discharge of its duty to itself, the duty that it owes to the state and the duty that it owes to the people, is to investigate the fact of whether the witness has been guilty not only of the high crime, but of the highest contempt of this tribunal.

Why is it that we cannot bring out the facts that we allege? This witness has not only been coached as to what he is to say when on the stand, but has been given a written memorandum so that he cannot forget what to say. The Court owes a duty to itself to investigate the violation of the solemn admonition of the Court that the witness is not to talk of the case or suffer himself to be talked to of the case, either before or after testifying. That admonition, we claim, John Seward has violated, after being sworn and admonished as to his duties as witness.

The counsel for the other side objects to the question in cross-examination because he was disappointed in the testimony elicited from the witness, but I do not doubt but that he was misled as to what the witness would testify to, and I want to reiterate my statement that the counsel on the other side was not a party to the conspiracy. Why cannot we ascertain as to an attempt to suborn the witness and get him to testify in this case to that effect? That would be in the nature of an investigation, and I want to repeat that the Court owes it to itself to make such an investigation.

When Nelson concluded, the courtroom was a sea of bewilderment. Faces were blank with incomprehension over what happened. Despite Nelson's revelations, Judge Helm sustained Crawford's objection saying the matter may come up before the court in another shape. The letter from Seward to Dayton was not read in court.

Mr. Crawford rose to speak:

Before the court calls the jury, I wish to make a statement which I think it my duty as an officer of the court to make, also my duty as an attorney for the defendant. In the assumptions of Colonel Nelson, he has done me the justice to state what he believes to be my position; but as an officer of this court, and as attorney for the prisoner, it is my duty to say to your Honor, that one of the most difficult things is to discriminate as to what evidence I should produce and what evidence I should not. It seems that this trial has stirred up many people with illusions. I have a letter written to me by a person who says that he is the man who has done this thing, and from that on down I have all the shades.

I desire to call a witness next the falsity or truth of whose statements my client knows nothing of. But, sir, the statement is a remarkable one. If he shall not tell the truth and it shall be proven that he is not telling the truth, I shall be as glad as anyone to see him punished. But when he comes to me with a story so directly in this case, even touching the jurisdiction of the court, I feel it is my duty as an officer of the court to put him on the stand.

With that, Crawford called William Frankly Trusty, Jr. to the witness stand. Trusty had shaved and put on a clean suit, but his big hands were stained with the grease and grit of the rail yard. If he understood Crawford's introduction, it had no effect on his testimony. In the witness chair, the broad-shouldered brakeman towered over the attorneys who questioned him, but his ruddy countenance and rural dialect expressed the sincerity of a farm boy.

He said he came to Cincinnati on January 31, to look for work. On George Street, he met up with a woman he knew whose friend, a doctor, offered him $10 to drive a cab over the river. He accepted the deal and met them back at the George Street house at 10:00 p.m. His friend made sure the coast was clear then helped the doctor and another man bring the body of a dead woman out of the house and load her into the cab.

"She was dead if ever I seen a dead person," Trusty said.

He drove alone with the corpse over the bridge into Newport. In downtown Newport, under a jeweler's sign, he met another man who joined him on the seat of the cab and directed him down Alexandria Pike. When they reached their destination, the man paid Trusty the $10, threw the corpse over his shoulder, climbed the rail fence, and disappeared into the woods. Trusty drove back to the bridge where he met one of the men from George Street, who took the cab back from him.

He slept that night in Grand Central Depot, and the next day Trusty returned home to Urbana, Illinois. After reading of the headless corpse found near Fort Thomas, he was convinced it must have been the dead woman he drove from Cincinnati. He told his father, who told Captain Seward, who urged him to come forward.

Nelson began his cross-examination with some cursory questions about the events of January 31, but he was more interested in the circumstances that brought him forth to testify.

"What is your relation to John Seward?" Nelson asked.

"I ain't any." Trusty sat up straight and appeared nervous for the first time.

"Are you sure?"

"No, my father and him are third cousins, he tells me."

"You'd be fourth cousins then," said Nelson.

"Well, I guess I would."

"How did you happen to come to Newport?"

"John Seward sent me a ticket."

Nelson went after Seward's reputation. "Wasn't he in the Kentucky Penitentiary?"

"Yes, I know he has been there once."

"What is John's business?"

"He says he is a detective."

"Have you been employed in this case?" Nelson asked.

"No, sir."

"Has Seward?"

"I don't know."

Nelson had Trusty verify that he and Seward had been living at Herman's Hotel in Newport since early April, and they had been meeting regularly with George Dayton. Colonel Nelson was now the smartest man in court, and the room was silent as he pulled the truth from the witness.

He handed Trusty a letter and said, "Look at this paper and say if you saw it before."

Trusty examined the envelope and said, "No, sir, I don't think I have."

"Open it and look inside. Can you identify the handwriting?"

Trusty pulled the letter from the envelope, scanned it, and said, "That's my father's handwriting."

It was a letter from Trusty's father to Alexander Bryan, Pearl Bryan's father. Nelson read the letter in court, slowly and clearly. The letter was later shared with reporters who published it with Trusty Sr.'s semi-literate spelling uncorrected.

A. S. Bryan
Greencastle, Ind.

Dear Sir:

I have Read the Cincinnati Papers closely. Reading the murder of your daughter, my object in writing this you is as a father of grown daughters and a friend to Justus, to say to you and put you on your guard, to my sirtain knollege Wallings friends Has one of the Best Detectives in America working on the case, and I know that man well, and Have his intre confidence, and I know the he has undisputable evidence that your daughter was murdered in Cincinnati, Ohio. You see the point By which tha Hope to Askape Jestus By proving Beon a question at thare trial in Kentucky that it was don in Ohio. This Detective can and will produce the man that Holled your daughter to ft. Thomas ded when she left Cin, and he knows the Room the owner and he rented. I write you this letter, not for publication but to put you on your Gard, and I hope this letter will Bee strickley confidently, for I am a poore man, and I do not want the man to think that I would Betray His confidence, so if you want to see me, or have your attorney see me, I can be at my Home in Urbana Ills., 1309 Hill and Romine, or at any other place that you may disgnate at your expense for time and traveling. I know a grate deal more than I Have writing and it I think wil pay you to see me, for I would love to know of just such fellows to Get what tha orto have, and that would be the Rope.

Very Respectfully yours,
Wm. Trusty

P.S. this detective was Heare and I saw Him myself that is the reason, so I hope you will keep this confidently.

When he finished reading, Nelson opened and read a second, very similar letter from William Trusty Sr. to Silas Hayes, Mr. Bryan's attorney, this one explicitly offering his services for reasonable wages to bring out all the facts.

Nelson turned to the witness. "Do you know William Trusty well?"

"He's my father," Trusty said

"Are your relations intimate and close?"

"He is my father."

"I didn't ask you that," Nelson said.

"I don't understand you," Trusty said.

Nelson asked the court stenographer to read the question. He was taunting the ignorant railroad man. The stenographer read back what Nelson asked.

"I don't understand it yet," Trusty said, frightened.

"Are you close in your social relations with your father?"

"Why certainly."

"Are you and your father warm friends?"

"Yes, sir."

"Do you exchange confidences?"

"We do, sir."

"Do you talk freely and fully of your affairs?"

"Yes, sir."

"Then as soon as you arrived home and had your supper, you told your father all about your midnight trip to Fort Thomas?"

"Yes, sir."

"Did you and your father talk freely about this murder?"

"Yes, sir, when I told him about it, and that was the only time we talked about it...." Trusty's voice trailed off.

Crawford called from the defense table for the witness to speak louder.

"Yes," Nelson said, "speak loud as if you were on a freight train."

The testimony continued with questions about Trusty's fourth cousin, John Seward. Nelson had another back-and-forth with the witness when he asked Trusty whether he knew of a publication written by Seward. The problem was Trusty did not know the meaning of the word "publication." Finally, Nelson asked him if he knew that Seward published a book. Trusty said no.

Then, over Crawford's objection, Nelson had Trusty identify Seward's picture on the back cover of a book entitled *John Soard's Confession*. The book documented the history of the murder of an unknown man in Rich Hill, Casey County, Kentucky, in 1877.

"Where did you live in Kentucky, Mr. Trusty?" Nelson asked.

"Casey County."

"Were you a witness for John Seward in the United States Circuit Court in Louisville or Covington?"

"No, sir."

"Against him?"

"Yes, sir, I was against him."

The questioning continued for some time, but no new ground was covered. When the witness was excused, Colonel Nelson gave him notice that he would likely be recalled.

Crawford believed the witnesses brought to him by Walling's attorneys were unknown to anyone outside of their circle, but the law was onto Seward's conspiracy before the trial had even begun. Maybe it was the letters from Trusty's father to Alexander Bryan, or maybe it was just Seward's lack of discretion, but detectives Crim and McDermott uncovered the plot to present perjured testimony by George Dayton, William Trusty, and Carrie Evans, instigated by Captain John Seward, alias Soard, ex-convict, private detective.

Carrie Evans, alias Georgie Baker, the woman Trusty said he met on January 31 was not called to testify. Seward coached her to say that Pearl Bryan died in her apartment at the hands of the anonymous doctor. Seward bought her shoes and clothes, and she allowed him to use her apartment to prepare the charade. When the detectives confronted Miss Evans, they persuaded her to tell all.

Reluctantly, she allowed Crim and McDermott access to her apartment where they could watch and listen as Seward rehearsed the play they were to stage at Jackson's trial. From behind a partition, they heard Seward coach Dayton to testify he helped Miss Evans and the doctor load Pearl Bryan's corpse into the cab. When the detectives later confronted Dayton, he had little choice but to agree to join the counterplot.

The police were more secretive than Seward was and revealed nothing before the trial. Captain Seward sat in the courtroom that Monday confident that his witnesses would deliver testimony that would turn the case around and earn him a nice reward. Seward's surprise at Dayton's failure to testify was only surpassed by that of Leonard Crawford, who truly believed Shepherd gave him a team of witnesses with a story at least the equal of George Jackson's.

Sheriff Plummer arrested Seward and Trusty in the courtroom for perjury and subornation of witnesses. Captain Seward admitted all and threw himself on the mercy of the court. Trusty, free on bail, lit for the rail yard, caught the first train out of Kentucky, forfeited his bond, and became a fugitive from justice.

The effect of Seward's conspiracy devastated Scott Jackson's case. Colonel Nelson's insistence of the defense attorney's ignorance of the plot saved Crawford's reputation, but now Scott Jackson's defense was dead in the water. Crawford was building his case so skillfully that even this hostile jury showed signs of doubt. His experts cast doubt on the notion that Pearl Bryan was decapitated while alive. Will Wood was shown to be a foul-mouthed, womanizing braggart with little regard for decency, and by contrast, the defendant, through his testimony and his letters, was portrayed in a whole new light and for the first time shown to be a man who might be worthy of sympathy. George Jackson's story was challenged from every angle, and serious doubts raised as to his character and credibility, and Trusty's testimony would have offered a reasonable alternative. But now that Seward's plot was uncovered, everything presented by the defense seemed tainted by fraud, and George Jackson's story, by default, was once again gospel.

Crawford took a gamble on witnesses provided by attorney Shepherd and lost. Shepherd, however, hedged his bet by giving the witnesses to Crawford. If they helped acquit Jackson, Walling would likely be acquitted as well. It turned out they were no help to Jackson, and Shepherd would need another strategy for Walling, but at least he would not be the one caught in open court with perjured witnesses.

21 THE VERDICT

Crawford rose to his feet before the session began on Thursday, May 8, and spoke in a manner more gentle than his usual address to Judge Helm.

"If the Court please, before going into this case, I have a statement I desire to make. On last Saturday, I was so annoyed by an expression of Colonel Nelson of the other side, that I gave expression to a nasty threat. I was led into making this threat in court when I should not have done so, and I desire here, in the presence of the Court, to make an apology to the court. I have been prevailed upon by a large number of my friends, of which I am proud to say Your Honor was one, to adopt this course, and realizing how injurious the strained relations between myself and Colonel Nelson is to both of us and to the court I desire to withdraw that threat."

Colonel Nelson looked up at the first mention of his name and kept his eyes riveted upon the speaker during his remarks. When Crawford had finished, Colonel Nelson rose in turn.

"It gives me a great pleasure to hear the gentleman from the other side make a public expression of his sentiments," said Nelson, "and in justice to myself, to him and this honorable court, I desire to also make an apology to this court. I desire to say that there are times when a man says some things upon which a false construction is placed. That was where the learned counsel on the other side, for once in his life, erred. The remark I made was merely while in a heated debate, and for a mere pleasantry during, as I thought, a harmless repartee.

"I intended no reflection on the attorney for the other side, and, fearing at the time my remark had been misunderstood, I hastily apologized, but I have since been informed that he did not hear my apology. His threat drove me to a position that I could not say anything, especially after the occurrence had been so freely chronicled by the newspapers, not only in this vicinity but all over the length and breadth of the land. For the past 20 years I have reckoned as my best friends the family of Mr. Crawford, and I take this opportunity of saying that not only in my estimation, but in the estimation of the entire community, no gentleman stands higher professionally or socially than Mr. Crawford. I think this statement is due the court and public, and I sincerely hope that no further difference may ever arise between Mr. Crawford and myself, especially in this honorable court."

As Colonel Nelson resumed his seat, Mr. Crawford arose, bowed, and smiled. Judge Helm looked down on them both like a beaming father on two deserving children.

"Gentlemen," he said. "This is very gratifying to me and also to the friends of both of you, and I assure you that I appreciate fully the manly sentiments that prompted this action."

And so ended the great feud of Scott Jackson's trial. The *Cincinnati Tribune* reported, "Colonel Crawford stepped over and shook hands with Colonel Nelson, while the little birds sang in the trees, and the cartridges in the dueling pistols unloaded themselves and lay down to rest in the shot bags."

The judge's statement notwithstanding, many viewed Crawford's apology as less than manly. That Nelson's apology was twice as long and far less conciliatory did little to improve Crawford's public image. More than that, Crawford's apology had the ring of a concession speech not only in the matter of Crawford vs. Nelson but in the Commonwealth vs. Scott Jackson.

The defense rested on Tuesday without calling many of their scheduled witnesses. Carrie Evans, and the rest of Seward's witnesses were, of course, not called, but neither were the wife and daughters of Dr. Wagner. It was not clear whether Crawford intended to link the two, making Dr. Wagner the mystery physician at Carrie Evan's George Street apartment, or whether he intended to open another alternative theory, but Trusty failed him so miserably there seemed little to gain by pursuing alternatives. Despite setbacks, Crawford remained confident that some of the seeds of doubt he sowed would take root, and Jackson would be acquitted.

Colonel Nelson showed no indication that he thought the trial was over, and he launched a vigorous rebuttal, but a weariness was descending on the courtroom. The *Cincinnati Enquirer* commented on the "ennui" of lawyers and officials: "Judge Helm talked to District Attorney Smith, of Louisville, while the trial was going on, and on several occasions, the attorneys had to wait for his attention. Sheriff Plummer put his feet out, rested his head on his chair back, and buried himself in the pages of Puck. The attorneys shot witticisms at each other to break the monotony of the proceedings, and some of the spectators went to sleep."

The main objective of the prosecution's rebuttal testimony was to repair the damage the defense did to the story of George Jackson. In court, an Associated Press reporter who had been in the circle when George Jackson identified the prisoners testified that the identifications were made without prompting. A woman testified to seeing the Caldwell Guards drill on the night of January 31, and George Jackson's employer testified to Jackson's honesty. But the real blow to the defense was inflicted by the parade of Caldwell Guards, the same ones deposed by Crawford, now testifying in person, saying, in contradiction to their sworn statements, that the guards had, in fact, drilled that Friday night. While Leonard Crawford was unable to convince any of the black men to cross the Ohio River and contradict George Jackson, Detective Cal Crim had no trouble persuading eleven of them to come across and testify in his favor.

Crawford was under siege. Sworn statements by credible witnesses read to the Court and now back in his portfolio were challenged in court by their flesh and blood authors. Crawford cried perjury, but each man had an answer—denied making the statement, didn't know he was under oath, had a lapse of memory. One man was too nervous to sign his name on the stand, but the rest, rattled or not, knew their presence was sanctioned by the law and they stood fast. No one ever made clear how these men were persuaded to cross the river to another state and contradict their own sworn testimony.

Nelson recalled Mayor Caldwell and the lawmen, Crim, McDermott, and Plummer to contradict what Scott Jackson said about his arrest and questioning. The prosecution brought in the detective from New Jersey who arrested Scott Jackson for embezzlement and told a more damning story than Jackson had.

Nelson was revisiting every aspect of his case and addressing every challenge. Will Wood was recalled to contradict what was said about him by Greencastle deponents. The medical men once again described the brutal nature of the killing, the journey from Wallingford's saloon to Lock's farm retraveled. To remind the jury of the depraved side of Scott Jackson's "Jekyll and Hyde" personality, several Cincinnati prostitutes testified that Jackson was a regular customer. And, still careful not to impugn Jackson's attorney, Nelson used Seward and Trusty to smear the entire defense effort with the taint of fraud. By the time the prosecution rested, there was little doubt that Scott Jackson would hang.

The following day Judge Helm gave his formal instructions to the jury prior to closing arguments of the prosecution and defense.

> If the jury believe from all the evidence, beyond a reasonable doubt, that the defendant, Scott Jackson, in this county and state, before the 14th day of February, 1896, did willfully, feloniously and with malice aforethought, with a knife or other sharp instrument, cut the throat of Pearl Bryan so that she did then and there, and because thereof, die, they will find said Scott Jackson guilty of murder.
>
> If the jury believe from all the evidence, beyond a reasonable doubt, that one Alonzo Walling, in this county and state, before the

14th day of February, 1896, with a knife or other sharp instrument did cut the throat of Pearl Bryan so that she did then and there, and because thereof, die, and also believe from all evidence, beyond a reasonable doubt, that the defendant, Scott Jackson, was there present and willfully, feloniously and with malice aforethought aided or abetted said Alonzo Walling in cutting her throat, intending that said Alonzo Walling should thereby kill the said Pearl Bryan, they will find said Scott Jackson guilty of murder.

If the jury believe from all the evidence, beyond a reasonable doubt, that Scott Jackson, willfully, feloniously and with malice aforethought himself administered, or aided, or abetted, counselled, or procured another to administer a drug, or drugs, to Pearl Bryan for the purpose of producing an abortion, she being then in a condition as to make the same necessarily dangerous to her life, or the drug, or drugs, begin in themselves, or in the quantities or manner of giving necessarily dangerous to her life, and that the said Scott Jackson in this county and state, before the 14th day of February, 1896, believing that said Pearl Bryan had been thereby killed, for whatever purpose, cut her throat with a knife, or other sharp instrument, so that she did then and there, and because thereof, die, they will find the said Scott Jackson guilty of murder.

Judge Helm's instructions to the jury continued with a litany of murderous scenarios, including nearly every combination of cutting and drugging involving Scott Jackson, alone, together with Alonzo Walling, or together with anyone else, for the purpose of aborting an unborn child or any other purpose.

Seven of the scenarios instructed the jury to find Jackson guilty of first-degree murder. Five more instructed them to find him guilty of voluntary manslaughter—if they believed that the cutting had been done "in a sudden heat and passion or in a sudden affray, but not in malice," or if Pearl died from the effect of drugs administered in a manner not necessarily dangerous for life. Involuntary manslaughter was an option if Jackson did not administer drugs which killed Pearl, but believing Pearl to be dead, removed the head not intending to kill her but for the purpose of concealing her identity. Crawford, whose own set of proposed instructions was rejected by Judge Helm, took formal exception to the instructions as read.

The closing arguments followed. Colonel Nelson spoke for five and a half hours retelling the now-familiar story of seduction and betrayal of the innocent girl by the unscrupulous scoundrel from the East. He reminded the jury of the eyewitnesses who saw Pearl Bryan with Scott Jackson on both sides of the Ohio River. He reviewed, link by link, the chain of testimony that took Pearl and her killers from George Street in Cincinnati to Lock's farm in the Highlands of Kentucky.

Amid a blizzard of objections, threatening to reignite their feud, Nelson dismissed the bulk of Crawford's case as perjury and attempted subornation. He lamented the good reputations of Mayor Caldwell, Colonel Deitsch, and Sheriff Plummer were called into question by a man so heinous and obviously guilty as Scott Jackson.

Crawford spoke himself hoarse the first day of his closing arguements. He systematically attacked the credibility of each prosecution witness with special emphasis on George Jackson and his history of fraud and perjury. He decried the tactics of the prosecution who searched for sympathy and not for truth. Once again, he attacked the Cincinnati Mayor and police department for ill-treatment of his client and accused them of using threats to force the Caldwell Guards to cross the river and perjure themselves. The next day, he talked until early afternoon.

Prosecutor Lockhart then spoke, rebutting the charges Crawford had made, and summarizing the prosecution's case once more until, at last, there was nothing left to say.

"Gentlemen of the jury," said Judge Helm, "you have heard the evidence in this case, you have heard the instructions of the court and you have heard the arguments. You will now retire to your room and arrive at a verdict."

Sheriff Plummer led the jury out of the Courtroom, and the Judge retired to his chambers. Gradually the din of the room returned to the level it was before the judge's arrival. There was an air of informality not seen in court before, but there was a different kind of tension in the courtroom that morning. Groups gathered to converse throughout the room, and people milled from one to the other in search of the latest gossip. When a group became too loud, the Sheriff and his men would escort them out. In the corridor and stationed around each door and window of the courtroom were Newport and Campbell County law officers in plain clothes, standing strong and stoic, prepared to foil any assassination attempt should the verdict come down in Scott Jackson's favor.

Scott Jackson sat seemingly oblivious to any threat, nervously giving his views to the newsmen crowded around him.

"I tell you," he said, "I am getting tired of this, and I am glad it is almost over. Let me see...," taking out his pencil and figuring on the edge of a newspaper, "I have been in jail just 99 days, and you can imagine that I am sick of the confinement."

"The funniest thing about this trial," he added with a laugh, "is the story of George H. Jackson. That fellow is one of the most accomplished liars I ever came in contact with. He is not the only one who testified falsely in the case either, but I guess it is all right.

151

"Will you excuse me for a few minutes," he said to jailer Bitzer, "while I go over and get a drink?" He laughed heartily. "Some of the papers have tried to make a drunkard of me. Why, do you know, I haven't had a drink of whiskey since I was arrested."

Jackson took a cigar when it was offered and puffed leisurely as he continued to speak about dentistry and other matters unrelated to the case. He laughed and joked, spoke pleasantly to everyone who addressed him. In another room of the building, twelve men were discussing whether Scott Jackson would hang, and here the subject of their debate sat, laughing and smoking, to all appearances the most unconcerned man in the world.

The jury deliberated for just under two hours. When it was announced that they reached a verdict, everyone hurried back into the courtroom and packed it to capacity. Jackson sat with Crawford on his right, and they were flanked on all sides by the vigilant plain-clothes officers. In the corridor and halls of the courthouse, the remainder of Newport's 40 policemen, most of them in uniform, stood guard on the chance that an unpopular verdict might incite mob violence.

At exactly noon Judge Helm took the bench.

"Mr. Sheriff, is the jury ready to report?"

"Yes, sir," responded Plummer.

"Then let them be brought in."

The deathly stillness of the courtroom was broken only by the bell of the clock tower tolling twelve as the jurors entered the Court led by their foreman, Murty Shea. They formed a semicircle facing Judge Helm.

"Gentlemen of the jury, have you arrived at a verdict?"

"We have, sir," replied Shea.

"I desire to say to the audience," Judge Helm intoned clearly, "before the verdict is announced, that there must not be the least indication of approval or disapproval. There are officers in the courtroom, and if there is any unseemly disturbance, they will at once arrest the disturbers for contempt of court. Mr. Shea, you may hand up the verdict."

Mr. Shea handed the paper to a deputy, who handed it to Judge Helm, who passed it to the clerk. The clerk read aloud.

"We, the jury, find the defendant, Scott Jackson, guilty of murder and fix the punishment at death. Murty Shea, Foreman."

Despite the judge's warning, a murmur of approval traveled around the Court, and an old man near the bench clapped his hands. The news spread into the corridor, and several people shouted.

"Mr. Sheriff," the Judge said, "send some of your men out and arrest those persons."

Scott Jackson sat straight, clearly in a state of shock as the reality of his situation sank in. His face was entirely drained of color, and his lips twitched nervously.

"The clerk will call the names of the jurymen," the judge said.

Clerk Reuscher directed the usual question to each juror asking him if the verdict was his verdict. Each man answered firmly, "Yes."

"Now, gentlemen of the jury," Judge Helm said, "without expressing an opinion as to your verdict, I wish to tender you the thanks of the court for the patient, upright and honest manner in which you have performed your onerous duties. The little compensation which the Commonwealth allows you for your services will be paid you by the clerk. The jury will now be discharged."

The trial was over, but Crawford's fire was still burning.

"If Your Honor pleases," Crawford said, "the code requires that a motion for a new trial must be made before the term of courts expires."

"I should think it sufficient to be made within three days," Lockhart said.

But Crawford would not wait and Judge Helm, with resignation, said, "The court will adjourn until 2 p.m., and I will then hear motions on this matter."

Six burly policemen took Jackson back to his cell. He lost the jaunty step and carefree attitude that brought him into the courtroom, and he seemed, at last, fully aware of his fate.

"It was horrible," Jackson told a reporter from his jail cell. "I don't understand it. I never thought that Murty Shea would bring in such a verdict as that. Why, you know that there was no evidence upon which to convict me. I don't know where they got the line of proof. After all the liars that went on the stand, after all the effort to prove that I lied, there was nothing shown that I killed Pearl Bryan, to say nothing of the fact that a man can be hanged only for premeditated murder. Yes, I am sure that the court of appeals will reverse this Judgment."

Alonzo Walling was housed in the same corridor of the Newport jail as Jackson while awaiting his trial. The guarding of both men had to be intensified now, and it would be easier and cheaper if they were jailed together. When Walling arrived at his new quarters, he already heard the verdict and did nothing to acknowledge it as he greeted Jackson. He just nodded carelessly and said, "Hello, sport."

After the guards had left, Walling spoke to reporters.

"Jackson got what he deserved," he said quietly. "He's guilty."

That afternoon, Alexander Bryan visited the jail with his son Fred and Sheriff Plumber. They came to see the facilities, assure themselves the prisoners were well guarded, and that justice would not be cheated. He walked by Jackson's cell without the slightest glance at the prisoner. Fred, however, glared, trying to catch the eye of Scott Jackson, who sat on the edge of his cot, head in his hands.

The Bryans stopped to speak briefly with Walling. Mr. Bryan asked him when he had last seen Pearl.

"I only saw her once," Walling replied.

"What do you think of Scott Jackson in connection with this case?" Mr. Bryan asked him.

"Jackson killed Pearl, and I think he ought to be hanged," Walling said.

"Well, if you are telling the truth and had nothing to do with the murder, you are in an unfortunate position," Mr. Bryan said.

Fred snorted. "I wouldn't give him that much satisfaction,"

"I am not giving him any satisfaction," his father replied, "I am simply telling him what I think."

PART THREE

22 FADING HOPE

In February 1897, the Cincinnati press marked the anniversary of Peal Bryan's death with illustrated Sunday feature stories summarizing the circumstances of the murder and chronicling events in the case from that time until the present. Jackson and Walling were both convicted of first-degree murder, all appeals failed, and Governor Bradley set March 20 as the date of the double execution.

The trial of Alonzo Walling began twelve days after Scott Jackson's conviction. It followed the same course as Jackson's with many of the same witnesses giving now familiar testimony but with a few notable exceptions. Allen Johnson, who since the arrests said that he saw Jackson, Walling, and Pearl get into a cab, but did not see who was driving, testified that he recognized the driver as Jackson and Walling's friend, Fred Albion. This cleared up a problem that was not addressed at Jackson's trial. Johnson saw them enter the carriage at around 6:00 p.m., but George Jackson said he was not hired to drive until after midnight. The question of who drove them away from Wallingford's remained.

Did Albion hire the carriage and then get cold feet? Fred Albion was not called to testify, but in a sworn deposition, he said he was with Walling on Friday night until 11:00 when Walling went to bed, contradicting Johnson's assertion that he drove the cab.

Two clerks from Heider's hotel also changed their stories. They previously confirmed Walling's assertion that he checked in around 3 a.m. the morning of Friday, January 31, but altered the testimony to say it was the morning of Saturday, February 1. This implied that Walling went to the hotel after committing the murder. Walling still maintained that it was Friday morning, and Albion's deposition corroborated him. The matter was further confused by the fact that the clerks previously claimed that Walling did not signed the register when he checked in. When Colonel Washington entered the register into evidence, it appeared to have Walling's signature on the morning of January 31, but Detective Crim swore that the signature was not there when the register was examined by the police in February. Heider himself concurred, saying the signature was not there before he lent the book to Walling's attorney, W.T. Shepherd.

Walling testified in his own defense, and his story changed somewhat. When first arrested, he said that he met Pearl Bryan on Tuesday with Scott Jackson and saw her for the last time on Wednesday at Fourth and Race in Cincinnati and did not stop to talk to her. He later testified that he spoke with Pearl for the first and only time on Wednesday at Fourth and Race to deliver a message for Scott Jackson. He saw her again at the post office on Thursday but did not stop. Regardless of what others testified, Walling denied going to Wallingford's or anywhere in Kentucky that week.

Colonel Nelson cross-examined the defendant thoroughly, but was not able to change his testimony. Walling consistently stated that he did not know how Pearl Bryan died, but he believed Scott Jackson killed her.

With very little direct evidence against Walling and no motive beyond his friendship with Scott Jackson, Walling stood a better chance of being acquitted, but, in truth, Walling's conviction was a foregone conclusion. The Commonwealth, the Bryan family, and the people of Campbell County wanted both men to hang. Walling was also sentenced to death, but both executions were suspended pending their appeals.

At the beginning of Walling's trial, Jackson and Walling were both confined in the Newport jail. After sentencing Jackson, Judge Helm visited the aging wooden structure and declared the facility inadequate to house capital prisoners. Sheriff Plummer was no longer supervising their confinement, and visitors now came and went at will. The judge feared the Newport jail offered little protection should Jackson conspire to escape, and it offered Jackson even less protection against assassination. He ordered security doubled, but Newport Mayor Bilts refused, saying that Jackson was the Commonwealth's prisoner now, and the town could barely afford to protect its own citizens.

As Walling's trial commenced, Jackson was transferred to the jail in Covington, Kentucky. The Covington jail was a cold, dark, stone prison where the convicted were known to die of tuberculosis well before their sentences were up. After his sentencing, Walling too was transferred there and put in the cell next to Jackson's.

Since their arrests in February 1896, Jackson and Walling were housed in the Cincinnati jail, the Hamilton County jail, Newport jail, and now the Covington jail. Jackson declared Covington the worst of the four, but he got used to it, and over time he and Walling came to be viewed as model prisoners.

As their lawyers worked on appeals, Jackson and Walling found what distractions they could in Covington. Walling even found an opportunity to practice dentistry when a Covington citizen with a severe toothache in desperation brought his pain to the prison. Both Jackson and Walling became prison snitches and testified to conversations of another inmate whose case went to trial. They received nothing in return but a brief time away from prison, a welcome break, even if all they saw was the inside of another courtroom.

During that summer, there was a jailbreak in Covington. An inmate got hold of the jailer's keys and unlocked the cells. The prisoners escaped the building out of a second-story window using a rope made of bedsheets. Jackson and Walling, sensing a trap, remained in their cells. They had nowhere to run to, and at least until hanging day, jail was the safest place they could be.

Scott Jackson was sentenced to hang on June 30 and Alonzo Walling on August 7, but both sentences were delayed pending the outcome of their appeals. Colonel Washington joined Leonard Crawford in preparing a case for each man to take to the Kentucky Court of Appeals. The trials were appealed separately, but the issues were the same for both—errors in the indictment, Sheriff Plummer's role as bailiff, use of tickets to limit attendance, rulings on admissibility of evidence, and improper instructions to the jury.

The most interesting point, and the point most aggressively pursued by the defense, concerned Judge Helm's instructions to the jury. Specifically, they challenged the instruction ascribing first-degree murder to the situation where Pearl Bryan was given poison in Cincinnati but did not die until she was in Kentucky. The argument was simple. Crawford asserted that the Kentucky court had no jurisdiction over matters occurring in Ohio. If Pearl were poisoned in Cincinnati but did not die there, the crime would be attempted murder in Ohio, but Jackson and Walling could not be charged with murder in Kentucky.

The appeals were filed, and the cases argued in early October. In December, the court of appeals denied the requests for new trials. The court upheld both verdicts, unwilling to create a new class of murder not punishable in either jurisdiction.

All hope of a judicial reprieve was gone, and on February 16, Governor Bradley signed the death warrant, which called for a double hanging on Saturday, March 20, to be administered by Sheriff Plummer. When they learned the news, both Jackson and Walling did their best to hide their intense emotions, and each spent the afternoon alone in gloomy contemplation. But by dinnertime, both seemed to be in better spirits, and after eating, they were laughing and chatting as usual as they played cards in Walling's cell. The men had grown accustomed to bad news, and other than putting a date on it, the governor's warrant did nothing to change their fate.

In the Covington jail, Jackson and Walling did not receive casual visitors as they had in Cincinnati and Newport. In addition to being more isolated than the other jails, Covington had two jailers—one for the city and one for the county— and each viewed himself as the one in charge of Jackson and Walling. City Jailer Joseph Wieghaus was more amenable to allowing visitors, but County Jailer John McKnight viewed Jackson and Walling as his personal prisoners and refused all requests to see them. To McKnight's great frustration, those who needed to see the prisoners soon learned to approach Wieghaus.

Despite the confusion, certain visitors were always allowed in. Attorneys Crawford and Washington met with their clients. Mrs. Walling came often to visit her son. A persistent young minister, Reverend James A. Lee, of the Third Baptist Church of Covington, became a regular visitor.

Reverend Lee was about the same age as Scott Jackson. Gaunt and lanky like a young Abe Lincoln, he would stand outside between their cells and lead them in song and prayer, then sermonize on forgiveness and the power of confession. Scott Jackson, who considered himself a man of faith, at first was more welcoming than Walling, but before long, Reverend Lee was paying more attention to Alonzo Walling.

The reverend was offering the condemned men hope of redemption, and not just in the hereafter. He was convinced that coming clean and telling the whole truth would not only please God but lead Governor Bradley to clemency, saving them from the gallows. Scott Jackson enjoyed Lee's visits and was an enthusiastic hymn singer, but he could not entertain the notion of telling any more than he already had. He saw no advantage in deviating from the story he told all year. Walling, though, was looking for any ray of hope and listened quietly to the minister.

Mrs. Walling agreed with Reverend Lee, and at her urging, Alonzo finally acquiesced and wrote the confession that he was pressured to write and gave it to Reverend Lee in a sealed envelope. Lee felt the best course of action was to take Walling's confession to Mr. and Mrs. Bryan. If the Bryans were good Christian people as everyone maintained, they would understand that Lon Walling was not a killer, but just another victim led astray by Scott Jackson. Surely, they would forgive him his mistakes, and thus so would Governor Bradley.

The reverend needed an entrée to the Bryans, and he knew the perfect man for the job. He went to Newport to seek out Louis Poock, who enjoyed a close relationship with the Bryan family since he provided the clue, through her tiny boot, that led to Pearl's identification.

Poock's fascination with the Pearl Bryan case bordered on obsession. The investigation took him away from his shoe store, as had testifying in two trials. Inattention in bad economic times took a toll on his business, and the store was now in receivership with creditors fighting with wholesalers over ownership of his remaining inventory. But Poock was distracted by the writing of a book about the solution of the Fort Thomas mystery, which was almost completed. The book, he believed, would reverse his fortunes.

In Greencastle, the Bryans were still suspicious of people from Ohio and Kentucky, still afraid their daughter would be denied full justice there, but they viewed Louis Poock as the salt of the earth. He, on his own initiative, identified their daughter's corpse, kept correspondence with them, and opened his home to the Bryan family when they came to Newport for the trial. Louis Poock was the only man in the Ohio Valley that the Bryans fully trusted. Reverend Lee knew this and persuaded Poock to use his influence to bring Walling's confession to the Bryans.

On February 26, 1897, Poock and Lee traveled by train to Greencastle. Trying to remain incognito, they registered at the Commercial Hotel under the names Dr. L.C. Abbott and Joseph A. Lyons, but Poock was recognized, and it was soon common knowledge that Mr. Poock was in town with a Kentucky minister. It did not take much guesswork to figure out why they were there.

By the next day, the telegraph confirmed their guesses. When Lee and Poock arrived at the Bryan home, several local reporters were already there waiting for them. As Reverend Lee waited at the gate, Poock started up the path alone,

Fred Bryan rushed out to stop him, telling Poock that his parents were not taking callers. Poock tried to explain that Reverend Lee had a message to deliver, but Fred already knew what they wanted and would not allow it. Lee came through the gate, holding the sealed envelope addressed to Fred's father. He joined the conversation, but as hard as they tried, Lee and Poock could not persuade Fred to let them in. Fred offered to take the envelope to his father, but Lee had promised Mrs. Walling he would hand the letter to Mr. Bryan and no one else.

When Fred proved unyielding, they went to the office of Silas Hayes, the Bryans' attorney. It was another dead end. Like Fred, Hayes was willing to deliver the letter but would not arrange a meeting. With nowhere else to turn, Poock and Lee left Greencastle that evening, their mission unsuccessful.

Not long after the Greencastle trip, the *Cincinnati Tribune* reported that Reverend Lee had offered to sell them the unopened envelope for $3,000. They declined because they felt the offer itself was a bigger story than what the envelope might contain.

The following Sunday, the *Cincinnati Enquirer* printed Walling's "confession" in full on their front page. There was nothing new in it. Walling wrote that Jackson planned from the start to murder Pearl, but he convinced Jackson that abortion was a better solution. He offered to help with the arrangements, but Jackson decided to go it alone. Though Walling had no part in Pearl's death and was not there when it happened, he speculated that Jackson had given her a drug that killed her, and then taken her body to Kentucky. Walling's only regret was that he did not immediately tell the Bryans of his roommate's plan to murder their daughter.

Walling's confession changed no opinions in Greencastle or Frankfort. It became increasingly clear that nothing short of a full confession from Scott Jackson exonerating Alonzo Walling would have any effect.

23 ALEXANDRIA

With the execution less than a month away, Sheriff Plummer appointed a deathwatch—guards to watch over the condemned men to prevent them from taking their own lives and cheating the gallows. The addition of a new faction of guards from another jurisdiction exacerbated the already chaotic administration at the Covington jail. This, together with the discovery that a reporter entered the jail without authorization and held a private conversation with Scott Jackson, convinced Sheriff Plummer to move the prisoners once more.

On March 3, Jackson and Walling were moved to the jail in Alexandria, Kentucky. Their trip took them down Alexandria Pike, past the site where Pearl Bryan's body was found.

"Do you recognize this place, boys?" Sheriff Plummer asked as the wagon passed the spot.

"I never was here before in my life," said Jackson.

"Neither was I," said Walling.

The jail in Alexandria was part of an old fort and consisted of two large rooms meant to hold multiple prisoners. Before the arrival of the Covington prisoners, the current inmates were moved to another prison. One large room was lined with steel panels with steel bars on the door and windows. Within this room, a large steel cage was constructed with a divider down the middle to make two compartments. Jackson and Walling each shared a compartment with one of the deathwatch guards. Alexandria was more isolated than Covington, and the prisoners would see even fewer visitors here.

From the beginning of their incarceration, Jackson and Walling were visited by groups of young women who were fascinated by the prisoners and fully convinced of their innocence. Jackson basked in the attention and was never too downhearted to entertain a young lady. Walling was sometimes moody and did not always welcome the girls, but he had his followers as well.

With each new jail, access to the prisoners became more difficult, and the ranks of their admirers began to dwindle until only the most dedicated came to see Jackson and Walling. Since the move to Alexandria, reporters were able to put names to the faces they had seen around the jails for months.

A tall brunette named Katherine Storey visited Jackson and Walling frequently since their arrest. At the Covington Jail, she wore a veil when she called and told reporters she was "actuated solely by charity." Scott Jackson was the focus of her attention, and she believed him to be innocent. After the move to Alexandria, the papers referred to Kate Storey as Jackson's sweetheart, and she was always allowed to visit him.

Walling had a sweetheart as well. Emma Roberts, a young woman who knew him from childhood was living in Cincinnati and regularly visited him in jail. It was reported that prior to his arrest Alonzo Walling and Emma Roberts were engaged to be married, but this was unlikely. It was well known that in the months before the murder, Walling was seeing May Smith, and when he could afford it, would join Jackson at the brothels on George Street. But in Alexandria, Emma and Alonzo appeared to be lovers—more so than Scott Jackson and Kate Storey—and would have hushed conversations while holding hands through the bars.

Emma Roberts sometimes visited the jail with Alonzo's mother, Sarah Walling, who took up residence in Alexandria at the home of Mrs. T.H. Orr. They shared the belief that Alonzo could save his life if he told all that he knew away from the influence of Scott Jackson. They were pressuring authorities to have the prisoners completely separated.

Sarah Walling was a frail, delicate, silver-haired woman whose face bore signs of anxiety and emotional pain when she met with a *Cincinnati Enquirer* reporter in early March. In the rare interview, she echoed the sentiment many expressed since the arrests—that Scott Jackson had hypnotic control over her son.

"I have hoped and prayed every hour for months, that my son would be spared me," she told the reporter. "This has been a most unfortunate affair for Lonnie. He has a weak boyish mind, and Jackson has made him his tool. Anyone can see the strange influence Jackson has over him. I don't know whether it is hypnotism or what the name of it is, but I know—I know—that this is the influence which Jackson holds over my son. Oh, if they could only be separated; if I could talk to my boy when he is free from Jackson's influence, we would certainly be able to learn something which would save Lonnie. I am going to see Lonnie this afternoon, but it is perfectly useless for me to attempt to influence him in Jackson's presence. He does not seem to be able to think for himself if Jackson is near him."

Scott Jackson's mother was also staying at the home of Mrs. Orr. Sheriff Plummer arranged for both mothers to stay at one of the finest residences in Alexandria. Mrs. Jackson, a large motherly woman, also named Sarah, became warm friends with Sarah Walling, despite Mrs. Walling's animosity toward Scott. Both women were widows who raised their sons alone, both were Methodist, worshiping together in Alexandria's little Methodist church, and they understood each other's grief as no one else could.

Sarah Jackson also spoke with the press in Alexandria in her first public statement since the arrest of her son. She spoke bitterly of the treatment received by Scott and herself and made the only negative comment yet spoken about Pearl Bryan:

> When I first heard of my son's arrest for this awful thing, I was crushed and horrified. For five weeks I lay without sleep and without a tear. I said if my son has done this awful thing, I ask only that he receive justice, tempered with mercy. We have received neither from press or people. I am 64 years old, a woman alone in the world, without an earthly one to support me. I have prayed that I may live to lay my son down. After that, the sleep of death will be most welcome. After the cold, inhuman persecution we have suffered, I can only say that the blood of my son and myself will be upon the heads of the people who have maligned us unless God makes bare his arm, stretches forth His hand, and rescues us from the civil persecution we have endured for many months.
>
> It has been made to appear that the unfortunate girl who was the victim of this tragedy was the pure and innocent object of the villainy of one as black as Satan. I have seen her on the streets of Greencastle, and I did not wish my son to associate with her.

The two mothers remained friends, but sometimes their goals were at odds. On March 9, Mrs. Walling left Alexandria to catch a train for Greencastle, Indiana, and did not tell Mrs. Jackson. She was going to visit the Bryan family and plead for the life of her son and was afraid it would anger her new friend. But Mrs. Jackson planned her own trip to meet with Governor Bradley and did not begrudge Mrs. Walling any attempt to save her son.

Though Reverend Lee was unable to meet with the Bryans, Mrs. Walling was convinced that her mission would be successful. She would meet with Mrs. Bryan as one mother to another; they would share each other's sorrow. Alonzo had been a victim of Scott Jackson's evil, no less than Pearl had been, and she was sure that Mrs. Bryan would understand and forgive her son's weakness.

Mrs. Walling was welcomed inside the Bryans' home, and Pearl's parents listened politely to her appeal for mercy. She told the Bryans that her son Lonnie did not kill their daughter. It was Scott Jackson who did the deed. Like their daughter, Lonnie was led astray by Jackson. He was guilty of bad judgment but not of murder.

The two mothers wept together over Pearl's tragic death and Alonzo's dire fate and even shared a tearful embrace. But in the end, Mrs. Bryan could not bestow her mercy. Though it may have been Scott Jackson who wielded the knife, she could not exonerate those who abetted him. Calamity was forced upon her, she said, and one word from Will Wood when he took Pearl to the station in Greencastle, or one word from Alonzo Walling when he met Pearl in Cincinnati would have averted the awful crime. Then she asked Mrs. Walling the one question whose answer could save her son's life—where is the head of her poor daughter? But Mrs. Walling did not know. She asked Alonzo many times, and he could not tell her. That ended any hope of mercy. Mrs. Walling brought with her a formal document, drawn up by her attorney, proclaiming the Bryans' forgiveness of her son. She returned to Cincinnati with the paper unsigned.

As the execution day drew nearer, it looked as if there was no hope to save Scott Jackson, but there was a growing sentiment that Alonzo Walling was not guilty of first-degree murder and should not hang beside the man who manipulated him. Sarah Walling, Emma Roberts, and Reverend Lee remained convinced that he did not tell all that he knew and pressured him to tell the whole story. Even his attorney, Colonel Washington, believed there was a chance for clemency if Walling told the whole truth.

But Walling refused to say any more. Scott Jackson told him the previous July that if every chance to save their lives was gone, he would tell enough in three minutes to save Walling's life. Walling took Jackson at his word, and his trust in his friend's promise did not waver, but if Jackson had anything to tell, now was the time to tell it.

24 CONFESSIONS

Three days before the scheduled execution, most of the country, and much of the world, had its attention focused on Carson City, Nevada, where "Gentleman" Jim Corbett would be defending his heavyweight championship, fighting "Ruby" Robert Fitzsimmons. Billed as the fight of the century, there was bad blood going in. Corbett had been refusing Fitzsimmons' challenges for several years and at one point had nearly retired without defending his title, but Fitzsimmons had raised the necessary cash and Corbett finally accepted the challenge.

The fight provided a rare point of disagreement between Jackson and Walling while in the Alexandria Jail. Walling rooted for the challenger while Jackson supported Gentleman Jim, claiming to have met the champion several years earlier in New Jersey.

In February of 1896, Jackson and Walling both met Jim Corbett when he visited them in the Cincinnati Jail. The jail was open to anyone who wanted to see the accused murderers and prominent Cincinnatians of all types had visited, including sports stars Buck Ewing, Bug Holliday, and Bid McPhee, of the Cincinnati Reds baseball club. Corbett was in town starring in a theatrical production, The Naval Cadet, and out of curiosity went to see the accused killers. Jackson charmed the fighter as he did most everyone who visited him in his cell, and he told Corbett they met before at his training camp in Asbury, New Jersey. Corbett did not remember and was skeptical until Jackson described some of his training procedures that would only be known to someone who saw them firsthand.

The Corbett-Fitzsimmons fight was held on St. Patrick's Day, and the prisoners listened intently as updates from the fight were received by telegraph and relayed to their cells. The bout lasted fourteen rounds and ended in Walling's favor. A blow to the stomach knocked the wind out of Corbett and he hit the canvas; ten seconds later, Bob Fitzsimmons was the new Heavyweight Champion.

The fight was a welcome diversion for the prisoners, but they soon returned to the dire urgency of their impending executions. All hope appeared to be gone for Scott Jackson but Walling's people—his mother and brothers, Emma Roberts, Reverend Lee, Colonel Washington—and a growing segment of the population thought Alonzo Walling did not need to hang.

Walling's role in the murder was shadowy from the beginning. His arrest the night of Jackson's arrest was an afterthought initiated by a reporter. He had no direct connection to Pearl Bryan and no motive for killing her. With the exception of Allen Johnson, who saw Walling nearly every night at Wallingford's Saloon, all who identified him did so after his picture and description were published again and again in the papers. Walling clearly hid the truth out of misplaced loyalty to his roommate, and to the bitter frustration of all who cared for him, it was too late now to tell it.

Any meaningful confession had to come from Jackson himself and would need Walling's corroboration. Nothing said by Walling alone would be sufficient to stop the execution. A confession from Jackson alone could not be trusted either, but it had to come from him first and it had to explain what had really happened to Pearl Bryan. Everyone was convinced that there was more to the story than had yet been told.

Walling was still counting on Jackson to honor the promise he made to save his life, but his family had lost faith in Jackson. Clint Walling, Alonzo's brother, confronted Jackson saying, "We want you to help us save Lonnie."

"All right, I'll do the best I can," was Jackson's less than reassuring response.

What happened next surprised everyone.

Attorneys Crawford and Washington agreed that there was no hope of either escaping the gallows unless both men now told the whole truth and nothing but the truth. They went to Alexandria jail on Thursday morning to meet separately with each prisoner.

The meeting with Walling lasted only a few minutes but they spoke with Jackson for over an hour. The lawyers emerged from the meetings and announced publicly that the prisoners agreed to tell all and would issue two concurring written confessions. Officials made immediately to put Jackson and Walling in a cell together with paper and pens and an almanac to verify dates.

The work began on Wednesday, March 17, and continued into Thursday afternoon. Conferring when necessary to confirm their facts, Jackson and Walling produced two separate documents, which were sent by train to Frankfurt and in the hands of Governor Bradley by late Thursday night. By previous arrangement, for an undisclosed sum to be paid to the mothers of the condemned men, the confessions were also given to the *Cincinnati Enquirer*, where they appeared in full the following morning.

The first was Scott Jackson's:

To Hon. William O. Bradley, Governor, State of Kentucky

Your Excellency,

I hereby present to you for your consideration and attention my appeal to you for executive clemency in the case of the Commonwealth of Kentucky vs. Scott Jackson.

The so-called evidence as presented by the prosecution, does not show any of the facts in the case – or very few, at least. I hereby give you in a very few words, the main points in the case at the request of my friends and ask you to give these your attention and humbly beg of you to grant to me my life. God did not demand of Cain his life when he slew his brother Abel.

Pearl Bryan came to Cincinnati, Ohio, by direction and advice of her seducer, William F. Wood, and with the desire on her part to have an operation performed to relieve her of her burden and to get out of her trouble. I had many letters from Will Wood telling me of his trouble and begging me to tell him how to get out of it, and what to do to help him and relieve her. I sent him all of the information I knew or heard about such matters in order to help them both. He finally became so anxious owing to her condition that he said he would send her to Cincinnati and wrote to me to get someone to perform the operation and thereby save them both from disgrace.

I showed those letters to Alonzo M. Walling, my roommate and fellow classmate, and he said he thought he would be able to get someone to perform the operation and said he would look up someone and try to secure a room for her.

On Monday afternoon, January 27, 1896, I received a postal card from William Wood, saying this: "Baggage was en route and to look out for it and fix things O.K. for him." Walling had not yet made any preparations for receiving Miss Bryan and hadn't secured anyone to attend to her, for we did not expect her so soon.

She arrived at Cincinnati on Monday evening and went to hotel (Indiana House) and sent a message to us on Tuesday that she had arrived and for us to call and see her as soon as possible. We went to the Indiana House on Tuesday just before noon and told her that Walling was in communication with a friend to secure a place for her to go and obtain medical treatment. She asked me to take her valise and relieve her of the trouble of caring for it, and I did so. This was partly filled with clothing. I took it to my room and left it there. On Tuesday I took Miss Bryan out for a walk and ride in the car, and she returned to the Indiana House for the night.

I arranged with Miss Bryan to meet Walling on Wednesday at Fourth and Race Streets, Cincinnati, shortly after dinner about 1 o'clock and he was to tell her if possible, where to go and that when I heard from her again, I would go to her with the clothing. Walling received information by mail on Wednesday morning and went to see her as arranged. I saw Walling at the college in the afternoon and he told me he had sent Miss Bryan to a doctor. Intended to go see her that evening but did not.

On Thursday Walling received word by mail from Dr. Wagner to come out, and in the evening we both went to Bellevue and met Dr. Wagner on the corner by Foertmeyer's drugstore. We walked down to his house on Ward Street and stood outside for about half an hour but we did not go inside, but made arrangements to be out again on the next evening (Friday). Walling had an engagement and so I did not hurry home to meet him, but it seems he did not keep it. I went to my room and called downstairs on Miss McNevins and then went to my room, remaining there until about 11 o'clock, waiting for Walling, and as he did not come, I went out as quietly as I could and went to Bellevue to the doctor's house.

I met Walling looking for me, entered the house (front room). Wagner was excited and told one of us to go at once to the drugstore and get him some ergot. I ran there and told Foertmeyer to let me have it quickly for Dr. Wagner. He did so and I hurried back. The doctor gave a dose of it to Miss B. and after a few minutes' talk I noticed she was in great pain. Wagner at once opened her dress and gave her an injection of some medicine, clear in color (I know not what it was.) He also gave her some whiskey. She seemed easier for a few minutes, and then suddenly fainted or became unconscious. Dr. Wagner tried to bring her to herself again, but was unable to do so, and exclaimed, "She's gone, boys, and we must get her out of here quick." He told us to stay there for a short time and he would "fix things or else we would all be in a big hole, and I must get her away."

Walling and myself remained in the house. I am sure she died of the medicine given her to produce abortion. Dr. Wagner returned in a few minutes – maybe half an hour – when he came in the back door, and said, "Get her ready, quick, and we will take her away." She was on a sofa, or couch, with underclothing and light wrapper on. I put a cloak about her, and Walling and Wagner carried her out to a cab in the alley back of the house. I carried the two bags belonging to Pearl Bryan, and her hat; these were all put in the hack, Walling and myself getting inside and Wagner drove down the alley and out into the country. We talked the thing over and tried to think of something, and as a result did not do anything. He stopped and said, "Have you fellows any idea what to do now?"

I said I did not know but did not want to ride any more that I could help in the cab. He said, "Well, we must leave it somewhere, but I don't know where." I said, "Well do it quick." Walling said, "You must get this thing out of sight, or we will all be in trouble."

Wagner drove to the lane between Stone's and Lock's farm (I afterward learned.) He stopped the cab on the Alexandria Pike and said, "Let's leave it here – down there."

All were excited and I cannot say just how we removed the body from the cab. We carried it over the fence and a short way up the lane behind some bushes. Dr. Wagner then took off her corset and listened to hear any heart action and said, "This is a hell of a case and it is the first time I ever knew of anyone going under in that way and, by God, boys, you must not betray me for he would be damned if he was going to be caught."

And with that he took out his dissecting knife and told me to take hold of her head. I did so, and he severed the head from the body and threw it into the cloak and wrapped it up. The body was then under some bushes, but as I let go of it, it fell forward. Walling picked up the cloak with the head in and we all hurried to the cab. Wagner put the head inside and we all rode to Newport Bridge where Walling and I left and went to Cincinnati.

Wagner drove away. Walling left me to go to Heider's Hotel. I went to my room taking the valises with me and threw the clothing into the river as I was going over the bridge. She wore a sack over the wrapper. This became discolored when the head was severed by the blood, and as it was put in the valise it must have caused the inside to become stained. The head was not in the valise at any time.

Trusting you will see I am not guilty of any attempt to destroy life and that you will grant me your clemency,

I am, very humbly yours,
Scott Jackson

Next ran the confession of Alonzo Walling:

To the Governor of Kentucky,

I have always said that I know nothing more of the death of Pearl Bryan because I had made up my mind that I would rather hang than have disgrace on my family. I had expected a statement from Scott Jackson, which would show that I was not guilty of murder. Now, I make a clean breast of it, because I cannot help acting upon the advice of my friends who do not wish to see me hang, and who know the part I took in the case. I think that any man might have done the same with his life at stake.

The first intimation I ever had that there was such a girl living as Pearl Bryan came from a letter received by Scott Jackson from Will Wood stating that he had a girl by the name of Pearl Bryan in trouble and that he was compelled to have something done to relieve her and save himself. This was, I think, some time in November 1895.

After this, I saw several letters begging Jackson to help him out of his trouble, but I was not asked by Scott Jackson or Will Wood to assist them in any way until Scott Jackson returned from Greencastle after the holidays, at which time Scott Jackson asked if I know of anyone who could perform an abortion. I told him I did not, but that I would try to find out for him if he wanted me to. He said for me to find out if I could.

On January 27, 1896, I wrote a letter to a friend of mine by the name of May Smith, asking her if she knew of anyone who could perform an abortion. On Wednesday, January 28, I received a letter from her stating that she would advise me to talk to a Dr. Wagner, whom she knew and that she would send a letter to him, having him call at the college and see me. On Wednesday, Dr. Wagner called at the college and inquired for me. After finding me, he showed me the letter May Smith had written to him asking him to call and see me.

We had a little talk, after which he said he would perform the operation. He gave me his address and I said I would send Pearl Bryan out to see him. After dinner I went to the corner of Fourth and Race Streets where I met Pearl Bryan, as Jackson had made arrangements to meet her there, and I instructed her to go to this Dr. Wagner and he would arrange for her and relieve her disgrace and told her Jackson would be out to see her in the evening and bring her clothes as he said he would do after making arrangements for her to go there.

Thursday, January 30, I received a note at college from Dr. Wagner asking me to bring Pearl Bryan's clothes out to him as she was under his care and for us to meet him in front of Foertmeyer's drugstore. We went out that evening and found him there and walked down to his house, but I did not go inside, stood on the outside for a short time and made arrangements to come out on the following night, Friday, January 31. This evening Jackson and myself made arrangements to go to Dr. Wagner's house together and arranged to meet at the room at 7:30 o'clock. I waited there till 8 o'clock. Jackson did not come, as I concluded he had gone out and I immediately took a car and went out by myself. When I arrived, Jackson had as yet not been there. I waited awhile and about 10:30 o'clock, Jackson came, and we were all in the parlor together, when suddenly Pearl was taken with severe pain and Dr. Wagner asked Jackson to go over to Mr. Foertmeyer's drugstore and get some medicine for her. He said he was going to change the medicine, that the medicine he was using was not producing the desired effect, and that he wanted to get through with the case.

Jackson returned with the drug and Dr. Wagner gave a large dose of it and in a short time she became unconscious. Dr. Wagner then gave her a hypodermic injection of some clear liquid. This did no good and she was apparently dead. The doctor said she was dead and said for us to stay there for a while until he went out and made arrangements to take her away from the house. In a short time, he came in through the back way, saying "Boys, help me get her out to the wagon." We all got her in the wagon and Wagner drove off. I did not know where he was going and when he stopped, we were somewhere in the country. I do not know how we got the body out of the wagon for I was too much terrified, but I do know that Dr. Wagner and Jackson removed the head.

We all got into the wagon and rode to the Newport Bridge and Jackson and I walked across the Newport Bridge to Cincinnati, and I stayed all night at Header's restaurant for I was so tired I could go no further.

Alonzo M. Walling

The story was not new, rumors of Dr. Wagner's involvement circulated in Campbell County since the beginning and nearly made it into Scott Jackson's trial. Crawford had listed Anna, Maude, and Nellie Wagner as potential witnesses but never called them to testify. In many ways the confessions were more satisfying than the official story. To some, a botched abortion seemed more plausible than cold-blooded murder by decapitation.

It was a familiar story in Campbell County, but it would be all new to Governor Bradley. With the scheduled execution just a day away, would the governor be convinced of its truth? Would it be enough to halt the hangings?

25 ANOTHER STORY

The confessions sent reporters scrambling for confirmation. Jackson and Walling named names, and those in a position to verify what was written made themselves available.

The often-elusive May Smith was easily found, accompanying Walling's mother to the Alexandria Jail. She corroborated all that was said about her in the confessions and shared with reporters a letter which she sent to Governor Bradley in support of the prisoners' statements.

> Dear Sir—I have come to the conclusion to make a statement of the condemned men, Scott Jackson and Alonzo Walling, held for the murder of Pearl Bryan, for which they are sentenced to be hanged March 20, 1897.
>
> I was in Louisville and on Monday, January 27, I received a letter from Alonzo Walling asking me if I knew a doctor who would perform an abortion. I answered Tuesday, January 28, telling him Dr. Wagner, of Bellevue, could do the work. I wrote Dr. Wagner also to call and see Mr. Walling at the college. He did so, and Dr. Wagner did the work.
>
> I will make affidavit of this statement at any time.
>
> May Smith

The confirmation by May Smith of her role in the abortion was essential to the confessions, but at this point, it is uncertain what an affidavit from May Smith would be worth. She had changed her story several times, and although this one was more probable than her last story, she always followed Walling's lead. It was hardly conclusive that she followed him now.

William Foertmeyer was a different story. A disinterested party with no connection to Jackson or Walling and no reason to lie, he confirmed what was said in the confession and gave his own account of what transpired the night of Pearl Bryan's death. The absent-minded German druggist had been part of the prosecution's case, testifying that Jackson, Walling, and Pearl

Bryan went to his store, though the day in question was still unresolved. Questioned a year later, in light of the two confessions, Foertmeyer had much more to tell. And he corroborated everything in the confessions.

In Jackson's trial, Foertmeyer testified to receiving a telephone message to his store from Scott Jackson but did not elaborate. He said several messages were sent and received between Scott Jackson and Maude Wagner. One afternoon Miss Wagner was in his store with a strange young lady "of the blonde type" and telephoned a drug store on Ninth and Elm in Cincinnati. Later in the week, the blonde lady telephoned the same drug store, giving her name as Pearl Bryan. Every message received was from the same drug store and was signed Scott Jackson.

As many druggists did, Foertmeyer kept his door unlocked and kept a light burning in the store window all night. He slept in a room behind the counter to be on hand for any late-night emergencies. He recalled a man coming in that Friday night around midnight asking for ergot, which Foertmeryer sold him. About 4:00 a.m., another man, identified by Foertmeyer as Alonzo Walling, came in to buy a pint of whiskey. He was not licensed to sell whiskey alone, so Foertmeyer suggested a preparation including ginger. After some argument, Walling agreed, took the bottle, and hurried out of the store.

On Sunday, after the body was found, Foertmeyer received a message from a drug store in Cincinnati requesting that Maude Wagner meet the caller that night at Ninth and Race. When Foertmeyer asked what name he should sign to the note, the caller said no name was necessary.

Foertmeyer formalized his statement in a letter handed to Jackson's brother-in-law, Edwin Post, who then forwarded it to Governor Bradley.

To the Hon. W. O. Bradley,
Governor State of Kentucky

Dear Sir:

Having waited until the present moment for some word from the two young men, Scott Jackson and Alonzo Walling, that should substantiate my opinion and feeling that they were withholding certain facts that would bring about a commutation of their sentence, by reason of their having given an oath that they would not disclose the connection of the third party in the case, I now make it known to you:

On the last Friday night of January 1896, Scott Jackson appeared at my store a few minutes before 12 o'clock, and told me that he had been sent by Dr. Wagner of this town for some Fld. Ex. Ergot. He seemed to be in haste and came behind the prescription case where the light of the store was burning. Thinking that the doctor was so taken up with the case that he had no time to write a prescription for the medicine, I gave him a 1 ounce bottle of the same and then retired for the night.

Between the hours of 12 that midnight and 6 A.M. that Saturday morning, February 1, on which the death of the girl was supposed to have occurred, I was awakened four times. I think Scott Jackson was the first caller but what he got at that time I have never been able to recall. The last of these callers, to the best of my knowledge was Alonzo Walling. He remained in the front part of the store where the light was dim but at that time, I recognized him as the man I had seen with Scott Jackson on several occasions before. He stated that he had been sent by Dr. Wagner for some whiskey for a very sick person.

I objected to giving him that, stating the reason that I had no state license to sell liquor, but knowing that the saloons were all closed, and fearing that delay might prove injurious to the patient, I finally consented. I told him if he allowed me to add some medication to the whiskey that would destroy its identity as a beverage, I would give him a little until the saloons opened. He demurred at first saying that in that shape it might not serve the purpose, but finally consented. I gave him 30 cents worth of the mixture, and he offered me a fifty cent piece in payment. I found I had taken all my small change upstairs as is my custom and told him I had nothing but pennies to give him. He said, "Never mind, I will call in the morning for the change," and left hurriedly, but never called back for it, and I do not recall seeing him again until I went to identify him in the jail in Cincinnati.

Other incidents that convince me that some things occurred in this town that ought to be considered are the facts that numerous remarks were overheard on the streets connecting the doctor before mentioned with this case long before I made known the circumstances of receiving telephone calls from Scott Jackson to a member of the doctor's family, also the persistent denial on the part of that same family that they had received any telephone messages from any one from my store although my clerk and errand boy state emphatically that they have received and delivered several messages to them other than those received from Scott Jackson to that same family.

I am also willing to take an oath that the mother and daughter were at my store and called up Scott Jackson a day or two before the finding of the body of Pearl Bryan.

There are other circumstances that I will not now disclose until I am confident that these young men make a confession.

The foregoing facts I have just related I had told to Crim the detective a year ago, but those engaged with prosecuting this case were in fear that these facts, if offered, might seriously detract from the weight of the evidence of the colored coachman.

Hoping you will give this consideration, I remain yours respectfully,

W.L. Foertmeyer, Druggist

Neighbors of Dr. Wagner previously reported seeing a pretty blonde girl in the Wagners' yard the week before the murder. They said that before he was committed, Dr. Wagner could be heard raving about the murder, and some claimed to have seen him digging in his backyard looking for the head.

Mrs. John Riordan, who lived around the block from Dr. Wagner, and a year earlier reported a disturbance the night of January 31, steadfastly refused to speak to reporters, echoing her husband's advice to stay out of other people's affairs. The *Enquirer* printed her story secondhand, "according to one who has heard of it."

The day preceding Pearl Bryan's death, Mrs. Riordan noticed Dr. Wagner sharpening knives and surgical instruments on a stone in his rear yard. That night at a late hour, she heard a scream, as if of terror, coming from the doctor's house, followed a few seconds later by a second cry of alarm. Later on, she heard the rumbling of a vehicle from the Wagner house, down Ward Avenue. The next morning, she found a photograph which she thought resembled pictures she had seen in the newspapers of Will Wood. She took the photograph to the Cincinnati Police, and now more than a year later, it was unknown what became of the photograph.

The Wagner family denied everything Foertmeyer said and dismissed his story. They said it was driven by years of bad blood between Foertmeyer and Dr. Wagner that began when Foertmeyer challenged a prescription Wagner wrote for a cholera patient. Foertmeyer said it was the wrong medicine and referred the patient to a doctor in Cincinnati. It was ridiculous to claim that Wagner sent someone to Foertmeyer's to fill a prescription. He had not done so in years.

Responding to the neighbors' suspicions, Mrs. Wagner said that they probably mistook her niece, Mrs. Strobridge, for Pearl Bryan. Mrs. Strobridge was also blonde and had visited the Wagners at the end of January.

"My father is innocent," said Maude Wagner, "and on the night that the tragedy occurred, he was not at home. It is hard for a daughter to say that her father is insane, but I must admit that he had lost his reason at that time. I have never received any telephone messages from Foertmeyer's drugstore, nor have I ever used his telephone."

She was deeply offended that Jackson's confession asserted that her father said "hell" and "damn." It was proof enough for her that the story was untrue. Beyond that, she would say nothing.

By afternoon, the Wagners produced a postal card they claimed proved the doctor was not at home when Pearl Bryan died. As with all evidence in the case, it was vague and ambiguous. Postmarked Camp Washington, Cincinnati, Ohio, Jan 23, 1896, it read:

> Arrived here last night, all right. Found Bro Wagner in a very critical condition. I think the best thing to do is to bring him home with me for a few days. A doctor here thinks it is the best we can do for him at present. I shall be at home tomorrow or the next day.

> Walter Hendren.

Walter Hendren, who lived in Nicholasville, Kentucky, was Mrs. Wagner's brother. The message dated more than a week before the body was found implied Hendren was taking his brother-in-law to his home in an interior Kentucky town. Mrs. Wagner explained the Cincinnati postmark by saying she had an aunt who lived there, and her brother stopped for a visit. The postal card indicated Hendren's intention but was hardly proof of his brother-in-law's whereabouts the night Pearl Bryan died.

At the Eastern Kentucky Asylum for the Insane, Dr. Scott, who was treating Wagner, said publicly that even in his wildest hallucinations, Wagner never mentioned Pearl Bryan or made reference to any event that may be even remotely connected to the murder. Scott declared that Wagner "regained his mind" and was anxious to return home to defend himself.

"That is the biggest falsehood ever told on top of earth," said Dr. Wagner when an *Enquirer* reporter showed him a copy of Jackson's confession. "I do not now, nor at any other time did I know Scott Jackson or Alonzo Walling. I never knew Pearl Bryan, and she was never at my house, to my knowledge, while I was there or away from there."

Wagner was insulted when the reporter asked if he ever performed abortions. "What do you mean, sir?" Wagner cried, approaching the reporter with clenched fists. "Would you dare insult a gentleman? Do you know, sir, that performing such an operation is committing murder? Do you, too, accuse me of murder?"

Reaction from Greencastle was swift and unyielding. The Bryan family now asserted that Pearl's sole reason for traveling to Cincinnati was to convince Scott Jackson to marry her. She never intended to undergo an abortion. Fred Bryan called the confessions admissions of guilt and nothing more. To Alexander Bryan, the statements revealed the "fine Italian hand of the legal fraternity." The family was confident that Governor Bradley would not deprive them of the justice they had so long awaited. Even the disposition of Pearl's head, now that her mutilated body was peacefully interred, was of secondary importance to the punishment of those responsible. They were content to let the criminals take that secret with them, as long as they left soon.

The confessions of Jackson and Walling were not what Colonel Washington expected, and they put him in an uncomfortable position. In addition to being Alonzo Walling's attorney, he was the Wagner family's attorney, and he previously dismissed allegations against Dr. Wagner as "Too absurd to talk about."

Washington sent a letter to Governor Bradley, which, without making reference to the confessions, humbly requested that he delay the executions. His lengthy appeal in support of Alonzo Walling ended with a list of reasons that his client should not hang:

> Without necessarily extending this communication, I appeal to Your Excellency along the lines suggested to bear in mind in connection with this application the following facts:
> 1. That Alonzo Walling was totally without motive.
> 2. That he never saw Pearl Bryan until two days before her death.
> 3. That his previous character was good.
> 4. That he was young and relatively without experience.
> 5. That he was, and is, mentally weak and without will power.
> 6. That it was his misfortune to be under the domination of an older man, of strong will, of vastly superior intelligence and of greater experience.
>
> The last three affirmations involve matters of which, I do not doubt, the Almighty Ruler will, in His infinite mercy, surely take cognizance. And if He will do so; then they can not be inappropriate to an application of the nature of this one.
> Finally, even if Your Excellency should by any possibility err, you will always have the proud satisfaction of knowing that it was on the side of mercy, and as I may safely add, in conformity with a desire upon the part of the public, which is as earnest and as universal among all classes and conditions as anything that has ever fallen under my observation.
> And now, trusting that Your Excellency may overlook anything contained in this application which may seem to you not altogether proper and attribute it to the haste with which I have been forced to prepare it, I beg you leave to subscribe myself, with great respect.

A cold rain on Friday, March 19, was not enough to deter the crowd that gathered to await the news from Frankfort. To those fiercely opposed to capital punishment, the confessions printed in the morning papers just compounded fears that two men would be killed in error. A growing faction was content to hang Jackson alone and let Walling, his innocent tool, escape the noose. But most of those waiting in the rain were satisfied that both verdicts handed down nearly a year earlier were correct and that the hangings were long overdue. The mob was ready to address any change in plans.

At 3:00 that afternoon, Governor Bradley's response arrived by train in Newport. The answer was clear before the statement was read. The train also carried the McCreary Guards, a company of the state militia, who, with the tattoo of drums, amassed in front of the courthouse. Some took positions guarding the perimeter of the courthouse yard where the hanging would take place, while the rest set up camp and awaited their watch.

The governor was not moved by the confessions or Colonel Washington's plea for mercy. As the Bryans had, he saw the confessions as admission of guilt to a capital crime and showed that Jackson and Walling are equally guilty. He released the following statement:

> The common law concerning the crime admitted to in the confessions to have been committed is in force in this state. The confession shows that Pearl Bryan was killed by drugs administered to produce an abortion. If this be true, she being quick with child as shown by the evidence, the child was killed also. Her death was caused by drugs deliberately administered, the effect of which clearly manifests an utter disregard for human life. The agency employed was not one from which death or great injury would probably result, but from which, considering its rapid operation, death would necessarily result. Either the physician who administered the drug knew or had every reason to suppose it would cause death; or should have known it. Under either state of the case, he was guilty of murder, and Jackson and Walling were and are equally guilty under the statute of Kentucky. All this must be considered if the confessions are true.

> The confessions, however, are inconsistent and contradictory, utterly at war with every statement that each of the defendants made on the witness stand.

> It is urged that this should be overlooked, because they were swearing for their lives.

> Conceding that their false statements were made to escape danger then pending, it may well be asked how much greater is the danger that now confronts them when they stand in the shadow of the gallows.

> If they are excusable for false swearing then, how much more are they excusable, and how much more likely is it that they would speak falsely now?

> One of them says the body was taken away in a cab; the other that it was taken in a wagon.

> This conflict would be quite immaterial but for the fact that Jackson

says they got inside the cab while Wagner drove. The contradiction, therefore, becomes material. Walling says that Wagner and Jackson removed the head, while Jackson says that Wagner did it. The removal of the corsets might have taken place to distribute the blood more generally through the system, or they may have loosened when the injection was administered, and fallen when the girl was being conveyed to the place.

The whole confession bears a striking similarity to the testimony of George Jackson, for it is now admitted that the body was removed by both Jackson and Walling, and both were present when the body was decapitated, thus destroying the defensive theory on the trial that the tracks were made by others than Jackson and Walling. The note or letter said by Walling to have been received from Dr. Wagner asking that the clothes of Pearl Bryan be sent to him, and stating that she was under his care, is not produced, nor is its absence in any way accounted for.

Not only is the confession a contradiction on the evidence of both defendants, but a flat contradiction of the letter of Walling, sent me only a few days since, and claimed to have been written by him under sense of rapidly approaching and impending death.

These men have not only trifled with human life, but have trifled with the Courts, trifled with the execution and set at defiance the laws of God and man. If it is established that one criminal, after such conduct as this, can by a mere pretended confession obtain respite, then every other is entitled to lied treatment, and this would result in frustrating justice and bringing the execution of laws into contempt. The wounded hand of Pearl Bryan solemnly and surely points to the fact that she was not dead when beheaded. That wound could have been inflicted only when during the terrible agony of her decapitation she raised it on order to ward off the cruel knife.

Dr. Wagner is in the asylum, and is the man of all others, by reason of his condition, at whose door the defendant would most naturally lay this terrible crime.

To grant a respite in order that the defendants might be used as witnesses to procure his conviction would result in a delay of at least a year, as experience in the trial for the defendants have demonstrated. In view of the various conflicts in the defendants' statements no jury would or could, believe any statement that either of them might make, and, consequently, Wagner would not be convicted.

Such delay could do no good and would only add fuel to the flames and furnish a further incentive to mob violence in this state.

The claim that Walling is under the influence of Jackson and therefore deserves clemency cannot be considered. He shows himself the willing and ready assistant.

Each of them clearly exhibited a reckless disregard for human life.

Their confessions taken in connection with the facts and circumstances proven in the case show that they committed an atrocious crime. Life is precious to them, but no more so than it was to their victim.

Their poor mothers are entitled to sympathy, but no more so than the mother of Pearl Bryan.

The law has been set at defiance, and the fair name of Kentucky stained with another terrible murder.

Twelve men have passed upon the guilt of each. The Circuit Judge and Appellate Judges have affirmed their action.

My oath is that "I will see that the laws are faithfully executed."

The jury has fixed the penalty. I have plain duty to perform. It is not my province to make laws, but to enforce them. Neither is it my province to fix the death penalty, nor is it proper that I should intervene to prevent its infliction when the law and evidence authorizes it.

Respite refused.

William O. Bradley,
Governor of Kentucky.

SO FAR FROM HOME

26 DIE GAME

The McCreary Guards were deployed to Newport to prevent a recurrence of the mob violence that occurred at the public hanging of Robert Laughlin in Brookville, Kentucky, the previous January. Laughlin had confessed to attempting to rape his young niece, and when his wife tried to stop him, he beat them both to death with a poker, and then set fire to the house to hide the crime. Public animosity toward Laughlin was high, and after his arrest, he was moved several times to escape lynching. After his conviction in July 1896, he was moved to the Covington Jail, where Jackson and Walling were already under heavy guard.

At Laughlin's hanging, a crowd amassed outside the fence at 7:30 that morning. When the doors were opened at 9:10, the mob pulled down the fence in a mad rush into the jail yard. A deputy sheriff managed to subdue the crowd and prevent a full-scale riot by mounting the scaffold and asking for quiet. It was not clear that Sheriff Plummer would have that calming ability, but the guards, carrying rifles with fixed bayonets, would do the trick.

Sheriff Plummer brought Jackson and Walling back from Alexandria on Friday afternoon shortly before word arrived that Governor Bradley denied the request to delay the execution. The sheriff placed little value on the recent confessions and had no doubt that the governor would ignore their plea.

Loved ones said their final farewells to the condemned men in the jailer's living room in Alexandria, Thursday night. Jackson met with his mother and his sister Minnie, but he requested that they not bring his little niece Ruth. He did not want this to be her last memory of him. They cried and embraced but spoke few words. Mrs. Jackson uttered a fervent prayer for the soul of her son, then mother and sister left, weeping bitterly.

Mrs. Walling met her son with a heart racked with grief. "No tears coursed her furrowed cheeks," said the *Cincinnati Enquirer*, "Her wound was too deep to bleed." They had a long, quiet talk, then Walling knelt at his mother's knee while she prayed for God to have mercy on his soul.

Sarah Walling's last words to Alonzo were, "My son, if we cannot be together in this world, we can in the next."

Emma Roberts bade her final farewell to her sweetheart earlier that afternoon. It was reported that she and Walling planned to marry in the

Alexandria Jail with Reverend Lee officiating, but the wedding was called off when Mrs. Walling did not approve. Instead, they parted with a simple handclasp. Walling returned a photograph of Miss Roberts, and at his request, she agreed to send him a note of farewell when they were back in Newport.

The sun shone brightly that first day of spring, Saturday, March 20, 1897. A tall stockade fence built the week before around the courthouse yard cast long shadows across the yard. The McCreary Guards stationed outside the fence to make sure no one entered the yard except those with a professional interest—lawmen, attorneys, clergymen, and reporters. The guards were joined by Sheriff Plummer's deputies, who limited admittance to those holding tickets issued by the Sheriff's office.

The air smelled of sawdust from the still-fresh construction of a double gallows behind the courthouse. The structure was painted white with black outlines on the trapdoors. Noosed ropes were wrapped around the joist above the platform and oiled by Plummer's men so the long knot would tighten gracefully when pulled. They tested the ropes and traps with sandbags and bundles of pipe. Sheriff Plummer himself conducted the execution. There was no room for error.

Inside the jailhouse, the scene was chaotic and frenzied, in stark contrast to the calm spring weather outside. "It was a morning of shifting, dramatic, uncertainty," said the *Cincinnati Enquirer*, "when fiction played frolic with facts and rumor ran its unceasing rounds."

Reporters from several newspapers were already there, vying for Sheriff Plummer's attention. But the Sheriff, hurriedly attending more pressing matters, had no comment for them.

Reverend Lee, in full vestment, carrying Bible and hymnal, checked his watch. Colonel Washington stood anxiously near the hall of the prisoners' cells, ready to spring at the slightest hint that Jackson would honor his promise and exonerate Walling.

Deputies went to officially wake the prisoners, though it was doubtful they did much sleeping that night. They had breakfast and met in one cell so Reverend Lee could work on their souls.

The strains of "In the Sweet Bye and Bye" echoing throughout the jailhouse and out into the street were irreverently raucous. The reverend had his work cut out. They sang several more hymns, and then finally all fell quiet as Reverend Lee led the men in prayer. He then left, and the deathwatch took over.

At 8:00 a.m., Sheriff Plummer told the prisoners to be dressed in their good suits and ready in one hour. At that time, they would be brought out into the yard, and the hanging would commence. Colonel Washington requested more time to pressure Scott Jackson once again for a full confession that would exonerate his client, but Sheriff Plummer was reluctant. He was not interested in anything more Jackson might say.

From outside the jail, friends of Walling sent a message to Colonel Washington to pressure Jackson to say that Walling was not present when Pearl Bryan was killed. The governor would have to respite Walling. A few simple words could save Walling's life, but when the proposition was put to Jackson he refused.

"I can't say that, it's a trap," said Jackson, "I can't say that Walling was not there without admitting that I was there."

That seemed to clinch it. There was nothing to do but wait. At three minutes to nine, as the Sheriff gathered those who would lead the prisoners to the scaffold, a jailer hurried into the room, and said Jackson wished to make a statement regarding Walling. Sheriff Plummer went to the cell and asked Jackson what he wanted to say.

"I do not believe that Alonzo Walling is guilty of the death of Pearl Bryan by premeditation," Jackson responded.

Walling, in a frenzy, pressured Sheriff Plummer to telegraph the governor so he could grant a reprieve.

"It is not sufficient," said Plummer, "Mr. Jackson does not even say that he knows you are innocent. He merely says that he does not believe you are guilty."

Walling asked him to summon Colonel Washington, and together, Walling, Washington, and Rev. Lee urged Scott Jackson to say more. Jackson asked for a private conversation with Rev. Lee. The sheriff was reluctant, but Lee implored him to consider the grave responsibility he had, holding a man's life in his hands.

Plummer relented, and Jackson and Lee spoke alone for several minutes. Then Jackson returned and said, "Mr. Sheriff and gentlemen present, I know that Alonzo M. Walling is not guilty of murder."

Walling again implored Sheriff Plummer to send Jackson's statement to the governor, but Plummer said it would be of no avail. Jackson gave no facts or details as to how and when, and where Pearl Bryan died. Plummer told him that only a circumstantial and complete confession would be of any value, but Jackson had no more to say. Colonel Washington and Sheriff Plummer debated what the governor needed from Jackson to exonerate Walling. By that time, they accepted the assumption of Walling's innocence. The question was how much Jackson needed to say to convince the governor. Walling thought Jackson said enough and finally persuaded Plummer to telegraph Governor Bradley:

> Hon. William O. Bradley. Governor, Frankfort, Ky.:
> The execution was to take place at 9. At three minutes to 9 Jackson made this statement: "I know that Alonzo M. Walling is not guilty of murder." I agreed to send you telegram. Shall I proceed? Wire answer

at once.

Jule Plummer.

Everything paused while they waited for Governor Bradley's response, but when it came, Sheriff Plummer was not pleased.

Jule Plummer, Sheriff, Newport, Ky.:
Have received telegram purporting to have been sent by you, in which it is alleged that Jackson says he knows Walling is not guilty of murder.
If this telegram was sent by you, you can proceed with his execution, and if he makes a statement on the gallows that acquits Walling, suspend his execution until you telegraph me, and receive instructions.

William O. Bradley

Outside, the jail yard was filled with spectators straining the surrounding fence. The sheriff issued fifty tickets, but deputies learned too late that counterfeit tickets were sold outside the gate all morning. And many of those with legitimate tickets passed them through or over the fence to allow their friends entrance. By 9:00 a.m., there were at least 300 people inside the stockade, and the fence itself was giving way to pressure from both sides. In the street outside the stockade hundreds more hoped to see or hear or just be present at the execution.

After 10:00 a.m., the crowd, inside and out, became loud and restless. Plummer knew that if he took two men outside and did not hang two men, the crowd would riot. He told his deputy to contact Judge Helm. He would not do this alone.

They contacted Judge Helm by telegram, and he traveled to the jail as quickly as he could from his home in the Highlands. He held a brief but intense discussion with Washington and Plummer. The three men left for the Covington law offices of Harvey Meyers, an associate of Judge Helm's, where they called the governor by long-distance telephone. Governor Bradley held to the romantic notion that Jackson, on the scaffold, confronted by the noose, would confess all and clear his roommate.

The Newport men convinced him that if it did occur, and Walling was taken down from the gallows, the crowd would be enraged and would almost certainly try to intercede. They decided that Jackson should be given one more chance to spare Walling before being taken outside.

The men hurried back to the jail and met again with Scott Jackson. Judge Helm tried to impress the gravity of what was about to happen. Jackson was about to meet his God, and if he could save the life of an innocent man, it was certainly his duty to do so. But, the judge continued, he ought not to die with a falsehood on his lips.

Judge Helm suggested they give Jackson some time to ponder his situation. Plummer told Jackson that it was now six minutes to 11:00. They would return for his answer at 11:00. They left the door ajar so they could see Jackson and make sure he did not use the time to try and kill himself.

The judge left Jackson with a dilemma; he had a duty to save an innocent man but should not die with a lie on his lips. If Jackson, himself, was truly innocent, the only way to exonerate Walling was to lie about his own involvement.

"I have nothing further to tell you." said Jackson when they returned, "I have nothing to say."

Sheriff Plummer telephoned Governor Bradley once more and relayed Jackson's statement. The governor reverted to his original order—proceed with the double hanging, if Jackson, on the gallows, exonerates Walling, suspend Walling's execution but continue Jackson's.

At that, as if awakened from a stupor, everyone sprang to life. Events moved quickly again. The prisoners were brought out, and the black caps were placed on their heads, the hoods rolled up.

Deputy Maurer handed Walling a letter from Emma Roberts. The brief note sent Walling her love and told him to "die game." She wanted her sweetheart to remain stoic and face his doom like a man.

The death procession formed. Reverend Lee was followed by Jackson, then Walling, each man with a deputy to his left. They stood at the door of the jail as Sheriff Plummer walked alone outside. Shouts and whistles rose from the crowd as he emerged, climbed the stairs of the platform and strode across to the center. The noise subsided when the Sheriff rapped on the balustrade of the gallows. When the crowd had quieted, Plummer began to speak, loudly addressing the sea of anxious faces.

"Gentlemen, I want to ask you, while the execution is taking place, to observe the utmost quietude and make no demonstrations of any kind upon such a solemn occasion as this. You may agree and be assured that the law will be properly complied with, but I ask you to make no expression of any kind. It is a hard duty for me to perform. Especially has it been so the last two hours. At 11:30 o'clock, we expect to have this execution take place. I will ask you to show the reverence that ought to be shown in the presence of death."

The procession moved into the quieted yard. A brief murmur spread through the crowd as all saw that both men were wearing death caps. Rumor spread through the yard that Walling would be exonerated. Once the truth was acknowledged, the crowd went quiet again.

The prisoners were led across the platform to the spot traced in black below his noose. They remained quiet and unmoving as deputies bound their ankles with straps of leather and strapped their wrists behind their backs. Sheriff Plummer was standing between and in front of the condemned men.

He turned and faced them. "Scott Jackson and Alonzo Walling, I am here for the purpose of carrying out the mandate of the governor of this state, as expressed in the death warrant, which I read to you on last Tuesday. Scott Jackson, have you anything to say?"

Jackson's hesitation was noticeably long, and Walling turned to him, terror in his eyes. Jackson ignored Walling and the crowd. He turned his eyes upward and said, loudly enough to be heard clearly by those in the front section of the crowd, "I have only this to say. That I am not guilty of the crime for which I am now compelled to pay the penalty of my life."

Sheriff Plummer turned to Walling. "Alonzo Walling, have you anything to say?"

"Nothing. Only that you are taking the life of an innocent man, and I call upon my God to witness the truth of what I say."

Plummer took a step back and said, "Brother Lee, you will conduct the services."

Before the silenced crowd, Reverend Lee solemnly sang "I Save my Soul in the Haven of Rest." He then read from Isaiah, "Look unto me and be saved, and all the land of the earth; for I am God, and there is none else." Then from John, "For God so loved the world that he gave His only begotten son that whosoever believeth in Him should not perish but have everlasting life." From Matthew, "Come unto me, all that labor and are heavy laden, and I will give you rest." From Revelations, "And the Spirit and the bride say, come. And let him that heareth say, come. And let him that is athirst come. And whosoever will, let him take the water of life freely."

The Reverend turned to Sheriff Plummer who, again, addressed the crowd.

"Reverend Lee will now invoke a divine blessing."

Reverend Lee prayed in his full Sunday cadence.

"Our Father, our Savior, our God, we pray You that You shall receive the souls of Scott Jackson and Alonzo Walling and save them, that they may be worthy of Thee, and salvation. O Lord, O Christ, Thou who didst save the thief who died on the cross, be with them today. Oh, admit these boys in Thy life, in Thy mercy, we ask, and rely upon Thee, Jesus Christ, today and forever. Amen."

The Reverend then turned to the condemned men.

"Scott, goodbye. Lonnie, goodbye. I ask in the name of the Lord, right now, that you engage in a secret prayer that your souls may be saved." And the clergyman walked slowly to the rear of the platform.

After a silent moment, deputies Moore and Hindeman came forward and placed the nooses around the necks of Jackson and Walling. Deputy Moore seemed excited and pulled the noose so tightly that Jackson could be heard to exclaim. It was the first time Jackson betrayed any fear. His face grew ashen, and his eyes rolled back in terror.

The deputies quickly rolled down the black hoods to cover the prisoners' heads and faces and walked off the platform. Sheriff Plummer followed them. The crowd was charged, but the yard was so quiet boats on the Ohio River were heard in the distance.

Plummer sprung the traps. All gasped in unison as the men fell through and hung below the platform, their shoes not two feet from the ground.

The crowd thought it was over, but as the suspended bodies twisted slowly and their backs came into view, the mob could see their fingers twitching wildly below their bound wrists. Their legs, too, were jerking, as if trying to shake off the straps. The crowd in front was silent as, horrified, they watched the bodies jerking just enough to prove that life remained. Further back, people clamored, anxious for confirmation that the deed was done.

But it was not done.

Neither man's neck had been broken, as anticipated, by the fall. Jackson and Walling were slowly strangling to death. They were clearly in agony, but not a sound came from under the black hoods.

Walling's body became still first. Doctors Pythian and Caruthers went to check for a pulse. At 11:55, fifteen long minutes after the fall, Alonzo Walling was pronounced dead. Six minutes later, Scott Jackson was officially dead. They had both died game.

The news traveled back through the crowd, and for a moment, it was still again. The mob suddenly pushed forward, irrationally, toward the bodies. It was a feral pack, drunk with blood lust and triumph, and after the spoils. At the front, the McCreary Guards, bayonets drawn, stopped the advance, but further back, they still pushed. The doctors backed away and headed for the door of the jailhouse. The guards subdued the crowd just long enough for the deputies to carry the bodies inside. With nothing left for them, the crowd, at last, backed off and the yard was soon empty and silent.

EPILOGUE

Despite the excruciating delays and the unruly crowd, Sheriff Plummer was praised for his management of the hanging. Once it started, the execution went off like clockwork. The attendance was larger than anticipated, and the sheriff's men were not able to prevent non-ticketed witnesses from entering the jail yard, but the crowd remained calm almost until the end. The McCreary Guards, their bayonets fixed, stopped a mob from rushing the gallows, but beyond that brief incident, the Guards were not needed. The *Cincinnati Post* reported that the Guardsmen had been carrying unloaded weapons during their stay in Newport.

One brief controversy arose from the hanging. Why had the fall broken neither man's neck? Some said the platform was built too low, and consequently, the fall was too short to generate sufficient force. Others said the nooses were not correctly adjusted. The knot should have been positioned over the left ear to jerk the body sideways, snapping the spine at the neck for a quick, clean death. In both cases, the knot was behind the head when it tightened, suggesting that strangulation may have been intentional. Some went so far as to speculate that nails were inserted in the ropes to guarantee the nooses would not tighten. But the question was short-lived. The two murderers were dead. If the process was not perfect, the result was.

Some felt that three men should have hung that day, but for Will Wood, justice took another form. His notoriety in Indiana grew to the point where a normal life was impossible. A grand jury in Greencastle failed to indict him in connection with Pearl Bryan's death, but many in town were still ready and willing to string him up themselves. In Indianapolis, Wood applied to two medical colleges and was denied admission to both. His reputation was so bad that he could not even secure a room in a boarding house.

U.S. Postal Inspector Charles Salmon reviewed Will Wood's letters to Scott Jackson for possible prosecution. The letters' inherent obscenity and their specific references to drugs and procedures for abortion violated the Comstock Laws, which prohibited the transfer of such information by U.S. Mail.

But Wood found an escape from these charges as well. Three days before the hanging of his former comrade, Will Wood boarded the *U.S.S. Castine* as

SO FAR FROM HOME

a clerical yeoman in the United States Navy. The *Castine* left Newport News, Virginia, bound for the South Atlantic as war with Spain loomed.

The case finally closed, but several mysteries surrounding the death of Pearl Bryan remain unsolved. The paternity of Pearl's unborn child is still uncertain. Most assumed it was Scott Jackson, but he said it was Will Wood, and Walling said they did not know which was responsible. The urgent efforts of both Scott Jackson and Will Wood to end the pregnancy would indicate that Walling was right. The Bryan family held Will Wood equally responsible for Pearl's death, and although they never said as much, the extreme animosity they had for Will Wood implied that they were not sure either.

It was never determined where Pearl Bryan slept on Wednesday night and Thursday night prior to her death. She checked out of the Indiana House on Wednesday morning, but she did not register in any other hotels. Witnesses claimed to have seen Pearl in Cincinnati and in Northern Kentucky on those two days, but nothing beyond her visit to a Cincinnati piano store could be verified, and where she slept those nights was anybody's guess.

To the police, it did not matter. They had witnesses who saw Pearl with Jackson and Walling, on Friday night, leaving Cincinnati and arriving in Kentucky. But without the two previous nights, the story is incomplete, leaving police assumptions open to challenge.

Lulu Mae Hollingsworth never made good on her promise to save Jackson and Walling from the gallows. By the time of the execution her story was forgotten but, in February 1896, it was taken seriously. The press and some in law enforcement were prepared to believe that on Thursday, Pearl traveled with Walling to Indianapolis, where Lulu Mae Hollingsworth attempted to induce an abortion. If her story had not ventured into the fantastic, Miss Hollingsworth would have been charged with the crime and prosecution moved to Indiana.

Pearl may have slept both nights in Jackson and Walling's room, which could be the reason Walling slept at Heider's Hotel on Thursday night. Maybe, as May Smith and Lulu Hollingsworth had suggested, Pearl died in Scott Jackson's room, but could he have kept her death a secret from his ever-vigilant landlady?

From the beginning, Jackson and Walling each maintained that on Wednesday, Pearl went to the place where the abortion was to be performed. Each said Pearl went in the other's company, and neither man could give the destination. In their last confessions, they declared that Pearl had stayed in Bellevue, Kentucky, at the home of Dr. Wagner, whose attempted abortion killed her. Wagner had an alibi, and the Wagner family's proof that the doctor was out of town on the night of the murder was sufficient to satisfy Sheriff Plummer and Governor Bradley, but the claim was credible enough to cast more doubt on the official story.

Determining what really happened on the night of January 31, 1896, is hampered by the number of people who lied about it. George Jackson gave the most important testimony in both trials, but by the time of the execution, his story was almost universally regarded as false. The convoluted route, the improbable timeline, the unlikelihood that the killers would hire a stranger to drive them combined with George Jackson's reputation as an attention-seeking fabricator, caused many, even in the law enforcement community, to doubt his story. At the time of the execution, George Jackson was on trial in Springfield, Ohio, for perjury in another, unrelated case.

Others who testified in support of the "unbroken chain" of evidence told stories that were inconsistent at best. Dave Wallingford and Allen Johnson said they saw Jackson, Walling, and Pearl the night of the murder. The three of them were in Wallingford's saloon, but there were reasons to believe the night was not Friday. Wallingford and Johnson were both fringe characters, often at odds with the law. It would take little coaxing to make their stories align with the official one.

In Cincinnati, a dozen or so members of the Caldwell Guards gave Leonard Crawford sworn depositions that the guards did not drill on the night of January 31. When the Cincinnati Police persuaded these men to travel to Kentucky and testify, they all denied their previous statements and swore they did drill that night. Both statements were made under oath, but both could not be true.

At the time of the execution, Captain John Seward and William Frankly Trusty, Jr. were serving time in a Kentucky penitentiary for perjury in Scott Jackson's trial. Seward pled guilty to the charge of suborning perjury. Trusty admitted he lied on the witness stand but still maintained he had firsthand knowledge of the case. While at the house of a lady friend in Cincinnati, Trusty saw the body of a young woman who turned out to be Pearl Bryan. He now told reporters that the head was severed in Cincinnati; his lady friend wrapped it in her cloak and took it away. Walling drove the carriage carrying the body to Kentucky, while Jackson went in a separate buggy with the so-called doctor.

"I do not know the cause of Pearl Bryan's death," said Trusty as the execution approached. "I do not know where she died. This I do know, that Alonzo Walling and Scott Jackson never committed the crime for which they are sentenced to hang. Neither did the negro George Jackson ever drive the rig that took Pearl Bryan to Fort Thomas, either dead or alive."

The last confessions of Scott Jackson and Alonzo Walling were quickly deemed fabrications calculated to forestall the execution. They would be easy to dismiss, but for corroboration of the druggist, William Foertmeyer, a disinterested third party. Foertmeyer claimed he filled a prescription from Dr. Wagner for Alonzo Walling on the night of January 31. In addition, he claimed to have taken telephone messages between Scott Jackson and Maude Wagner earlier that week. He said he gave this information to Detective Crim and Sheriff Plummer but was never asked about it in court.

Dr. Wagner's family claimed that he was not in town that night and that none of them ever heard of Pearl Bryan, Scott Jackson, or Alonzo Walling before the murder. No one in the family ever sent or received telephone messages through Foertmeyer's store. Either Foertmeyer was lying, or the Wagners were.

May Smith also corroborated the confessions, but she already told one story about Pearl Bryan's death that she later admitted was untrue. No doubt, she had knowledge of the case, but nothing she said could be trusted.

It is impossible to piece together a reliable story of Pearl Bryan's death because there is no firm foundation to build it on and no reliable testimony to confirm it. Even cherry-picking the most convenient "facts," as the prosecution did, will result in a story fraught with contradictions.

The greatest mystery is why Alonzo Walling became involved at all. He only knew Scott Jackson well for four months and never met Pearl Bryan or Will Wood. By his own admission, Walling agreed to help procure an abortion for Pearl, putting himself at risk of arrest for the sake of his roommate.

When he was arrested, Walling placed the blame squarely on Jackson, but he never told all that he knew. He never provided enough detail to charge Jackson with a crime. Had he chosen to testify against Scott Jackson, Walling could have saved his own life. Instead, he kept quiet and took Jackson at his word, believing to the end that Jackson would save him.

Some said Scott Jackson had a strange power to manipulate others—his "evil eye." Mrs. Walling believed Jackson controlled her son through hypnosis and believed that Lon would only tell the truth if they were separated. Will Wood testified that Scott Jackson had significant influence over everybody he knew. "It was an influence I cannot explain," he said, "I did about whatever he wanted me to. I was always trying to keep up my end of the string with him." It seems that Walling was trying to keep up his end of the string as well. To his own detriment, Walling always deferred to Scott Jackson, taking his advice over that of his mother and his attorney.

Alonzo Walling's prosecution for the murder of Pearl Bryan was the merest chance. The police dismissed him until an offhand remark by Scott Jackson sent reporter Ed Anthony back to the rooming house to make the arrest.

In a *Cincinnati Enquirer* story many years later, Detective Cal Crim said of Alonzo Walling, "I am glad that I did not instigate his arrest, and I have always felt that he was only a simple country boy who fell under the blighting influence of an older and much more sinister man, for whom he became a willing tool. His weakness was his enemy. Though his part in the gruesome crime, however incidental and subordinate cannot be condoned, and he deserved severe punishment for it, I have always felt that his execution was a grave miscarriage of justice."

Walling stuck with his friend, and even when he was angry with Jackson, he never wavered in his belief that Jackson would save him from the gallows. Jackson could have saved Walling's life, but he knew the only way to do it was by confessing that he murdered Pearl Bryan in cold blood by severing her head. This he could not do.

The one indisputable fact is that Scott Jackson was responsible for the death of Pearl Bryan. She traveled to Cincinnati to see Jackson, either for an abortion or, as her family would assert, to persuade him to marry her. Whatever happened to Pearl the night of January 31, 1896, was instigated, if not perpetrated, by Scott Jackson.

But was Jackson capable of first-degree murder—did he sever the head of a living woman in the Kentucky Highlands? Scott Jackson was a rogue, a self-serving liar, manipulator, libertine, and deceiver who traveled easily in many worlds, but he was not a likely suspect of a violent murder. He was small in stature and had no history of violence, and while Jackson often found himself in trouble, he was always able to talk his way out. If he were the one responsible for Pearl Bryan's pregnancy, it is hard to imagine that he would choose murder to solve his problem.

More likely, the death was the result of a botched abortion—whether performed in Bellevue, Kentucky, in a George Street apartment, in Scott Jackson's room, or somewhere else is impossible to say. Though it would have meant a prison sentence, Jackson could have saved his life by telling the truth when first arrested. Perhaps he naively believed that he could not be found guilty of first-degree murder, so was unwilling to admit any culpability in any crime. Whether the story he finally told—of Dr. Wagner performing the abortion—had any truth did not matter. Jackson had denied his involvement for so long that nothing short of a full and damning confession would be believed.

For all his faults, Jackson was also an intelligent and congenial young man, and despite charges of hypocrisy, a religious man who viewed himself as a good Christian. As seen in his letters to Pearl Bryan, Scott Jackson was capable of expressing sincere emotion. The night before his execution, he spent his time writing farewell notes to those closest to him, including deathwatch guard Dan Veith:

Newport,
3-20-97

Dear Friend Dan:

I will try and say a few words of farewell to you but they must at this time be few. I want to thank you for all of your kindness to me during my stay with you. You have been a good friend to me, and you have my heartfelt thanks. May God bless and keep you. I trust you may ever be true to yourself and all mankind.

Yours,
Scott Jackson

Sarah Jackson hoped to bury her son in Greencastle Cemetery where she could visit his grave but fearing her request would be denied, she planned instead to bury his body in the town of Wiscasset, Maine. It was her hometown and the place where Scott himself spent his early childhood before Commodore Jackson moved the family to New Jersey. She had to look a long way back in his life to find Scott Jackson a peaceful resting place.

Reporters and curiosity seekers determined the train necessary to begin the journey to Maine, and they waited at the Newport depot for the body's arrival. But they were disappointed; Scott Jackson's body was secretly taken by wagon back to Cincinnati, to the Clifton Crematory where, without services or ceremony, it was reduced to ashes.

The cost of transporting the body was too great, and the family feared that his body might be stolen during the long trip back east, and that any grave, even one as far away as Maine, was likely to be desecrated. Cremation seemed the most merciful course.

Those who stayed at the station long enough did see Walling's coffin loaded into a train for Hamilton, Ohio. There his brother Clinton would handle the arrangements to send the body to its final resting place, a private cemetery in Mt. Carmel, Indiana, where the family owned a plot. Alonzo would be buried near his father, who had died seventeen years earlier.

As her father had feared, Pearl Bryan is remembered only as the murdered girl buried without her head. Her grave became an attraction for souvenir hunters, who chipped off pieces of the headstone until her family had it removed, leaving only the un-engraved stone base. Visitors today leave coins on the stone, heads up, in remembrance.

Through years of retelling, the history of Pearl Bryan's death has lost much of its detail and nuance. In song and story, her experience became a cautionary tale, warning against the trust of a false-hearted lover, until the century that should have been hers found such stories hopelessly quaint.

Pearl Bryan's head was never found.

BIBLIOGRAPHY

Akron Beacon Journal (Akron, OH), 1896.

Alton Telegraph (Alton, IL), 1896.

American Nonconformist (Indianapolis, IN), 1896.

Biographical and Historical Record of Putnam County, Indiana. Selby Pub. & Printing, 1985.

Burt, Olive Woolley. *American Murder Ballads: And Their Stories.* Oxford University Press, 1958.

Chillicothe Gazette (Chillicothe, OH), 1896.

Cincinnati Daily Enquirer (Cincinnati, OH), 1896-1897.

Cincinnati Enquirer (Cincinnati, OH), 1896-1897,1946.

Cincinnati Post (Cincinnati, OH), 1897.

Cincinnati Tribune (Cincinnati, OH), 1896.

Cohen, Anne B. *Poor Pearl, Poor Girl!: The Murdered-girl Stereotype in Ballad and Newspaper.* Univ. of Texas Pr., 1973.

Courier-Journal (Louisville, KY), 1896.

Covington Friend (Covington, IN), 1896.

Daily Illinois State Journal (Springfield, IL), 1896.

Daily Leader (Lexington, KY), 1896.

DeCamp, Graydon. *The Grand Old Lady of Vine Street: The Cincinnati Enquirer: 150 Years, 1841-1991.* Cincinnati Enquirer, 1991.

Dellinger, Susan. *Red Legs and Black Sox: Edd Roush and the Untold Story of the 1919 World Series.* Cincinnati, OH: Emmis Books, 2006.

Eddy, Mary O., and D.K. Wilgus. *Ballads and Songs from Ohio.* Folklore Associates, 1964.

Grayson, Frank Y. *Pioneers of Night Life on Vine Street.* Cincinnati Times-

Star, 1924.

Greencastle Daily Greencastle Banner and Times (Greencastle, IN), 1896.

Greencastle Democrat (Greencastle, IN), 1896.

Indiana State Journal (Indianapolis, IN), 1897.

Indianapolis Journal (Indianapolis, IN), 1896-1897.

Indianapolis News (Indianapolis, IN), 1896-1897.

Indianapolis Sun (Indianapolis, IN), 1896.

Interior Journal (Stanford, KY), 1896.

Kentucky Advocate (Danville, KY), 1896.

Kentucky Post (Covington, KY), 1896.

Marietta Daily Leader (Marietta, OH), 1896.

Miller, Zane L. *Boss Cox's Cincinnati*. Oxford University Press, 1968.

Morning Herald (Lexington, KY), 1896.

Owensboro Daily Tribune (Owensboro, KY), 1896.

Owingsville Outlook (Owingsville, KY), 1897.

Pearl Bryan, Or: A Fatal Ending. A Complete History of the Lives and Trials of Scott Jackson and Alonzo Walling, Both Being Sentenced to Death. Barclay &, 1896.

Philadelphia Inquirer (Philadelphia, PA), 1897.

Phillips, Clifton Jackson., and John J. Baughman. *DePauw: A Pictorial History*. DePauw University, 1987.

Piqua Daily Call (Piqua, OH), 1896.

Plain Dealer (Cleveland, OH), 1896.

Police and Municipal Guide, 1901. Ebbert & Richardson Company, printers, 1901.

Poock, L. D. *"Headless, Yet Identified;": A Story of the Solution of the Pearl*

Bryan, or Fort Thomas Mystery, through the Shoes. Hann & Adair, Printers, 1897.

Public Ledger (Maysville, KY), 1896.

Reis, Jim. *Pieces of the Past 1.* Kentucky Post, 1988.

Reis, Jim. *Pieces of the Past 2.* Kentucky Post, 1991.

Repository (Canton, OH), 1897.

Richmond Climax (Richmond, KY), 1896.

Richmond Item (Richmond, IN), 1896.

Ross, Steven Joseph. *Workers on the Edge: Work, Leisure, and Politics in Industrializing Cincinnati.* Figueroa Press, 2002

Society, Kentucky Historical, James C. Klotter, and Hambleton Tapp. *Kentucky: Decades of Discord, 1865-1900.* Kentucky Historical Society, 1977.

South Bend Tribune (South Bend, IN), 1896.

The Mysterious Murder of Pearl Bryan, or, The Headless Horror: a Full Account of the Mysterious Murder Known as the Fort Thomas Tragedy, from Beginning to End: Full Particulars of All Detective and Police Investigations: Dialogues of the Interviews between Mayor Caldwell, Chief Deitsch and the Prisoners. Barclay & Co., 1896.

Weik, Jesse William. *Weiks History of Putnam County, Indiana.* B. F. Bowen & Company, 1910.

Williams' Cincinnati Business Directory. The Williams Directory Co., 1909.

ABOUT THE AUTHOR

Robert Wilhelm writes about historical true crime with a particular interest in nineteenth-century American murders. He is the author *Wicked Victorian Boston* which documents vice and crime in nineteenth century Boston and the efforts of reformers to control it, and *Murder and Mayhem in Essex County*, a chronicle of murders and other capital crimes in Essex County Massachusetts from the Puritans to the turn of the twentieth century.

His blog Murder by Gaslight (www.murderbygaslight.com), "A compendium of information, resources, and discussion on notable nineteenth century American murders," has been running continuously since 2009. In his weekly posts, Robert has written the stories of more than 500 American murders. In 2014 he published a compilation of fifty posts from Murder by Gaslight, entitled *The Bloody Century*.

Made in the USA
Coppell, TX
05 May 2022

77402709R10118